To the Federal employees
who tirelessly toil
preparing,
redoing,
defending,
and carrying out
Federal budgets.

Todd,
Hope The course was
useful.
Don Green

Understanding the Budget Policies and Processes of the United States Government

Fourteenth Edition

Michael J. O'Bannon
President, EOP Foundation

Donald E. Gessaman
Senior Vice President &
Principal Author

The EOP Foundation can provide training assistance to organizations by conducting a seminar on Federal Budget Policies and Processes. The EOP Foundation has published a case study that allows students to portray the roles of the participants in the budget process from developing a budget at the field activity level through passage of an appropriations bill on the floor of the House of Representatives. Interested parties should contact:

The EOP Foundation
819 7th Street, NW
Washington, D.C. 20001
(202) 833-8940

ISBN 9781453691762 (Soft Cover)

Table of Contents

Acknowledgements

Preface

Acknowledgments

The EOP Foundation wishes to thank principal author **Don Gessaman**, former OMB Deputy Associate Director for National Security, and **Chad Campbell**, a senior associate at the Foundation, for their tireless and unselfish work and expertise ensuring the quality of this publication. **Don Gessaman** continues to lecture to Government employees across the Government to teach both the historical context in which the budget is enacted and analytical techniques targeted in improving its quality.

The Foundation also wishes to acknowledge the contribution of the many Federal budget professionals and policymakers who have contributed practical data, case studies, and advice updating our knowledge of the Federal budget process. We continue to acknowledge the book's expanding readership. The book now reaches Federal executives, military academies, universities, Wall Street, corporate offices, public libraries, and many others. It is also important to acknowledge the Foundation's staff for assisting with research and contributions to the book.

Many of the concepts and subjects in the book were discussed and nurtured at *Smith & Wollensky's Restaurant* in Washington, DC, a well-known gathering place for former and current employees of the Office of Management and Budget, as well as Congressional Members and staff. This fixture of the Washington scene will never experience a budget deficit so long as executives of the Federal Government continue their patronage.

This fourteenth edition of The EOP Foundation's book on the budget has a slightly more descriptive title. We have added "Policies and Processes" to the title to reflect how the focus of the publication has evolved since the first edition. *Understanding the Budget Policies and Processes of the United States Government* reflects upon President Barack H. Obama's first year in office. The President's Budget will be acted upon by Congress during the upcoming months of this fiscal year. The new Budget proposes funding to stimulate the economy and to encourage new programs in energy, environment, health, education, and agriculture. These concepts will be energetically debated due to the historic realignments included.

We hope this year's edition will bring the deliberative process into focus for our readers.

Michael J. O'Bannon
Joseph S. Hezir

PREFACE

FY 2011 Budget

On February 1, 2010, the President submitted his budget for fiscal year 2011. A summary of President Obama's spending initiatives for FY 2011 follows[1]:

Department of Agriculture programs are to decrease from the FY 2010 level by $1 billion. The FY 2011 budget is aimed at creating new jobs and opportunities in rural communities, expanding opportunities for farmers, improving nutrition programs, and protecting America's natural resources.

- $429 million, the highest funding level ever, for competitive research grants through the Agriculture and Food Research Initiative.
- $418 million in loans and grants for rural communities to expand broadband access.
- $50 million for new "Healthy Food Financing Initiative" to bring grocery stores and other healthy food retailers to underserved communities.
- $1.2 billion, an increase of 37%, for the Environmental Quality Incentive Program.
- $54 million increase to promote U.S. agriculture exports.

Department of Commerce programs are to decrease by $5 billion from the FY 2010 level, primarily as a result of the census costs in the 2010 budget.

- $534 million increase, to the International Trade Administration.
- $712 million for the National Institute of Standards and Technology laboratories.
- $246 million to support economic growth programs at the Economic Development Administration.
- More than $2 billion to develop and implement NOAA's polar orbiting and geostationary weather satellite systems, satellite-born measurements of sea level and other climate variables, and other space-based observations.
- $1.3 billion to the Census Bureau.

The budget for the Department of Defense is increased to $548.9 billion, a 3.4 percent increase over the 210 enacted level.

- The funding increase allows DOD to reform defense acquisitions, develop a ballistic missile defense system that addresses modern threats, and continue to provide high quality health care to wounded service members.

---

[1] http://www.whitehouse.gov/omb/

- $159.3 billion is included for DOD's overseas operations in Iraq, Afghanistan and Pakistan.

The Department of Education programs increase to $49.7 billion for FY 2011, $900 million over the 2010 level.

- $3 billion increase for programs authorized by the Elementary and Secondary Education Act.
- $405 million to back successful and innovative pathways into teaching and school leadership.
- $1.8 billion investment in the Supporting Student Success initiative.
- $500 million to expand the Investing in Innovation Fund.

Energy programs increase to $28.4 billion, a $2 billion increase, to support scientific innovation, develop clean and secure energy technologies, maintain national security, and reduce environmental risks.

- $36 billion in new loan authority to support loan guarantees for nuclear power facilities.
- $4.7 billion in clean energy technology investments.
- $5.1 billion for the Office of Science.
- $2.7 billion, an increase of $550 million, to secure nuclear material, develop and field technology to detect and deter nuclear testing and smuggling, and support international nonproliferation treaties, regulatory controls, and safe-guards.

Health Care programs include $81.3 billion for the Department of Health and Human Services, a $1.7 billion increase from the 2010 level.

- $2.5 billion for health centers to provide affordable high quality primary and preventive care to underserved populations, including the uninsured.
- $25.5 billion for additional Federal Medicaid assistance to help states maintain their Medicaid programs and ensure access to health care.
- $32.1 billion for the National Institutes of Health.

The Department of Homeland Security programs are increased to $43.6 billion.

- $4.6 billion to support 20,000 Border Patrol agents and complete the first seg-ment of Customs and Border Protection's virtual border fence.

Housing and Urban Development programs are reduced to $41.6 billion, a $2 billion decrease from FY 2010.

- $19.6 billion for the Housing Choice Voucher program.
- $9.4 billion for the Project-Based Rental Assistance program to preserve approximately 1.3 million affordable rental units through increased funding for contracts with private owners of multifamily properties.
- $2.1 billion for HUD's Homeless Assistance Programs to implement the HEARTH Act.

The Department of Interior budget is $12 billion, the same as FY 2010.

- $73 million, a $14 million increase, to expand agency capacity to review and permit renewable energy projects on Federal lands.
- Nearly $620 million through the Land and Water Conservation Fund for DOI and USDA to acquire new lands for national parks, forests and refuges, protect endangered species habitat, and promote outdoor recreation.
- Nearly $2.6 billion for Bureau of Indian Affairs programs that invest in community infrastructure, education, worker training, and job opportunities along with initiatives to improve the quality of life in Indian Country.

The Department of Justice programs have increased to $29.2 billion for 2011, up from $27.7 billion in 2010.

- $600 million, an addition of $302 million, to support the hiring or retention of police officers in communities across the country.
- $538 million, an increase of $120 million, to support women victims of violence.
- $145 million for enhancements to the FBI's national security programs.

Department of Labor programs decreased to $14 billion, down from $14.3 billion in FY 2010.

- The budget will prepare workers for good jobs, guarantee fair, safe, and healthily workplaces, and secure retirement for workers.

International Affairs programs increase to $56.8 billion, a $6 billion increase from FY 2010.

- $4.0 billion for Afghanistan assistance and $3.1 billion for Pakistan assistance.
- $4.5 billion in FY 2010 supplemental funds to advance the President's strategy for Afghanistan and Pakistan and to help facilitate the military-to-civilian transition in Iraq.
- $8.5 billion to expand the President's Global Health Initiative.

Transportation programs increase by $1.8 billion from $77 billion in 2010 to $78.8 billion in 2011.

- $4 billion to create a National Infrastructure Innovation and Finance Fund.
- $530 million as part of the President's Partnership for Sustainable Communities to help State and local governments invest in transportation infrastructure that will be integrated with housing development and other investments.
- $1 billion for high-speed rail.

Treasury programs increase from $13.6 billion in FY 2010 to $13.9 billion in FY 2011.

- $250 million to support affordable lending in low-income communities.
- Eliminate $250 million in Federal subsidies to insurance companies for terrorism insurance.
- $2.3 billion to support IRS services.

Veterans Affairs programs increase to $60.3 billion from $56.1 in FY 2010.

- The increase will improve access to benefits and services and improve treatment and assistance for veterans with special needs.

Environmental Protection Agency has a budget of $10 billion, the same as in FY 2010.

- The budget will strengthen EPA's program implementation, research, regulation, and enforcement activities.
- The budget will provide more funding for state and tribal program implementation grants.

About this Book

The objective of this book is to present usable and relevant information about the budget and the budget process in a straightforward format. Our intent is to explain clearly the facts about the Federal Budget without making judgments on the political issues. With this information the reader should have a better foundation of knowledge to make judgments on current issues and policies.

Each edition of this book is published on the heels of the transmittal of the President's annual Budget proposal to Congress, which occurs in February. The content of the book focuses on reference material describing how the budget process works.

Although this book focuses on process, this edition contains some information on the current Budget proposal. **Chapter 1, The Economy and the President's Priorities**, discusses the current issues facing the U.S. economy how the President's past and proposed spending initiative interact with it.

Chapter 2 thorough Chapter 6 provide the reader with fundamentals needed to better understand the processes discussed later in the book. These fundamentals include a primer on **Federal Budget Law**, an overview of **Budget Concepts**, a summary of **Department and Agency Missions**, and a breakdown of **Key Players in the Budget Process**.

Chapter 7, **Chapter 8,** and **Chapter 9** get into the nitty-gritty of how the Budget process works by addressing the **Formulation of the President's Budget**, the **Congressional Budgetary Process**, and **Budget Execution**.

Chapter 10 through Chapter 15 get into specific issue areas including tricks of the trade, or **Budgetary Gimmicks**, a description of **Federal Financial Management Systems**, and a look at **Government Settlements with the Private Sector**, **Ethics**, **Regulatory Policy**, and **Politics.**

The remainder of the book, **Chapter 16 through Chapter 19**, gives the reader handy reference material including a list of **Internet Resources**, a **Glossary of Budget Terms**, a **Summary of Budget Documents** and where to find them, and a **Directory of Budget Officials** complete with contact information.

Finally, the Appendix provides a brief **History of Income Tax** in the United States.

Chapter 1

The Economy and the President's Priorities

The global economic crisis of 2008 and 2009 was the worst on record since the Great Depression in the 1930s. Even though the United States was squarely in the crosshairs of the meltdown, its economy remains by far the largest in the world. Gross Domestic Product (GDP)[1] is a common measure used by economists to compare the size of national economies in terms of goods and services produced and/or provided. In those terms, the GDP of the U. S. is about $14.5 trillion per year – almost twice that of China and over three times the output of Japan, the second and third largest national economies, respectively.[2]

The Recession

A majority of economists agree that a worldwide recession began in late 2007. Economists also agree, based on growth in GDP over the final two quarters of 2009, that the worst of it is now over. The official determination will come from the National Bureau of Economic Research which is the agency recognized as the authority on the economic climate. As of April, 2010, no such official proclamation had been made.

The Congressional Budget Office (CBO) defines a recession as a decline in overall business activity that is pervasive, substantial, and of at least several months duration. Historically, recessions have been identified by a decline in GDP (the total dollar value of all final goods and services produced for consumption in society during a particular time period) for at least two consecutive quarters.

---

[1] GDP is defined as the total dollar value of all final goods and services produced for consumption in society during a particular time period.
[2] Comparisons adjusted for Purchasing Power Parity per CIA World Fact Book.

The causes of the most recent recessions follow:

- **1973**: An embargo by the oil cartel OPEC and high spending on the Vietnam War led to stagflation (this occurs when a stagnant economy and high inflation occur simultaneously).

- **1980**: The Iranian Revolution of 1979 caused sharp increases in the price of oil.

- **1981 and 1982**: The U. S. adopted a tight monetary policy to control the rise of inflation.

- **Late 1980s to early 1990s**: The collapse of junk bonds and a stock market crash in the U.S. caused a recession in many of the western nations.

- **1990 and 1991**: A real estate bubble collapsed causing a recession in the U. S. and Japan.

- **2001 to 2003**: The terrorist attacks on September 11, 2001 and the collapse of the Dot-Com Bubble led to a mild recession in the U. S.

- **2007 to 2009**: The burst of a housing bubble following unprecedented Wall Street bets on mortgage-backed securities created tens of trillions of dollars of worthless paper threatening the viability of the global financial system.

Recent data released by the Bureau of Economic Analysis (BEA) influenced many economists' opinions that the recession ended between July and September of 2009.

- GDP increased at an annual rate of 5.6 percent in the fourth quarter of 2009 (i.e. the increase from the third to fourth quarter) compared to a 2.2 percent increase in the third quarter. The growth in GDP can be attributed to an acceleration in private inventory investment, and an increase in exports, personal consumption expenditures, and non-residential fixed investment. Although imports also increased in the fourth quarter, this growth was less than the growth in exports.
- The Consumer Price Index (CPI) increased 2.0 percent in the fourth quarter compared to an increase of 0.3 percent in the third quarter.
- U. S. exports of goods and services increased 22.8 percent in the fourth quarter, compared to a 17.8 percent increase in the third quarter.
- Corporate profits increased $108.7 billion in the fourth quarter, compared to a $132.4 billion increase in the third quarter
- Residential real estate investment increased 0.43 percent in the fourth quarter, compared with 0.10 percent in the third quarter. This is the first time since 2005 that housing sales have increased for two successive quarters.
- Sales of domestic products (reflected in private inventories) increased 1.7 percent in the fourth quarter, compared to a 1.5 percent increase in the third quarter.

In addition to the BEA data, the stock market has rallied 65 percent since its low point in March of 2009. All of these contributing factors led CBO to report that the economy is expanding at a 2.5 percent annual rate at the close of the first quarter of 2010.

Historical data also supports the theory that the recovery period after a recession can cause GDP to expand to a level far greater than when the recession started. The average pre-recession decline in GDP in the U. S. since 1950 has been 2.2 percent, while the average growth following a recession has been 8.8 percent. Economists have predicted that the U. S. GDP will increase by approximately 3.6 percent in 2010 and continue to grow in subsequent years. This trend will also be seen on a global scale, with the GDP of Asian and European economies expected to grow by approximately 6.8 percent and 2.5 percent respectively for 2010.

Stimulus and the Recovery Act

The President's FY 2011 Budget totals over $3.5 trillion, of which about $1.4 trillion would be deficit spending. The FY 2010 deficit was the largest in history and the FY 2011 deficit is only slightly less. Historically, two categories of Government action have shown positive results in reducing the effects of an economic recession: 1) increase Federal spending; and 2) reduce taxes. Both theoretically result in increased consumer spending, which accounting for 71 percent of the U. S. economy, is the most significant indicator of the economic climate.

While taxes have been reduced for certain types of taxpayers, the majority of economic stimulus legislation has attacked this economic problem by increasing Government spending.

The financial crisis came into full force in the waning years of President Bush's second term. His Administration worked with congress to pass three major economic stimulus packages aimed at avoiding a complete meltdown of the global financial system:

- The Economic Stimulus Act of 2008
- The Housing and Economic Recovery Act of 2008; and
- The Emergency Stabilization Act of 2008.

The banking crisis came to a head in the days leading up to the 2008 presidential election. While the candidates disagreed on exactly what to do, both recognized more legislation would be needed. Immediately following his inauguration as the 45th President, Barack Obama worked swiftly with Congress to enact the American Recovery and Reinvestment Act (Recovery Act), the largest economic stimulus effort in world history.

Through these four pieces of legislation, the United States committed to spend over $1.8 trillion to fight the global financial crisis. For perspective, this is 30 percent greater than the annual GDP of Canada.

The Recovery Act authorized $787 billion to achieve three immediate goals[3]:

- Create new jobs and save existing ones;
- Spur economic activity and invest in long-term growth; and
- Foster unprecedented levels of accountability and transparency in Government spending.

Funding under the Recovery Act was divided into three major investment categories:

- $288 billion in tax cuts and benefits for families and business of which $99 billion has been expended;
- $275 billion for Federal loans of which $86 billion has been expended; and
- $224 billion for entitlement spending to include education and health care of which almost $119 billion has been expended at the time of writing.

Figure 1-1 shows a breakdown of Recovery Act funds available per agency and the total amounts paid out to date[4].

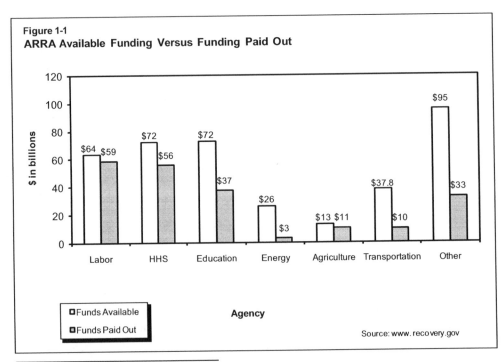

Figure 1-1
ARRA Available Funding Versus Funding Paid Out

$ in billions

	Labor	HHS	Education	Energy	Agriculture	Transportation	Other
Funds Available	$64	$72	$72	$26	$13	$37.8	$95
Funds Paid Out	$59	$56	$37	$3	$11	$10	$33

Agency

☐ Funds Available
☐ Funds Paid Out

Source: www.recovery.gov

---

[3] www.recovery.gov
[4] This table only includes funds that have already been paid to recipients and does not include any funding that may have been allocated but not awarded to different programs or projects.

4

Some examples of Recovery Act expenditures are:

- The Federal Highway Administration (FHWA) authorized a total of 12,160 projects costing a total of $26.2 billion. FHWA currently has 8,449 projects underway in all 50 states and the territories to which the Administration attributes 40,000 new jobs.
- The Department of Education is currently reviewing applications for the $11.5 billion State Fiscal Stabilization Fund and is expected to announce their Phase II decisions imminently. The Administration attributes 400,000 new jobs to this program.
- The Department of Labor has provided over $4 billion for Workforce Investment Act programs to which the Administration attributes 20,000 new jobs.
- The Department of Health and Human Services (HHS) spent over $50 billion to increase access to health care, expand educational opportunities, and provide immediate relief to states and local communities. The Administration tallied 30,000 new jobs due to these expenditures.

In all, the Administration claims 608,317[5] new jobs have been created by Recovery Act funding, with this number expected to continue to increase. By using numbers from similar (though smaller) historical policies, the Congressional Budget Office (CBO) estimates the Recovery Act's impact on job creation and economic output could be in the range of 600,000 to 1.6 million new jobs created.

The Recovery Act created an unprecedented level of accountability and transparency for funding expenditures. All recipients of Recovery Act funding, including not-for-profit, private companies, and individuals, are bound by law to report all funding received and how this funding is used to enhance the goals and objectives of the Act. The Government makes this information available to the public on the Internet (www.recovery.gov) and updates it frequently.

The Recovery Act also created an oversight committee comprised of the Inspectors General (IGs) of 28 Federal Agencies to oversee all agencies' management funding and to ensure that any uses of funding awarded is reported accurately and expeditiously.

National Debt

The national debt or Federal debt represents the accumulated balance of Federal borrowing of the United States Government.

The national debt is broken down into 2 main categories:

---

[5] www.recovery.gov

- **Debt held by the public**: Debt held by the public consists of debt held by individuals, corporations, and local or state governments, foreign governments, and all other entities outside of the U.S. Government less Federal Financing Bank securities. These can include Treasury Bills, Notes, Bonds and United States Savings Bonds.
- **Debt held by Government accounts**: This includes Federal securities held by Government trust funds, revolving funds, special funds, and Federal Financing Bank securities. A small amount of marketable securities are also held by Government accounts. This debt includes the Government securities held by Social Security and the military and civilian retirement programs.

At the time of writing, the Federal Debt stood at $12.2 trillion.

On December February 4th 2009, the United States Senate approved a $1.9 trillion increase in the statutory debt limit that Treasury said was needed by the end of the year to avoid a default and perhaps a shutdown of Federal operations. The statutory debt limit is the cap that Congress imposes on the amount of public debt that may be outstanding. When this limit is reached, the Treasury may not sell new debt issues until Congress raises the limit. The statutory debt limit now stands at $14.3 trillion.

Figure 1-2 shows the trend of the debt held by the public and the debt held by the Government in relation to the overall debt projected in the FY 2011 President's Budget. OMB projects that the debt held by the public will increase to $18.6 trillion by 2020, about 2.5 times the level in 2009.

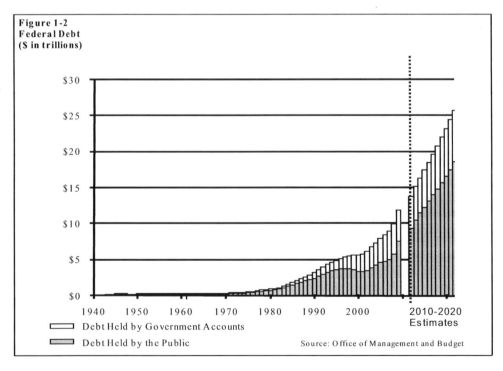

Figure 1-2
Federal Debt
($ in trillions)

According to the CBO, under current law, the Federal debt will continue to grow much faster than the economy over the long run. As a result of those deficits, Federal debt held by the public will increase from 53 percent of GDP at the end of fiscal year 2009 to 65 percent at the end of fiscal year 2010 and to 90 percent by 2020 under the President's Budget proposal.

Foreign ownership of Federal debt has become a growing concern among some Members of Congress because of the nation's large and rising trade deficit. During the past three decades, U.S. national savings has not been adequate to finance its capital investment needs and borrowing from abroad has covered the gap. In order for foreigners to invest in the U.S. economy on net, the United States must import more than it exports (run a trade deficit). When the Government runs a budget deficit, as it has done since 2002, it reduces the national saving rate. This implies that domestic investment must fall, unless private saving rises or borrowing from abroad increases.

The trade deficit occurs because foreigners must first purchase U.S. dollars before purchasing U.S. assets. When the demand for dollars increases, the dollar appreciates, making U.S. exports and import-competing goods relatively more expensive. Thus, foreign borrowing shifts production out of the trade sector and into the interest-sensitive sector.

A variety of factors are placing increasing pressure on the value of the U.S. dollar, increasing the risk of devaluation or inflation and encouraging challenges to the dollar's role as the world's reserve currency. If another currency replaced the dollar as the reserve currency, the U.S. would face higher interest rates to attract capital, reducing economic growth for the long-term.

Foreign ownership of public debt has dramatically increased over the past 40 years. During the 1960s, foreign holdings of debt were less than 5 percent of the total debt held by the public. At the end of 2008, foreign holdings of debt were $2.8 trillion, or approximately 48 percent of the public debt. The major owners of foreign debt are China and Japan which account for almost 45 percent of the total debt held by the public.

In terms of total U.S. debt (Government, business, and citizens), foreign interests held almost $9.7 trillion at the end of 2009. In contrast, U.S. entities held about $7.2 trillion of foreign debt at the end of 2008.

The Deficit Commission

With the U.S. deficit estimated to continue at high levels into the future, the White House and senior Democratic officials agreed on January 20, 2010, to create an independent budget commission to recommend fiscal alternatives to curb future deficits.

This follows increasing pressure from both the Democratic and Republican parties to create such a commission as the Senate did not do so as part of the recently passed debt-limit legislation.

The commission was created on February 18, 2010, by an Executive Order[6] from President Obama and is composed of eighteen members that will have autonomous powers to propose amendments to the tax code and entitlement programs. The commission comprises of the following:

- Six members appointed by the President, not more than four of whom shall be from the same political party – Erskine Bowles (Co-Chair), Alan Simpson (Co-Chair), Ann Fudge, David Cote, Alice Rivlin, and Andrew Stern.
- Three members selected by the Majority Leader of the Senate – Dick Durbin (IL), Max Baucus (MT), and Kent Conrad (ND).
- Three members selected by the Speaker of the House of Representatives,– John Spratt (SC), Xavier Becerra (CA), and Jan Schakowsky (IL).
- Three members selected by the Minority Leader of the Senate,– Judd Gregg (NH), Mike Crapo (ID), and Tom Coburn (OK).
- Three members selected by the Minority Leader of the House of Representatives– Dave Camp (MI), Paul Ryan (WI), and Jeb Hensarling (TX).

The commission is to propose recommendations by December 1, 2010, that would lead to a balanced budget (excluding interest payments on the debt) by 2015. At least fourteen members of the commission would have to be in agreement to propose any deficit reduction plan to the President.

While some believe that the commission is vital to ensure the economic stability of the country, others believe that this may just be a budgetary gimmick designed to disguise the actual cost of certain Government programs.

The majority of Democrats believe that the creation of the commission is vital to solve the nation's growing deficit predicament. It was originally proposed by Senate Majority Leader Harry Reid, House Speaker Nancy Pelosi, and House Majority leader Steny Hoyer. Senate Budget Committee Chairman Kent Conrad, a long time campaigner for such a commission, believes the panel "…goes to the country's credibility with managing its own finances. This is essential for the nation[7]." The commission, therefore, is expected to be the centerpiece of the Democratic Party's endeavor to reduce the deficit.

In general, the Republican Party is skeptical about the commission. Congressman Pence, Chairman of the House republican Conference, called the commission "a guard dog with no bite[8]." Republicans are wary that the commission would just be an excuse to

---

[6] Executive Order – National Commission on Fiscal Responsibility and Reform
[7] http://www.washingtonpost.com/wp-dyn/content/article/2010/01/19/AR2010011903310.html
[8] http://www.gop.gov/press-release/10/01/21/pence-calls-president-s-deficit

raise taxes and that the panel would have no authority to recommend cuts in discretionary spending. Senator Judd Gregg, who was a co-sponsor with Senator Conrad forwarding legislation to create a deficit commission by law, has stated that he believes a presidentially created commission would serve purely as a political cover for the Democratic Party.

Independent groups, including some unions and the AARP, have also expressed their concern that the commission does not have any legal authority to change the way the Government spends taxpayer money. Further, many people are of the opinion that the set-up of the commission with ten Democrats and eight Republicans is a recipe for political deadlock on any issues brought before the commission.

Healthcare reform

Although concerns about the deficit and debt have been the focus of much debate about the budget, healthcare reform has been the focus of most of the debate on Federal policy and is the single issue with the largest budgetary implications.

President Obama made healthcare reform his key policy proposal. The stated goals were as follows:

- Make insurance more affordable by providing the largest middle class tax cut for health care in history, reducing premium costs for tens of millions of families and small business owners who are priced out of coverage today. This would help over 31 million Americans afford health care who do not get it today – and makes coverage more affordable for many more.
- Set up a new competitive health insurance market giving tens of millions of Americans the exact same insurance choices that members of Congress will have.
- Bring greater accountability to health care by laying out commonsense rules of the road to keep premiums down and prevent insurance industry abuses and denial of care.
- End discrimination against Americans with pre-existing conditions.
- Put our budget and economy on a more stable path by reducing the deficit by $100 billion over the next ten years – and about $1 trillion over the second decade – by cutting Government overspending and reining in waste, fraud, and abuse.

On March 21, 2010, the House passed the Senate version of a health reform bill and President Obama signed it the next day. Additional measures proposed by the House were adopted by the Senate a few days later.

The legislation would:

- Establish a mandate for most legal residents of the United States to obtain health insurance;
- Set up insurance exchanges through which certain individuals and families could receive Federal subsidies to substantially reduce the cost of purchasing that coverage;
- Significantly expand eligibility for Medicaid;
- Substantially reduce the growth of Medicare's payment rates for most services (relative to the growth rates projected under current law);
- Impose an excise tax on insurance plans with relatively high premiums; and
- Make other changes to the Federal tax code, Medicare, Medicaid, and other programs.

The budgetary effects of the Act have been the subject of much debate. According to estimates made by the CBO, the Act would reduce the deficit by $138 billion over the first ten years and by about $1 trillion over 20 years. The Democrats have used this estimate to argue that the act will help fix both healthcare and the Federal budget deficit and debt.

Republicans, on the other hand, argued that the estimate reflects a variety of budget gimmicks and that the act will actually increase the deficit and debt in the coming years. The most outspoken critic of the budgetary effects was Republican Representative Paul Ryan of Wisconsin, the Ranking Minority member of the House Budget Committee and a member of the House Ways and Means Committee. His arguments are summarized as follows:

- **Timing Gimmicks**

    - The legislation includes ten years of tax increases and ten years of Medicare cuts to pay for six years of spending.
    - The CBO cost estimate of the health care overhaul is derived from the March 2009 baseline – instead of the March 2010 baseline, which has already been released. The outdated cost estimate hides the true price tag.

- **Double-Counting**

    - Democrats claim that their Medicare cuts will extend the program's solvency and reduce the cost of the bill. If double-counting of Medicare cuts, the savings from Social Security payroll taxes, and the CLASS are eliminated, the deficit increases by $460 billion over first ten years – and $1.4 trillion over the second ten years.

- ○ $53 billion in "savings" is claimed by counting increased Social Security payroll revenues. These dollars are already claimed for future Social Security beneficiaries.
- ○ $70 billion in savings is claimed from the CLASS Act – long-term care insurance. These savings are not offsets, but rather premiums collected to pay for future benefits.
- ○ More than $500 billion in Medicare cuts cannot be counted twice. Using Medicare as a piggy bank, the legislation raids nearly a half-trillion dollars from retirees' health coverage to fund the creation of another open-ended health care entitlement.

- **Hidden Spending**

  - – The CBO estimate does not include at least $70 billion in appropriations that will be required to implement the legislation. In a letter to Senator Reid, the CBO Director said that discretionary appropriation costs "…would probably include an estimated $5 billion to $10 billion over 10 years for administrative costs of the Internal Revenue Service (IRS) and at least a similar amount for expenses of the Department of Health and Human Services (HHS)" and "…at least $50 billion in specified and estimated authorizations of future discretionary spending for a number of grant programs and other provisions of the legislation…"
  - – All early iterations of the health care legislation in both the House and Senate included the prevention of scheduled cuts in Medicare physician payments – known as "the doc fix." The OMB has estimated that the cost of the doc fix would add an additional $371 billion to the cost of the legislation. With the price tag beyond what most Americans could handle, the Majority decided to remove this provision and deal with it in separate legislation.

In response to the Republican arguments, the Democrats pointed to the CBO estimate as an independent assessment and generally did not respond to the specific complaints of the Republicans. However, on March 4, 2010, Peter Orszag, Director of the OMB, made the following comments about the Republicans' claim of the timing gimmick:

> "Recently, a lot of attention has been paid to a claim that this deficit reduction is achieved only through a business-as-usual Washington budget gimmick: paying for just a few years of costs with many more years of savings.
>
> This charge is simply false—and let's get the facts straight.

- First, it's true that loading savings upfront and costs in later years is a time-honored budget gimmick. It has a single purpose—to hide the ball and make programs look paid for in the near term that will in fact substantially add to the deficit over the long-term.

- Second, it's also true that some of the savings under the health plan start sooner than the major costs in the legislation. We can move quickly to begin identifying waste and improving quality in the current health care system, as well as make certain reforms to rebalance the tax code. But, the major coverage expansion does not occur until 2014, in part because we need to take time to establish a system of state-based exchanges through which private insurance companies will provide quality insurance to those not getting it through their employer.

- Third, this is not a budget gimmick. The purpose the tried-and-true gimmick described above is to make a proposal that adds to long-term deficits appear fiscally responsible. But if that were the course we were taking, we would expect to see a large fiscal hole at the end of the first decade and larger and larger deficits in the second decade. Instead, over the long-term, the savings under the President's plan are expected to *grow faster* than the costs. So, when the Congressional Budget Office is done with its scoring, we expect it will find that the President's plan reduces deficits by roughly $100 billion in the first 10 years and roughly $1 trillion in the decade after that. In other words, health reform should reduce the deficit by growing amounts over the long-term."

Since passage of the bill, some Democrats have claimed that passage of the bill was directed at wealth distribution as much as it was directed at healthcare. Health reform is "an income shift," Democratic Sen. Max Baucus said on March 25. "It is a shift, a leveling, to help lower income, middle income Americans."

Baucus explained that in recent years "the maldistribution of income in America has gone up way too much, the wealthy are getting way, way too wealthy, and the middle income class is left behind." The new health care legislation, Baucus promised, "will have the effect of addressing that maldistribution of income in America."

At about the same time, Howard Dean, the former Democratic National Committee chairman and presidential candidate, said the health bill was needed to correct economic inequities. "The question is, in a democracy, what is the right balance between those at the top ... and those at the bottom?" Dean said during an appearance on CNBC. "When it gets out of whack, as it did in the 1920s, and it has now, you need to do some redistribution. This is a form of redistribution."[9]

---

[9] Washington Examiner, Obamacare was mainly aimed at redistributing wealth By: Byron York Chief Political Correspondent, April 2, 2010

The arguments from both sides demonstrate how difficult it is to determine precisely what the long-term costs will be for a bill that includes many revenue and spending provisions.

Banking Regulations and the Fed

On January 21, 2010, President Obama announced his proposal for stricter regulations governing banks and other financial institutions in an attempt to curb or prohibit risky activities and to protect the nation's taxpayers. The proposal would affect some of the biggest banks, including bank of America Corp., Goldman Sachs, and Citigroup Inc.

Following consultation from former chairman of the Federal Reserve, Paul Volcker, former chairman of the Securities and Exchange Commission (SEC), Bill Donaldson, House Financial Services Chairman Congressman Barney Frank, Chairman of the Banking Committee, Senator Chris Dodd, and other members of the President's economic team, President Obama proposed his initiative that would further strengthen the financial reform package that is currently being discussed in the Senate. The proposal would include:

- Limiting the scope of banks or financial institutions to ensure that they cannot own, invest in, or sponsor a hedge fund or a private equity fund, or proprietary trading operations unrelated to serving customers for its own profit;
- Limiting the size of banks or financial institutions by placing broader limits on the excessive growth of the market share of liabilities at the largest financial institutions, and to supplement existing caps on the market share of deposits; and
- Banning banks that accept deposits from also trading stocks for their own profit. [10]

The proposal follows the recent passing of the *Wall Street Reform and Consumer Protection Act of 2009* (H.R. 4173) in the House of Representatives. Sponsored by House Financial Services Commission Chairman Barney Frank, the legislation would establish a new Consumer Financial Protection Agency to regulate products like home mortgages, car loans, and credit cards. It would also give the Treasury Department new authority to place non-bank financial firms such as insurance companies into receivership and regulate the over-the-counter derivatives market. In addition, it would direct the Comptroller General to audit and report to Congress on all actions taken by the Board of Governors of the Federal Reserve System. Further, it would establish a Financial Services Oversight Council, consisting of the heads of specified federal financial regulatory bodies and chaired by the Secretary of the Treasury, to oversee the following including but not limited to:

---

[10] Source: White House Statement on Obama Bank Regulation Plan, January 21, 2010.

- Resolving disputes among two or more Federal financial regulatory agencies in specified circumstances;
- Subjecting a financial company to stricter prudential standards;
- Requiring that a financial holding company undertake one or more mitigation actions to address any grave threat its activities pose to the financial stability or economy of the United States; and
- Directing the Federal Reserve Board to impose stricter prudential standards on a financial holding company in certain circumstances.

Democratic Party members have been strong advocates for the new proposals. The bill carried in the House of Representatives by a vote of 228 to 203. The Republican Party, however, has voiced its strong disapproval of the proposal. During the House vote, all Republicans voted against a section of the bill that would allow the Government to force healthy companies out of business if they were deemed a threat to the financial system. Further, strong opposition to the bill on the Republican side came from concerns over the creation of gigantic Government bureaucracies which they say will limit access to credit. Because of the lack of Republican support, it is unlikely that the bill will pass through the Senate, especially since the Democratic Party no longer holds the sixty seats necessary to stop a filibuster.

Chapter 2

Federal Budget Law

The Congress shall have power to lay and collect taxes, duties, imposts and excises, to pay the debts and provide for the common defense and general welfare of the United States; but all duties, imposts and excises shall be uniform throughout the United States.

U.S. Constitution, Article 1, Section 8

Origins of Federal Budget Law

Without the authority to levy taxes and generate revenues, the Federal Government under The Articles of Confederation was significantly restricted. The authority to develop and fund a Federal budget was first granted to the United States Congress in Article I, § 8 of the U.S. Constitution, making it the first U.S. budget law and the starting point for all U.S. budget legislation. Its simple language was interpreted to grant Congress the power to authorize expenditures of Federal funds. This authority is so important and ingrained in our understanding of the operation of the Federal Government that it is difficult to imagine how our government would function otherwise. For these reasons, the power to tax and spend is considered one, if not the most important, of all Congress' powers.

Funding levels, funding priorities, and approaches to developing a budget differ with each new Administration. The legislation associated with the budget process changes less frequently and is codified in various statutes governing the formulation and execution of the budget.

The Executive Branch initiates the formal budget process when it submits a comprehensive budget to Congress. There is debate about the degree of influence this version of the Budget has over the final product and many view the President's version as little more than an explicit view of the Administration's policy priorities. However, even though the President's Budget has no legally binding effect, the overwhelming majority of the President's Budget (typically, more than 90 percent) is appropriated as submitted. Meanwhile, changes to the President's Budget by Congress are typically associated with big policy issues and partisan concerns.

The following laws are considered the most influential legislation affecting the Federal budget process and are discussed in this chapter:

- Anti-deficiency Act. 31 U.S.C. §§ 1341-1342, 1349-1351, 1511-1519 (1994);
- Budget and Accounting Act. P.L. 67-13, 42 Stat. 20 (1921);
- Budget & Accounting Procedures Act. 31 U.S.C. 3512 et seq. (1950);
- Congressional Budget and Impoundment Control Act. P.L. 93-344 (1974);
- Balanced Budget and Emergency Deficit Control Act of 1985 and Budget and Emergency Deficit Control Reaffirmation Act of 1987. P.L. 99-177 and P.L. 100-119 (Collectively, the Gramm-Rudman-Hollings Act);
- Budget Enforcement Act, Title XIII of the Federal Credit Reform Act of 1990. P.L. 101-508, as amended by 2 U.S.C. 661, et seq. (1990); and
- Government Performance and Results Act. P.L. 103-62 (1993).

Several statutes, regulations, and guidance requirements that affect the formulation and transparency of the budget and accountability of the branches of the Government have a direct, albeit lesser, impact on the Federal budget process; they are summarized below. The following Table 2-1 provides a comprehensive, categorical summary of laws category that directly affect the Federal budget process.

Additionally, there are many laws indirectly impacting the formulation of the Budget. For example, certain labor requirements (e.g., Davis-Bacon) and environmental requirements (e.g., National Environmental Policy Act, NEPA) are applied to Government programs by statute or regulation. While laws that indirectly affect the Budget are beyond the scope of this chapter, it is important to note that their application has significant implications. Further, court decisions played a role in the development of Federal budget law but have been incorporated into applicable legislation. As such, while the impact of the judiciary on the Federal budget process is subsumed within the content of this chapter, this topic is not independently addressed.

Table 2-1
Federal Budget Laws

Budget Formulation Laws	
Budget and Accounting Act of 1921, as amended (P.L. 67-13) (31 U.S.C. 701, et seq.)	• Requires the President to coordinate the budget requests for all Government agencies and send a comprehensive budget to Congress. • Requires the President to include specified information in the Budget.
The Executive Reorganization Plan—1 (1939)	• Relocates the Bureau of the Budget from the Treasury Department to the Executive Office of the President (EOP). Using the Bureau of the Budget, the Executive's power over the budget increased.
Special Studies and Work (1970) (P.L 91- 412) (15 U.S.C. 1525, 1526, and 1527)	• Authorizes Commerce to make special studies on matters within its authority. • Provides that Commerce may engage joint projects and perform services on matters of mutual interest with non-profit, research, and public organizations/agencies if costs are equitably apportioned.
The Executive Reorganization Plan—2 (1970)	• The name of the Bureau of the Budget is changed to the Office of Management and Budget (OMB). • Requires all executive departments, agencies, and other bureaucratic units to funnel budget requests through OMB, centralizing the Executive Branch's budget process with the idea that the budget could be used as a management tool.
The Gramm-Rudman-Hollings Balanced Budget and Emergency Deficit Control Act of 1985 (P.L. 99-177) and Budget and Emergency Deficit Control Reaffirmation Act of 1987 (P.L. 100-119) (Collectively, the Gramm-Rudman-Hollings Act)	• Sets annual deficit targets facilitating a balanced budget. • Increases the statutory limit on public debt. • The enforcement mechanism was sequestration, which altered the budget schedule slightly and provided for OMB and CBO to examine the preliminary budget by August 15.[1]

The Budget Enforcement Act of 1990[2], Title XIII of the Federal Credit Reform Act of 1990 (P.L. 101-508, as amended by 2 U.S.C. 661, et seq.)	• Divides spending into two types – discretionary and mandatory.
	• Creates the PAYGO rule for mandatory spending and receipts.
	• Prescribes new budget treatment for Federal credit programs to manage f Federal credit program costs more accurately:
	  – Placed the cost of credit programs on a budgetary basis;
	  – Required calculation of subsidy elements of credit programs;
	  – Encourages improved effectiveness in delivery of benefits to beneficiaries; and
	  – Improved allocation of limited financial resources among credit and other spending programs.
	• This act was extended several times, expired in 2002, and is currently on President Obama's and the 111th Congress' agenda for renewal.
	• Resulted in the formation of the Credit Reform Task Force, a work group to address accounting, auditing, budgeting, and reporting issues encountered by agencies subject to the Federal Credit Reform Act of 1990.

Omnibus Budget Reconciliation Act of 1993 (P.L. 103-66)	• Limits spending by extending the 2% per year maximum increase on discretionary spending. • This is no longer applicable law; however, legislation is currently under consideration which may result in a similar approach under the Obama Administration.
Government Performance and Results Act of 1993 (P.L. 103-62)	• Creates requirement for performance goals to be included with the annual budget submissions and a report on actual performance in March each year after the end of the fiscal year. • The Act is intended to bring about fundamental changes in the way government programs and operations are managed and administered.

---

[1] Sequestration is when the Comptroller General (the Head of the GAO) recommends the President issue a percentage cut of all discretionary programs in the Federal budget to reach a deficit reduction goal.
[2] Title XIII of the Omnibus Budget Reconciliation Act of 1990 (OBRA).

Contract with America Advancement Act of 1996 (P.L. 104-121)	• Provides for an increase in the public debt limit.
Balanced Budget Act of 1997 (P.L. 105-33)	• Set caps on discretionary spending for fiscal years 1998 through 2002.

Congressional Budget Process Laws	
U.S. Constitution	• Requires that appropriations be enacted before outlays occur. • Requires that revenue legislation be initiated in the House of Representatives.
Congressional Budget and Impoundment Control Act of 1974 (P.L. 93-344)	• Creates the Congressional budget process and Congressional Budget Office (CBO), centralizing the Congressional budget process. This was preceded by the Joint Committee on the Reduction of Federal Expenditures which was created by the Revenue Act of 1941. • Establishes process to add up receipts and total spending in all the bills to reach the Federal Government's bottom-line.
Unfunded Mandates Reform Act of 1995 (P.L. 104-4)	• Intended to "curb the practice of imposing unfunded Federal mandates," the act results in information about potential Federal mandates on other levels of government and the private sector for Congress and agency decision-makers to consider proposed legislation and regulations.

Budget Execution and Accountability Laws	
U.S. Constitution	• Grants Congress the *power to lay and collect taxes, duties, imposts and excises, to pay the debts and provide for the common defense and general welfare of the United States.* Supreme Court interprets this to permit Congress authorization of Federal funds expenditures. • Requires the Executive to report on spending.

Anti-Deficiency Act (31 U.S.C. §§ 1341-1342, 1349-1350, 1511-1519 (1994))	• Prohibits:
	  – Making/authorizing/creating an expenditure or obligation under any appropriation/fund or apportionment/reapportionment exceeding the amount available unless authorized by law;
	  – Involving the government in any monetary obligation before funds have been appropriated for that purpose; and
	  – Accepting voluntary services for the U.S. or employing personal services not authorized by law, except in cases of emergency involving the safety of human life or the protection of property;
	• Establishes associated sanctions and reporting requirements.

The Economy Act of 1932 (31 U.S.C. 1535)	• Prescribes rules for purchase of supplies, equipment, or service by one Federal Government bureau/department from another.
The Legislative Reorganization Act of 1946 (P.L. 79-601)	• The first public law that explicitly calls for "legislative oversight," it directs House and Senate standing committees "to exercise continuous watchfulness" over programs and agencies under their jurisdiction. • Creates the Joint Committee on the Legislative Budget which was to meet at the beginning of each session of Congress and report a legislative budget for the ensuing fiscal year. No attempts were made to comply with the Act after 1949.

Accounting and Auditing Act of 1950 (P.L. 81-784) (31 U.S.C. 66A)	• Establishes Government-wide policies for accounting and auditing:
	  – Full disclosure financial operations results;
	  – Full consideration to the needs and responsibilities of the Legislative and Executive branches when setting accounting and reporting systems and requirements;
	  – Executive branch maintenance of accounting systems and production of financial reports on operations of agencies;
	  – Conduct of audits by the Comptroller General;
	  – Emphasis on simplifying and increased accounting, financial reporting, budgeting and auditing, effectiveness; and
	  – Continuous improvement of accounting and financial reporting.

Budget and Accounting Procedures Act of 1950, as amended (31 U.S.C. 3501, et seq.)	• Requires warrants from Treasury for appropriated funds. • Requires apportionment of appropriated funds. • Requires GAO to set accounting standards. • Directs the Comptroller General of the U.S. to prescribe the principles, standards, and related requirements for accounting to be observed by executive agencies after consulting with the Secretary of the Treasury and the President. • Sets the responsibility parties for establishing and maintaining adequate systems of accounting and internal control, and preparing audited financial statements of agency revolving and trust funds and other activities which involve substantial commercial functions. • Requires the use of accrual accounting, cost-based budgeting, consistent classification, simplifications of allotment structure, and adequate control of property.
Title V of the Independent Office Appropriations Act of 1952 (31 U.S.C. 9701)	• Authorizes Federal agencies to assess charges/fees for Government services and the sale/use of Government property/resources. • Requires fair and equitable fees with consideration of direct and indirect cost to the Government, value to the recipient, public policy/interest served, and other pertinent facts. • Designates that collected amounts be paid into the Treasury as miscellaneous receipts.
The Supplemental Appropriations Act of 1955 (31 U.S.C. 1501)	• Provides that an obligation is only enforceable when is in writing to avoid inappropriate spending based on oral obligations and the balance of an appropriation limited to a definite period is available only for payment of expenses incurred during that period.
Closing Accounts (31 U.S.C. 1551-1557)	• Provides procedures for closing appropriation accounts with defined end dates. • Establishes the availability of appropriation accounts to pay obligations. • Addresses audit, control, and reporting requirements applicable after an account's availability for obligation ends.
Federal Claims Collection Act of 1966 (31 U.S.C. 3701, 3702, 3716, 3719) (Note: also the Code of Federal Regulations, Title 4, Chapter II, Parts 101-105)	• Prescribes procedures for follow-up on claims against parties owing the Federal Government money, including amounts owed because of audit follow-ups.
Freedom of Information Act (1974) (P.L. 89-554)	• Establishes the public's right to obtain information from Federal Government agencies.
Federal Banking Agency Audit Act (1978) (P.L. 95-320)	• Amends the Accounting and Auditing Act of 1950 to authorize GAO to conduct independent audits of the Federal Reserve System, the Federal Deposit Insurance Corporation (FDIC), and the Office of the Comptroller of the Currency. • Prohibits the GAO from auditing specified transactions and documents.
Federal Managers Financial Integrity Act of 1982 (P.L. 97-255)	• Amends the Accounting and Auditing Act of 1950 to require Federal agencies to establish internal accounting and administrative controls to prevent waste or misuse of agency fund or property and to ensure the accountability of assets.
Prompt Payment Act of 1982 (P.L. 97-452)(31 U.S.C. 3901 et seq.)	• The Act calls for payment of bills not later than due dates based on the receipt of proper invoices and satisfactory performance, as well as payment of any interest and penalties. The Act also stresses the importance of taking cash discounts.
Cash Management Improvement Act of 1990 (P.L. 101-453) as amended by the Cash Management Improvement Act of 1992 (P.L. 102-589)	• Improves the transfer of Federal funds between the Federal Government and the States, territories, and the District of Columbia. (The goal was to minimize the time associated with transfers of funds and payouts for program purposes.)
Chief Financial Officers Act of 1990 (P.L. 101-576 (31 U.S.C. 501 et seq.))	• The Act requires long-range financial planning, audited financial statements, integration of budget and accounting data, and development of cost information. It also establishes the financial

The Government Management Reform Act of 1994 (P.L. 103-356)	• Limits annual cost of living adjustments for Members of Congress, the Vice President, senior Government officials, and Federal judges.
	• Eliminates unlimited accumulation of annual leave by members of the Senior Executive Service, with a limit on excess leave of 90 d/yr.
	• Authorizes the Director of OMB to publish annually in the President's Budget any recommendations for the consolidation, elimination, or adjustment in frequency and due dates of statutorily required periodic reports to the Congress or its committees.
	• Requires direct deposit of Federal wage, salary, and retirement payments by electronic funds transfer for recipients who begin receiving such payments on or after January 1, 1995.
	  – Authorizes establishment of a franchise fund in six executive agencies for equipment and computer systems for maintenance and operation of administrative support services.
	  – Authorizes the Director of OMB to consolidate/adjust the frequency and due dates of statutorily required, periodic agency reports.
	  – Requires financial statements audit prior to OMB submission.

Debt Collection Improvement Act of 1996 (P. L. 104-134) (31 U.S.C. 3332)	• Enhances debt collection Government-wide; • Mandates the use of electronic funds Transfer (EFT) for Federal payments; • Allows Federal Reserve Bank Treasury Check Offset; • Provides funding for the Check Forgery Insurance Fund; • Provides that any non-tax debt or claim owed to the U.S. and delinquent for greater than 180 days be turned over to the Secretary of Treasury. • Requires Treasury to use computer matching so those owed money by the government are not sent multiple checks simultaneously; and • Permits Treasury to deduct delinquent debt from government payments such as tax refunds, wages, and retirement and benefit payments.
Line-Item Veto Act of 1996 (P.L. 104-130)	• This act authorized the President to cancel line items in appropriations and tax acts, but was ruled unconstitutional by the Supreme Court of the United States in 1998.
Federal Financial Management Improvement Act of 1996 (FFMIA) (P.L. 104-208, Div A, Title I, sec. 101(f), [Title VIII, sec. 801 et seq.) (31 U.S.C. 3512 note)	• The Federal Financial Management Improvement Act requires that each agency implement and maintain financial management systems that comply with Federal requirements, applicable Federal accounting standards, and the Standard General Ledger at the transaction level.
Federal Funding Accountability and Transparency Act of 2006 (P.L. 109-282)	• Requires the Office of Management and Budget to make information on Federal contracts and grants publicly accessible through a searchable website.

Key Budget Legislation

The following is an overview of the major Federal budget legislation.

The Anti-Deficiency Act

The Anti-Deficiency Act is the primary statute through which Congress exercises its constitutional control of the public purse. This legislation primarily affects budget execution and accountability.

Its first version was passed in 1870 and it has evolved over the years in response to various real and perceived political abuses involving the budget process. This law made it a criminal offense for an officer or employee of the United States Government or the District of Columbia to make or authorize an expenditure or obligation exceeding available funds.

In its current form, the law prohibits:

- Making or authorizing expenditure from, or creating or authorizing an obligation under, any appropriation or fund in excess of the amount available in the appropriation or fund unless authorized by law;[1]
- Involving the Government in any obligation to pay money before funds have been appropriated, unless otherwise allowed by law;[2]
- Accepting voluntary services for the United States, or employing personal services not authorized by law, except in cases of emergency involving the safety of human life or the protection of property;[3] and
- Making obligations or expenditures in excess of an apportionment or reapportionment, or in excess of the amount permitted by agency regulations.[4]

Furthermore, this Act establishes sanctions and reporting requirements associated with its prohibitions.

The Government Accountability Office (GAO) compiles information on violations of the Anti-Deficiency Act arranged by fiscal year using reports received pursuant to section 1401 of the Consolidated Appropriations Act, 2005.[5]

An example of how the Anti-Deficiency Act comes into play in the conduct of Federal affairs can be found in a 1999 Department of Energy (DOE) memorandum which addresses the question of whether multi-year contracts are exempt from the full funding requirements of the Act.[6]

The Budget and Accounting Act

The Budget and Accounting Act was the first law to establish annual centralized budgeting in the Executive Branch. This legislation primarily affects budget formulation.

Before this law was enacted, Federal Government agencies sent budget requests independently to congressional committees with no coordination of the various requests.[7] Under the Act, the President alone is responsible each year for submitting a statement of the condition of the treasury, estimated revenues, expenditures of the Government,

---

[1] 31 U.S.C. § 1341(a)(1)(A).
[2] 31 U.S.C. § 1341(a)(1)(B).
[3] 31 U.S.C. § 1342.
[4] 31 U.S.C. § 1517(a).
[5] P. L. 108-447, 118 Stat. 2809, 3192 (Dec. 8, 2004)
[6] United States. Department of Energy. "Relationship of the Anti-Deficiency Act to Multi-year Contracts Under the Utility Incentive Program Authorized Under Section 152(f) of EPACT." Comp. Mark S. Schwartz. June 22, 1999.
[7] OMB Circular No. A-11 (2006).

and proposals for meeting revenue needs to Congress. The President coordinates budget requests for all Government agencies and sends a comprehensive budget to Congress annually. Current law requires the President to send his budget proposal to Congress no later than the first Monday in February.[8] It also requires the President to include certain information in the Budget—the requirements, as amended, are codified in Chapter 11, Title 31, U.S. Code.

Furthermore, the Act created two Government offices that play an integral part in the budget process:

- The Bureau of Budget (later renamed the Office of Management and Budget, OMB), which assists the President in preparing budget recommendations for submission to Congress.
- The GAO, which is the principal auditing arm of the Federal Government.

President Warren Harding, who signed the legislation into law, called it 'the greatest reformation in governmental practice since the beginning of the Republic." Though it is relatively simple legislation with few provisions its impact is significant. The Act is a component of the reform movement of the early twentieth century focused on creating neutral processes and agencies to perform public functions. The goal was then, as it is now, to reduce (or remove) politics from the administration and delivery of government services.

The Budget & Accounting Procedures Act

The Budget and Accounting Procedures Act of 1950 amended the Anti-Deficiency Act. This legislation primarily affects budget execution and accountability.
It required apportionment to be performed by the Office of Management and Budget (OMB) and a fund control system to be run by the Department of the Treasury. Further, it made GAO responsible for government-wide accounting standards. Civil and criminal penalties for violations to the Anti-Deficiency Act were enhanced.

This act directs the Comptroller General of the United States to prescribe the principles, standards, and related requirements for accounting by executive agencies subsequent to consulting with the Secretary of the Treasury and the President. The Act made each executive agency head responsible for establishing and maintaining adequate systems of accounting and internal control and preparing audited financial statements of agency revolving and trust funds and other activities which involve substantial commercial functions. The use of accrual accounting, cost-based budgeting, consistent classification, simplifications of allotment structure, and adequate control of property is required to establish and maintain adequate systems of accounting and internal control. Furthermore, accrual accounting enhances the ability of agencies to execute cost-based budgeting.

---

[8] 31 U.S.C. §1105(a).

The Congressional Budget and Impoundment Control Act

This act was Congress' response to growing tension between U.S. Executive and Legislative branches. The legislation they passed primarily affects the Congressional budget process.

Congress and the White House were conflicted over the exercise of authority via the U.S. budget. President Nixon's refusal to spend appropriated monies (called "impoundment") was a flashpoint, for example. Committees in both the House and Senate met and made recommendations that resulted in the Congressional Budget and Impoundment Control Act having three purposes:

- Reassert the congressional role in the budget process;
- Utilize a centralized congressional process to influence to the Federal Budget; and
- Constrain the use of impoundments.

To accomplish these goals, the Congressional Budget and Impoundment Control Act created the congressional budget process, the Congressional Budget Office (CBO), and the House and Senate Budget Committees. This act established annual, centralized budgeting in the Legislative Branch (previously, regular appropriations bills were acted on separately by Congress and changes in taxes were authorized in separate process with no established process to reach the Federal Government's bottom line by accounting for receipts and total spending across bills).

Section 300 of the this act provided a timetable for Congress to complete its budget work by the start of the fiscal year on October 1; however, Congress does not usually meet the deadlines in this timetable.[9] (Table 2-2)

Table 2-2
The Congressional Budget Process Timetable

Date	Action to be completed
First Monday in February	President submits Budget to Congress.
February 15	Congressional Budget Office submits economic and budget outlook report to Budget Committees.
Six weeks after President submits Budget	Committees submit views and estimates to Budget Committees.
April 1	Senate Budget Committee reports budget resolution.
April 15	Congress completes action on budget resolution.
May 15	Annual appropriations bills may be considered in the House, even if action on budget resolution has not been completed.
June 10	House Appropriations Committee reports last annual appropriations bill.
June 15	House completes action on reconciliation legislation (if required by budget resolution).
June 30	House completes action on annual appropriations bills.
July 15	President submits mid-session review of his Budget to Congress.
October 1	Fiscal year begins.

[9] Heniff, Bill, CRS Report for Congress, The Congressional Budget Process Timetable, July 17, 2003. 7 31 U.S.C. § 1341(a)(1)(A).

This act also codified the President's impoundment authority in Title X by dividing impoundments into two distinct classes with different procedures for congressional consideration:

- Rescissions (or permanent cancellations) of budget authority which would require congressional approval, and
- Temporary deferrals of expenditures, which would remain in force unless rejected by Congress.

Jurisdiction over both was assigned to the House and Senate Appropriations Committees.

The fallout from this legislation, though generally considered successful in reasserting congressional authority over the Federal budget, has not been entirely positive. Critics argue the act failed to:

- Bring order and timeliness to congressional budget action—i.e. deadlines for enacting budget resolutions and the passing of appropriation bills are often not met; and
- Decrease or maintain congressional budgetary conflict—with the addition of Budget Committees and centralized decision-making, authority and power are spread across additional layers of responsibility and procedures resulting in repetitious treatment of single issues.

The Gramm-Rudman-Hollings Act

The Balanced Budget and Emergency Deficit Act, commonly known as the Gramm-Rudman-Hollings Act, was passed amidst concern over large and growing Federal deficits during the 1980s and a failure by the Federal Government to raise taxes or cut spending sufficiently to resolve the problem. The legislation attempted to control deficits through spending cuts.

The act specified a schedule of gradually declining deficit targets toward a 1991 balanced budget. It also specified that if the Administration and Congress were unable to reach agreement on a deficit targets specified in the bill, automatic and across-the-board spending reductions would be implemented in all programs except Social Security, interest payments on the national debt, and certain low-income entitlements. This process of automatic cuts was known as sequestration.

Specifically, the Gramm-Rudman-Hollings Act:

- Established annual deficit targets leading to a balanced budget by 1991 and created a sequester process to eliminate excess spending;[10]
- Increased the statutory limit on the public debt;

---

[10] Sequestration is when the Comptroller General (the Head of the GAO) recommends the President issue a percentage cut of all discretionary programs in the federal budget to reach a deficit reduction goal.

- Set annual deficit targets facilitating a balanced budget; and
- Increased the statutory limit on public debt.

Two years later, Congress postponed the target year for balancing the Federal budget.

Budget Enforcement Act

Notwithstanding the Balanced Budget and Emergency Deficit Act, deficits continued at high levels. In 1990 Congress was faced with a deficit of $110 billion. It then enacted the Budget Enforcement Act (BEA) which made the deficit targets more flexible and extended the target date for balancing the budget until 1995. The Act was amended several times to extend the budget targets through 2002. The legislation primarily affects budget formulation.

The BEA had the following specific results:

- Divided spending into *discretionary* and *mandatory* and applied different rules to each;
- Set limits or caps on the amount of discretionary appropriations for fiscal years 1991 through 1995
- Created the PAYGO rule[11] for mandatory spending and receipts;
- Created the sequester process to remove excess funds if discretionary or mandatory spending exceeded the new limits; and
- Placed the cost of credit programs on a budgetary basis:
    - Required calculation of subsidy elements of credit programs; and
    - Required the Government to budget for the subsidy costs of credit programs.

As part of the BEA, the Federal Credit Reform Act of 1990 (FCRA) was enacted to provide a more realistic picture of the cost of U.S. Government direct loans and loan guarantees. Before this Act, loans and loan guarantees were accounted for on a cash flow basis. This cash basis of accounting made loans appear relatively costly due to the immediate cash payments required and conversely made loan guarantees appear inexpensive due to a lack of immediate cash payments. This approach did not yield meaningful comparisons of the costs of loans and loan guarantees, or comparisons to the costs of other programs.

New procedures in the FCRA allowed for these cost of comparisons. This was accomplished by a method where credit programs have budget authority to cover the net present value of their subsidy costs. For a loan, subsidy costs reflect the present value of the difference between the loan and expected interest, repayment, and other cash flows. For a loan guarantee, subsidy costs reflect the present value of expected default costs and other cash flows, such as a fee for obtaining the guarantee. Credit subsidy costs calculations occur when a new direct loan or loan guarantee is made, during annual re-estimates, and when other modifications to the loan or loan guarantee occur, including loan sales.

---

[11] The requirement that legislation increasing spending or decreasing revenues be on a pay-as-you-go basis.

Furthermore, the BEA resulted in the formation of the Credit Reform Task Force, a work group to address accounting, auditing, budgeting, and reporting issues encountered by agencies subject to the Federal Credit Reform Act of 1990.

The Accounting and Auditing Policy Committee (AAPC) and Credit Reform Task Force

The AAPC was organized in May 1997 by OMB, GAO, the Department of Treasury (Treasury), the Chief Financial Officers' Council (CFO), and the President's Council on Integrity and Efficiency (PCIE), as a new body to research accounting and auditing issues requiring guidance. The AAPC formed the Credit Reform Task Force, composed of members of Treasury, GAO, OMB, and representatives from all the credit agencies, as a work group to address accounting, auditing, budgeting, and reporting issues encountered by agencies subject to the Federal Credit Reform Act of 1990. The Chief Financial Officer (CFO) Subcommittee on Credit Reform and the Government-wide Audited Financial Statement Task Force Subcommittee on Credit Reform were merged into this group, which meets periodically to discuss and resolve credit-specific issues.

This act was extended several times, expired in 2002, and is currently on President Obama's and the 111th Congress' agenda for reconsideration.

Government Performance and Results Act (GPRA)

Enacted in 1993, this legislation requires agencies to prepare strategic plans and annual performance plans, as well as annual program performance reports to the President and Congress beginning with FY 1999. It mandates a link between program performance and budgeting.

GPRA is intended to bring about fundamental changes in the way Government programs and operations are managed and administered.

This act represents a shift the focus of Government decision-making and accountability on the results generated rather than the activities undertaken such as grants dispensed or inspections made. This means measurements of real gains in employability, safety, responsiveness, or program quality, for example.

Transparency and Accountability

The tension between the values of an open government and the values of privacy are especially acute. The cost of freedom of information laws at national and local levels has long been a matter of intense public debate. Budget transparency is necessary to keep the public informed and to facilitate intra-governmental debate. Tension over the level of budget transparency grew under the Bush Administration, which was viewed as one of the most secretive administrations to occupy the White House in decades. During that Administration, the congressional earmarking process dominated newspaper headlines and transparency became a talking point for nearly all domestic political campaigns.

Several statutes have been enacted and policies implemented to facilitate the dissemination of Government work product and information. Other laws have been passed that push for greater accountability in Government spending and loan programs (and loan guarantee programs). However, it seems likely that the demand for greater transparency and oversight will continue as long as allegations of waste, corruption, and pork-for-profit schemes surface. Enacted in 1966, The Freedom of Information Act is the key Federal statutory law that establishes the public's right to obtain information from Federal Government agencies.[12]

- **Freedom of Information Act (FOIA).** "Any person" can file a FOIA request, including U.S. citizens, foreign nationals, organizations, associations, and universities. In 1974, after the Watergate scandal, the Act was amended to force greater agency compliance. In 1976, Exemption 3 was amended as part of the Government in Sunshine Act. It was also amended in 1996 to allow for greater access to electronic information. In 1986, FOIA was amended to address fees charged by different categories of requesters and the scope of access to law enforcement and national security records. In 2002, in the wake of the 9/11 attacks, the FOIA was amended to limit foreign agents' ability to request records from U.S. intelligence agencies.

    FOIA applies to Executive Branch departments, agencies, and offices; Federal regulatory agencies; and Federal corporations. Congress, the Federal Courts, and parts of the Executive Office of the President that function solely to advise and assist the President, are not subject to the FOIA. Records obtainable under the FOIA include all "agency records" - such as print documents, photographs, videos, maps, e-mail, and electronic records - that were created or obtained by a Federal agency and are, at the time the request is filed, in that agency's possession and control.

    There are several exemptions that permit a Government agency to withhold information from the public. One such exemption is Exemption (b)(5) which denies public access to Inter- or intra-agency communication that is subject to deliberative process, litigation, and other privileges.

    This FOIA exemption and the Executive Privilege Doctrine provide a legal basis for the Executive Branch to withhold certain types of information. Many times, when information is not forthcoming the involved party will invoke FOIA exemption (b)(5) by claiming that the requested information is pre-decisional. Pre-decisional information and work product does not have be released under FOIA.

- **Federal Funding Accountability and Transparency Act.** A recent effort by lawmakers to force greater transparency upon the Federal Government occurred

---

[12] 5 U.S.C. § 552, as amended in 2002.

on April 6, 2006 when a bipartisan group of Federal legislators introduced the Federal Funding Accountability and Transparency Act (S. 2590). The Senators introduced the legislation because they believed the public lacked access to timely, accurate information about individual contracts, grants, and other forms of Government financial assistance. The bill was signed into law by President George W. Bush on September 26, 2006.

The bill requires the Office of Management and Budget (OMB) to make Federal contracts and grants information publicly accessible through a searchable website. The website would allow the public to search for information about Federal:

- Contracts;
- Grants, including block grants, formula grants, and project grants;
- Cooperative Agreements; Loans (including direct loans, guaranteed loans, and insured loans);
- Direct payments for specified (e.g., financial aid) and unrestricted use (e.g., pensions, veterans benefits);
- Insurance; and
- Indirect financial assistance.

Proposal for amending the Constitution—Balanced Budget Amendment

Deficit spending has many critics. Among those critics are those that claim that a system that allows for deficit spending is the result of unethical Government actors. Others consider it a policy issue. However, for the purpose of this chapter this subject is addressed on the assumption that a systematic change in the way the Federal Budget is developed (or, limits thereto) would yield more ethical spending practices.

Over the past 25 years, several of these critics and lawmakers have drafted various proposals for a Balanced Budget Amendment. Any one of these proposed amendments to the United States Constitution would have required a balance in the projected revenues and expenditures of the United States Government. Most of the proposals have contained a supermajority exception allowed for times of war or national emergency. Obviously, such an Amendment would constrain both the Executive Branch and Congress.

There is no one proposed Amendment to which all proponents have agreed, but all proposals would require balance in the Federal Budget and/or restrict the amount of Federal spending. There have been several significant attempts to move such an amendment through Congress, including:

- 1982 – An amendment approved by the Senate (by a vote of 69 to 31) but supported by an inadequate majority of the House (236 to 187);
- 1997 – 160 sponsors introduced an amendment version to the House;
- February 17, 2005 – A measure similar to 1997's was introduced with 24 sponsors; and
- July 13, 2005 – 123 Congressional sponsors endorsed a slightly modified version of the February 17th Amendment.

As a political issue, the deficit, Federal debt, and proposed Balanced Budget Amendment have undergone varying levels of discussion and support for the proposed amendment has varied greatly. No proposals have garnered the necessary support to date, but it seems likely the introduction of future proposals continue as long as a significant deficit remains on the U.S. Government's balance sheets.

Line-item veto

Presidents have sought authority to cancel specific provisions within a bill as a way to either end or reduce special interest "pork barrel" projects and special tax benefits included in bills passed by Congress. The line-item veto would be a very powerful "tool" for the Administration, so Presidential lobbying for this is not surprising.

Before 1974, Presidents sometimes did not apportion appropriations to departments for implementation of un-requested programs (primarily large public works investment programs). Congress took away Presidential authority to withhold appropriations, except under certain conditions, as discussed in the Impoundment Control Act of 1974 section of this chapter.

Since then, Presidents have sought legal authority to strike out line items in a bill. Because such authority involves constitutional issues, Congress spent a considerable amount of time crafting legislation that might pass constitutional muster. Such authority was given to the President in Public Law 104-130, which was signed into law on April 9, 1996, and went into effect on January 1, 1997. The act provided the following:

- Presidential authority to cancel provisions in bills or joint resolutions that were signed into law provided for cancellations that reduced the budget deficit if they did not impair essential Government functions or harm the national interest.
- The President was required to sign the complete bill. Then, the President could cancel items by transmitting that message to Congress within five calendar days of the law's enactment.
- The Congress had five days to introduce a disapproval bill to override cancellations.

The new authority was first used by President Clinton on August 11, 1997, when he cancelled two items in the Taxpayer Relief Act of 1997 and one item in the Balanced Budget Act of 1997. Subsequently, he struck 78 provisions in nine FY 1998 appropriations bills. The savings in calendar year 1997 from the proposed cancellations totaled $855 million.

In February 1998, the United States District Court for the District of Columbia struck down the act as unconstitutional because, in the court's view, it violated the Constitution's requirement that the President sign or veto bills as presented.

The Supreme Court affirmed the District Court's judgment, holding the procedure unconstitutional because it, in effect, granted the President unilateral power to amend or repeal legislation.[13] This decision was reminiscent of *INS v. Chada*, where the Court held a one-house legislative veto unconstitutional.[14]

The Court's problem with the Line Item Veto Act was that once the President signed the bill passed by Congress, the entire bill became law, and only further legislation by both Houses of Congress could amend or appeal it. The Court rejected the argument that the President was merely exercising delegated authority on the grounds that when the President cancels an item so soon after signing the bill, the President is rejecting Congress's judgment, not furthering Congress's policy.

The line item veto tool will continue to be pursued by presidents. President Bush requested such authority in the FY 2005 through FY 2009 Budgets. Whether a line item veto that is consistent with the constitution can be crafted is questionable. The Congress, however, could ease the restrictive law on rescissions to simulate this authority.

Conditions on Federal Funding for States

Another important issue involving spending power involves Congress' ability to place conditions on grants to states and local governments. The Supreme Court has held Congress can institute conditions as long as they are expressly stated and have some relationship to the purpose of the spending program.[15] Congress will deny states Federal funding if certain state laws do not conform to imposed Federal guidelines.

For example, the national 55 mph (89 km/h) speed limit and the national 21-year drinking age were imposed through this method; the states would lose highway funding if they refused to pass such laws.[16] In practice, this allows Congress to compel states to comply with Federal conditions by using the "carrot" of Federal funds, and the "stick" of their withdrawal (and possible civil penalties).

Unfunded Mandates

A final topic causing controversy between government actors is the use of unfunded mandates. An unfunded mandate is a statute requiring governmental or private parties to carry out specific actions without appropriating funds for that purpose.

Examples of unfunded mandates include:

- Provisions in the Emergency Medical Treatment and Active Labor Act requiring nearly all American emergency rooms to accept and stabilize a patient regardless of ability to pay without providing adequate reimbursement for indigent patients.
- Provisions in the Americans with Disabilities Act requiring nearly all American

---

[13] *Clinton v. City of New York*, 534 U.S. 417 (1998).
[14] 452 U.S. 919 (1983).
[15] *Oklahoma v. Civil Service Commission*, 330 U.S. 127 (1947).
[16] *South Dakota v. Dole*, 483 U.S. 203 (1987).

business owners to make their business premises available to disabled customers without providing funds for the cost of reconstruction or additional interior space.

The Unfunded Mandates Reform Act of 1995 was enacted following intense pressure from the National Governors Association (NGA) and others. This Act established procedural mechanisms aimed to prevent Congress from imposing costs on states without providing Federal funds.

The Act requires the Advisory Commission on Intergovernmental Relations, in consultation with the Director of CBO, to study the costs and benefits to state, local, and tribal governments for complying with Federal law, including Federal mandates.

When a House or Senate committee reports a bill or joint resolution including a Federal mandate, the committee report must contain:

- A description of the Federal mandates in the legislation, including the direct costs to state, local, and tribal governments and the private sector;
- An assessment of costs and benefits anticipated from the mandates, including the effects on health and safety and on protection of the natural environment;
- A statement of the degree to which a Federal mandate affects both the public and private sectors; and
- The extent to which certain actions would affect the competitive balance between public and private sectors.

This Unfunded Mandates Reform Act Amended the Congressional Budget and Impoundment Control Act of 1974 with respect to unfunded Federal mandates.

Chapter 3

Budget Concepts

There is a lot of jargon associated with the Federal Budget. Although the use of budgetary jargon has been minimized in this book, some concepts must be understood to make sense of the budget and the budget process. This chapter describes these "must know" concepts including a discussion on the budget deficit and the national debt. Chapter 17 contains a detailed glossary of budget terms.

Budget Year

The first point to note is that the Government's fiscal year (FY) begins on October 1st of the previous calendar year. That is, FY 2010 began on October 1, 2009, and will end on September 30, 2010.

Budget Authority, Obligations, and Outlays

Budget authority (BA) is the authority for Government agencies to enter into obligations to pay for the delivery of goods, services, employee salaries and benefits, grants, and subsidies. For example, the Government incurs an obligation to pay for a product when a contract is signed. Before an obligation can take place, the department or agency must have the budget authority to make that obligation. Entering into an obligation without the requisite budget authority is a criminal offense.

Budget authority is provided through legislation in four forms:

- **Appropriation**. This permits the Government to incur obligations and make payments from Government funds.

- **Permanent appropriations.** Programs with permanent appropriations are called direct or mandatory spending programs. Once initiated, these programs never require further appropriations action by the Congress. Annual spending levels are determined by program eligibility criteria set in substantive law. Unless no money is available for writing Government checks, this spending will occur forever. Examples of mandatory spending include Social Security, Medicare, Federal Government retirement programs, and interest on the Federal debt.

- **Annual appropriations.** Programs that require annual appropriations are called discretionary spending programs. Funds for these programs are provided annually in one of twelve annual appropriations acts and in supplemental appropriations acts. Examples of discretionary programs include national defense, the space program, housing assistance, and environmental cleanup.

- **Borrowing authority.** This permits obligations to be incurred from borrowed funds, usually funds borrowed from the general fund of the Treasury. This is often done for business-type activities that are expected to produce income and repay the borrowed funds with interest.
- **Contract authority.** This permits obligations in advance of an appropriation or in anticipation of receipts that can be used for payment.
- **Spending authority.** This permits the obligation of funds received from user fees, e.g., Medicare Supplementary Insurance.

Obligations are binding agreements that will result in outlays, immediately or in the future. Budgetary resources must be available before obligations can be incurred legally. In general, BA provided in a certain fiscal year must be obligated in that year. Exceptions are made in the appropriations acts for investment programs covering a period of years.

Outlays are the payments to settle or liquidate obligations.

- Unless stated otherwise, the term "spending" refers to outlays.
- Outlays generally reflect cash disbursements. They also include the accrued but unpaid interest on public issues of Treasury debt and cash-equivalent transactions such as the subsidy cost of direct loans and loan guarantees.

Outlays resulting from an obligation usually occur over several years. Rarely is the BA provided for a program fully spent in the year it is made available. Consequently, outlays in a given fiscal year are the result of budget authority provided both in the current year and in prior years for the following reasons:

- BA provided in a single year for a major construction or procurement project generally will cover the entire project cost even though the work and outlays will occur over several years.

- BA provided for subsidized housing covers contracts that may last up to 40 years.
- BA provided for most education and job training programs covers school years that do not coincide with Federal fiscal years.

The BA carried over from one year to the next, and the outlays from BA provided in prior years are substantial. In a given year, about one fifth of outlays will be from appropriations obligated in prior years and four fifths will be from appropriations authorized in the current FY. Figure 3-1, Relationship of Budget Authority to Outlays for FY 2011, provides a current illustrative example.

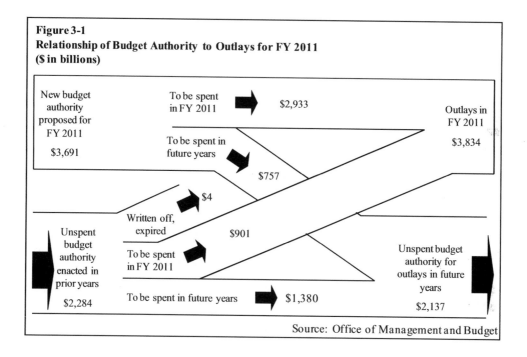

Figure 3-1
Relationship of Budget Authority to Outlays for FY 2011
($ in billions)

New budget authority proposed for FY 2011 — $3,691

To be spent in FY 2011 — $2,933

To be spent in future years — $757

Written off, expired — $4

Outlays in FY 2011 — $3,834

Unspent budget authority enacted in prior years — $2,284

To be spent in FY 2011 — $901

To be spent in future years — $1,380

Unspent budget authority for outlays in future years — $2,137

Source: Office of Management and Budget

Unified Budget (Federal Funds and Trust Funds)

The Federal Budget is presented as a unified budget combining two major components: Federal funds and trust funds.

- Federal funds include all taxes not designated in law as trust fund receipts, all expenditures except those from trust funds, and cash receipts from borrowing on the Federal debt.

  - About 91 percent of these receipts come from individual and corporation income taxes; the remainder includes excise taxes on alcohol and tobacco, customs fees and estate and gift taxes.
  - Except for FY 2000, the Federal funds have run annual deficits since 1960.

- Federal fund deficits are covered by borrowing from the public and from the trust funds.

- Trust funds are designated in law and receive receipts from which expenditures are made for specific purposes. Excess funds in the trust funds are invested in Federal securities (debt issued to cover the deficit in the Federal funds).

  - The largest trust fund by far is Social Security, which accounts for about two thirds of trust fund receipts. Federal civilian and military retirement, Medicare, and unemployment compensation are the other major components.
  - Except for five years, the trust funds have run annual surpluses since 1934.

Monies borrowed by the Federal funds from the trust funds will have to be repaid when expenditures from the Social Security and Medicare trust funds begin to exceed annual receipts in those funds.

Budget Deficit and Federal Debt

The deficit and the Federal debt are often confused.

- A deficit occurs when Government expenditures exceed the receipts in any FY. For example, in a given FY, if the Government spends $3.2 trillion but only collects $2.8 trillion from taxes and other sources, the deficit for that FY would be $400 billion.
- The debt is the cumulative effect of annual deficits and annual surpluses. Think of the national debt as the Government's "tab." Every time the Government closes out a year with deficit remaining (when it spends more than it brings in), the shortfall goes on its tab. If the Government runs a surplus in a year, the debt would decline. The Government pays interest on its debt just like a business or a person would. Just as in private business, there are valid arguments for maintaining debt and leveraging funds. This has been the Government's policy for decades and, as a result, its tab is equivalent to three or four years' worth of total expenditures.

Budget Deficits

Several factors can lead to larger than projected deficits:

- Congressional appropriations that are higher than the levels proposed by the President,

- Emergency funding for unforeseen circumstances such as an economic crisis, a natural disaster, or a war,
- A downturn in the economy leading to reduced receipts and additional expenditures such as unemployment compensation and food stamps,
- A downturn in the stock market leading to reduced receipts from capital gains taxes,
- An increase in inflation that can lead to higher costs for programs for which the expenditures are related to inflation such as Social Security, and
- An increase in interest rates that would increase the cost of borrowing funds from the private sector to finance the Federal debt.

On the other hand, several factors can lead to smaller deficits or move the annual result from a deficit to a surplus:

- An increase in the economy leading to increased jobs and receipts,
- An increase in the stock market leading to increased receipts from capital gains taxes,
- A reduction in inflation that can lead to lower costs for programs for which the expenditures are related to inflation such as Social Security, and
- A decrease in interest rates that would decrease the cost of borrowing funds from the private sector to finance the Federal debt.

Deficits are considered to consist of *cyclical deficits* and *structural deficits*.

- The observed total deficit is the sum of the structural deficit with the cyclical deficit or surplus.
- A cyclical deficit occurs because of the business cycle. At its lowest point, unemployment tends to be high, which means that tax revenues are low and expenditures (e.g., unemployment compensation and food stamps) tend to be high. At its high point the opposite is in effect. It is generally believed that the need to borrow money at the bottom of a cycle, the cyclical deficit, will be offset by a cyclical surplus at the top of the cycle.
- A structural deficit is the deficit that remains throughout the cycle because expenditures exceed receipts.

Chapter 4

Department and Agency Missions

This chapter summarizes the missions of each department and agency in the Executive Branch.

Department of Agriculture (USDA)

- Enhance economic opportunities for agricultural producers;
- Support increased economic opportunities and improved quality of life in rural America;
- Enhance protection and safety of the Nation's agriculture and food supply;
- Improve the Nation's nutrition and health;
- Improve import and domestic food safety; and
- Protect and enhance the Nation's natural resource base and environment.

Department of Commerce (Commerce)

- Advance economic growth and jobs and opportunities for the American people;
- Advance U.S. Competitiveness through Technological Innovation, Free Trade, and Intellectual Property Protection; and
- Observe and manage the Earth's environment to promote sustainable growth.

Department of Defense (DOD)

- Defend the United States and advance its interests around the globe;
- Train and equip military forces to deter aggression while protecting U.S. interests and promoting U.S. security objectives;
- Defeat terrorists and their supporters who threaten our freedom; and

- Prepare the Armed Forces and develop their capabilities to meet current and future threats.

Department of Education (Education)

- Promote student achievement and preparation for global competitiveness by fostering educational excellence and ensuring equal access;
- Promote educational excellence and access in elementary and secondary education through grants to states and local educational agencies;
- Conduct research and disseminate information on best educational practices; and
- Produce statistics on the condition of education in the United States.

Department of Energy (DOE)

- Advance the national, economic, and energy security of the United States;
- Maintain nuclear weapons stockpile and manage non-proliferation efforts to reduce threat from weapons of mass destruction;
- Support deployment and expansive research into green technology;
- Sponsor basic research that supports DOE programs and operate scientific facilities; and
- Advance environmental cleanup and nuclear waste management.

Department of Health and Human Services (HHS)

- Promote and protect the health and well-being of all Americans;
- Prevent and prepare the Nation for health emergencies, including pandemic influenza and bioterrorism;
- Expand and promote the use of health information technology and increase the transparency of health care price and quality information;
- Continue to assist low-income children, vulnerable populations, and families in need; and
- Provide world leadership in biomedical and public health sciences.

Department of Homeland Security (DHS)

- Prevent attacks on the United States from terrorists, both international and domestic;
- Minimize the damage and recovery from attacks that do occur;
- Protect the Nation's transportation systems to ensure the freedom of movement for people and commerce;
- Ensure the nation's digital information security (Cybersecurity);
- Uphold the nation's boarder security; and

- Provide a clear understanding of Nation's security responsibilities, including awareness of the full scope of potential risks, deployment of comprehensive prevention, protection and response activities, and organizational mandates to optimize performance and stewardship requirements.

Department of Housing and Urban Development (HUD)

- Increase homeownership, support community development and increase access to affordable housing free from discrimination;
- Subsidize housing for low-income households through rental assistance, construction grants, and loans;
- Embrace high standards of ethics, management and accountability; and
- Forge new partnerships—particularly with faith-based and community organizations—that leverage resources and improve HUD's ability to be effective on the community level.

Department of the Interior (DOI)

- Protect the nation's natural resources and heritage, honor its cultures and tribal communities, and supply the energy to power its future;
- Manage over 507 million acres of land (roughly one-fifth of U.S. land area), 700 million acres of subsurface minerals, and the Outer Continental Shelf;
- Protect much of the Nation's natural and cultural resources, including providing for their responsible use, and serve as the largest supplier and manager of water in the 17 western states;
- Meet many of the Government's trust responsibilities to Indian tribes and affiliated island communities; and
- Disseminate U.S. earth science information and research findings to the public.

Department of Justice (DOJ)

- Enforce the law and defend the interests of the United States;
- Ensure public safety against threats, foreign and domestic;
- Provide Federal leadership in preventing and controlling crime;
- Seek just punishment for those guilty of unlawful behavior; and
- Ensure fair and impartial administration of justice for all Americans.

Department of Labor (DOL)

Foster and promote the welfare of the job seekers, wage earners, and retirees of the United States by:

- Improving working conditions,
- Advancing opportunities for profitable employment,
- Protecting retirement and health care benefits,
- Helping employers find workers,
- Strengthening free collective bargaining, and
- Tracking changes in employment, prices, and other economic measurements.

Department of State

- Advance freedom for the benefit of the American people and the international community by helping to build and sustain a more democratic, secure, and prosperous world composed of well-governed states that respond to the needs of their people, reduce widespread poverty, and act responsibly within the international system;
- Provide development assistance through the U.S. Agency for International Development (USAID) and international finance through the Department of the Treasury;
- Promote exports through the Export-Import Bank, the Overseas Private Investment Corporation, and the Trade and Development Agency;
- Provide international broadcasting through the Broadcasting Board of Governors; and
- Provide for other functions, including the Peace Corps.

Department of Transportation (DOT)

- Ensure sufficient and safe roads, rails, airways and seaways to keep the economy growing;
- Improve transportation safety; and
- Work with state, local, and private sector partners to promote a safe, secure, efficient, accessible and convenient national transportation system.

Department of the Treasury (Treasury)

- Help maintain healthy and competitive U.S. capital markets;
- Regulate financial institutions and manage Government finances;
- Increase revenues through more effective tax collection; and
- Protect citizens from illegal drugs, financial crime, violence and terrorism.

Department of Veterans Affairs (VA)

- Operate the veteran's health care delivery system;
- Ease the transition for veterans as they leave active military service; and

- Administer veterans' benefits, including monthly disability payments, education assistance, life insurance, home loans, vocational rehabilitation and veterans' cemeteries.

Army Corps of Engineers

- Develop, manage, and restore water resources; and
- Help communities respond to and recover from floods and other natural disasters.

Environmental Protection Agency (EPA)

- Protect human health and safeguard the natural environment (air, water and land) through research, regulation development and enforcement, economic stimulation of environment-friendly initiatives, and proliferation of environmental information;
- Develop and enforce environmental regulations; and
- Collaborate with international and domestic partners to address energy and climate issues.

National Aeronautics and Space Administration (NASA)

- Pioneer the future in space exploration, scientific discovery and aeronautics research; and
- Pursue supporting capabilities such as space launch vehicles (e.g., the Space Shuttle) and orbiting platforms (e.g., the Space Station).

National Science Foundation (NSF)

- Advance science and engineering in the United States; and
- Make merit-based grants to individual researchers and groups at colleges, universities and other institutions.

Small Business Administration (SBA)

- Aid, counsel, assist and protect the interests of small businesses and help families and businesses recover from physical disasters; and
- Foster business-friendly environment that will allow American small business to excel on a global scale.

Smithsonian Institution

- Increase and diffuse knowledge through scientific research by operating 15 museums in New York City and Washington, D.C., as well as the National Zoo.

Social Security Administration

- Manage the Old-Age, Survivors, and Disability Insurance (OASDI) programs, known as Social Security;
- Administer Supplemental Security Income (SSI) program for low-income aged and disabled individuals;
- Increase program integrity efforts to ensure benefits are provided to the right beneficiaries— preventing improper payments; and
- Support the Medicare program on behalf of the Centers for Medicare and Medicaid Services.

Commodity Futures Trading Commission

- Regulate U.S. futures and options markets; and
- Protect investors by preventing fraud and abuse and ensuring disclosure of information.

Consumer Product Safety Commission

- Protect the public from unreasonable risk of injury connected with consumer products;
- Help develop uniform safety standards for consumer products; and
- Conduct and promote research into preventing product-related deaths, injuries, or illness.

Corporation for National and Community Service (CNCS)

- Provide service opportunities for more than 1.5 million Americans in educational, public safety, and environmental activities through AmeriCorps and the National Senior Service Corps (NSSC).

Equal Employment Opportunity Commission

- Enforce laws that prohibit employment discrimination based on race, sex, religion, national origin, age, or disability;
- Enforce the nation's equal employment laws through selective litigation, mediation, and alternative dispute resolution; and
- Strive to prevent employment discrimination through outreach, training, and technical assistance to promote employer compliance.

Executive Office of the President (EOP)

- Support offices, councils, and accounts dedicated to serving the President.

Federal Communications Commission (FCC)

- Regulate interstate and international communications by radio, television, wire, satellite and cable; and
- Encourage a fully competitive marketplace in communications and promote affordable communications services for all Americans.

Federal Deposit Insurance Corporation (FDIC)

- Maintain stability and public confidence in Nation's financial system through Federal deposit insurance, by insuring deposits in banks and thrift institutions for at least $250,000);
- Identify, monitor and address risks to the deposit insurance funds; and
- Limit the effect on the economy and the financial system if a bank or thrift institution fails.

Federal Election Commission (FEC)

- Monitor financing of election campaigns for the U.S. House of Representatives, the U.S. Senate, Vice Presidency and the Presidency.

Federal Trade Commission (FTC)

- Enforce consumer protection and antitrust laws that prohibit business practices that are anticompetitive, deceptive, or unfair to consumers; and
- Promote informed consumer choice and public understanding of the competitive process, without impeding legitimate business activity.

General Services Administration (GSA)

- Help Federal agencies by offering quality workplaces, expert solutions, acquisition services, and management policies at best value to tax payers and federal customers; and
- Provide or procure commercial services for Federal agencies on a reimbursable or fee-for-service basis.

Institute of Museum and Library Services

- Provide state grants and competitive awards to assist museums and libraries in expanding their services to the public; and
- Undertake research and policy development activities such as collaborative efforts with the National Science Foundation to share research information in digital library technology.

National Archives and Records Administration

- Safeguard records of all three branches of the Federal Government; and
- Ensure ready access to evidence that document the rights of American citizens, the actions of Federal officials, and the national experience.

National Endowment for the Arts

- Support efforts to enhance the availability and appreciation of the arts, both new and established.

National Endowment for the Humanities

- Support research, education, preservation, and public programs in the humanities; and
- Preserve America's cultural and intellectual resources.

National Labor Relations Board

- Regulate private-sector employer and union relations to minimize interruptions to commerce caused by strikes and worker-management discord;
- Oversee secret-ballot elections in which employees determine whether to be represented by a union; and
- Prevent and remedy unfair labor practices, by unions or employers.

National Transportation Safety Board (NTSB)

- Investigate the causes of domestic transportation accidents; and
- Issue safety recommendations aimed at preventing future transportation accidents.

Nuclear Regulatory Commission (NRC)

- Regulate nuclear material use in the United States to protect public health and safety, promote common defense and security, and guard the environment;
- Improve the control of radioactive material and strengthen security at NRC-licensed facilities in line with homeland security objectives.

Office of Personnel Management (OPM)

- Provide human resource management leadership to the Executive Branch;
- Advance the President's goal of recruiting, hiring and retaining the best and the brightest for Federal service;
- Oversee Federal civil service merit systems; and

- Provide retirement, health benefit, and other insurance services to Federal employees, annuitants, beneficiaries, and agencies.

Railroad Retirement Board

- Administer comprehensive retirement, survivor, unemployment, and sickness insurance benefits for qualified railroad workers and their families financed through railroad employer contributions, railroad employee payroll deductions, payments from Social Security trust funds, and taxpayer subsidies.

Securities and Exchange Commission (SEC)

- Regulate U.S. capital markets and the securities industry;
- Strive to protect investors by preventing fraud and abuse in U.S. capital markets and ensuring adequate disclosure of information; and
- Conduct compliance inspections and examinations in order to review and monitor the conduct and financial conditions of securities firms and their affiliates.

Tennessee Valley Authority (TVA)

- Promote economic development and flood control management;
- Generate and sell electric power; and
- Provide navigation, recreation, water supply and other environment friendly services throughout Tennessee and in six neighboring states.

Chapter 5

Overview of the Budget Process

At anytime, the Federal Government is working on three budgets:

- Execution of the budget for the current fiscal year that began on last October 1st;
- Congressional action on the budget for the coming fiscal year that begins next October 1st; and
- Formulation of the President's Budget that will be sent to the Congress next February.

For example, during calendar year 1, the agencies are executing the FY 1 Budget, Congress is working on appropriations for FY 2, and the Executive Branch is formulating the President's Budget for FY 3 (Figure 5-1).

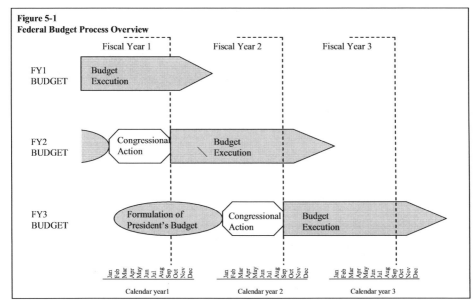

Figure 5-1
Federal Budget Process Overview

While the processes for making budget decisions appear unwieldy and excessively complex, they are, in fact, rather simple and straightforward. The complexity is attributed to the intricacy of the issues that require budget decisions, the amount of time the processes consume, the numerous actors involved in the processes, and the even larger number of stakeholders with a vested interest in the outcome.

Steps in the Process

A summary of the process follows. Subsequent chapters provide further details. Dates for key steps are set in law, though there are no legal penalties for delays.

- **Formulation of the President's Budget**. This Budget reflects the President's priorities on spending and revenue for the budget year and the four following fiscal years. The process starts about 12 months before the President must submit a Budget to Congress (the first Monday in February of each year). The Budget describes the President's priorities and includes details on each of more than 1,300 appropriation accounts. The President may submit amendments to the Budget to reflect new or changed conditions. The timing of this process may be somewhat different in transition years when a new President takes office. This is discussed in more detail in Chapter 1 of this book.
- **Congressional action.** This begins with receipt of the President's Budget and ends with enacted appropriations. The Congress can accept, modify, or completely disregard the President's request. Although it often does not happen, all action should be finished by the start of the fiscal year on October 1. Products include the following:

  - **Concurrent Budget Resolution (CBR).** The CBR is the master plan for Congressional action and is due by April 15th. It is an agreement between the House of Representatives and the Senate specifying spending for the entire Government by individual budget function, e.g., national defense, energy, housing, etc., and the expected revenue for the budget year and the four following fiscal years. The resolution does not require Presidential approval. Work on the CBR begins with a budget baseline calculated by the Congressional Budget Office (CBO). This baseline estimate starts with the last enacted appropriations, adds inflation to all discretionary programs, and projects entitlement program spending based on likely use of the programs, and projects revenues at the current rates in law.
  - **Reconciliation bills.** These bills change existing revenue and direct spending laws to make them consistent with the spending and revenue provisions in the CBR. The reconciliation bill does not address the spending included in the annual appropriations bills described below. Normally, one omnibus reconciliation bill includes all of the spending changes required by

the CBR while a separate bill addresses tax matters. Reconciliation action is to be complete by June 15th.

- **Authorization bills.** An authorization bill provides the legal basis for a program and establishes program requirements. Some programs have permanent authorization; and others require new authorization each year or every two or three years. Generally, the Congress authorizes a program before providing appropriations. Funding for mandatory (direct spending) programs is generally included in the bills authorizing the programs. Mandatory spending, which accounts for almost two-thirds of total spending, does not require annual appropriations. The largest components of this spending are Social Security, Medicare, and net interest on the Federal debt.

- **Appropriations bills/acts.** Annual appropriations acts provide funding for those programs that require annual funding. These appropriations, termed discretionary spending, account for a little over one-third of total spending. Funding in the bills cannot exceed the limits set in the Budget Resolution unless Congress passes a waiver, deems the spending to be emergency spending, or changes the limits. The House is supposed to complete action on all annual appropriation bills by June 30. When an annual appropriations bill is not finished by the start of the fiscal year, Congress must pass and the President must sign a Continuing Resolution to provide funding until a bill can be enacted.

Each house of Congress performs each of the above steps independently and differences are resolved in conferences of key House and Senate members. After both houses agree to the conference bill, the result is termed an enrolled bill and is sent to the President for approval. The President can approve the measure or veto it and send it back to the Congress for reconsideration.

- **Program Execution.** This phase begins at the start of the fiscal year and ends when the appropriations are spent or expire, which can take several years. Subject to certain limitations, some departments can transfer appropriated funds between programs and accounts and all departments may reprogram funds within programs permitting them to respond to changes in program performance and requirements. The President can and does request supplemental funds if necessary to meet changed conditions. Routinely, supplemental funds are requested for natural disaster response and recovery and for military actions.

Scorekeeping

Scorekeeping guidelines have been adopted to make certain the costs and receipts associated with the President's Budget, proposed legislation, and enacted legislation are measured in a consistent manner. This practice, known as budget scorekeeping, uses the guidelines issued as part of the Budget Enforcement Act of 1990.

- President's Budget

    - OMB uses the guidelines to project the costs and revenues of the President's Budget that is submitted to Congress in February each year.
    - CBO uses the guidelines to prepare its estimate of the financial effects of the President's Budget.

- Proposed Legislation

    - CBO, using guidance from the House and Senate Budget Committees, estimates the cost of each bill (appropriations and direct spending authorization) that provides money before the bill goes to the floor of each House (2 USC 602).
    - The Joint Committee on Taxation (JCT) estimates the effects of revenue legislation (2 USC 601(f)).
    - These scorekeeping estimates provide the basis for potential points of order during floor discussion in the House or Senate. A point of order is a formal objection to a measure that violates a budget rule, such as exceeding a level established in the Congressional Budget Resolution.

Both the OMB and the CBO estimate outlays by year from proposed and enacted appropriations using outlay (spendout) rates based on historical spending trends for a specific appropriation or for similar appropriations in the case of a new appropriation.

Because scorekeeping will always require some judgment, there can be significant differences between Congress and the Administration over how certain items should be scored. Resolution of scorekeeping issues when the differences are great may require consultation between the President and congressional leadership. The House and Senate Budget Committees can direct the CBO to project BA or outlays in certain ways. This can include directing CBO to use the same estimates used by OMB if OMB and CBO have differing estimates.

Application of Guidelines during the Budget Process

The scoring guidelines in the conference report (H.R. 105-217) accompanying the Budget Enforcement Act of 1997 are summarized below:

- Classification of appropriations

    - Appropriations are classified as either mandatory or discretionary. A list of appropriations classified as discretionary is included in the 1997 conference report (H.R. 105-217).

- Estimates of outlays from prior year appropriations

    - Outlays from prior-year appropriations are classified as mandatory or discretionary consistent with the classification of the account from which the outlays occur.

- Direct spending programs (entitlements and other mandatory programs including offsetting receipts)

    - These are scored at current law levels, unless congressional action modifies the authorizing legislation.
    - Direct spending savings included in both an appropriations bill and a reconciliation bill are scored to the reconciliation bill and not to the appropriations bill.

- Transfer of Budget Authority (BA) from a mandatory account to a discretionary account

    - The receiving discretionary account will show an increase in discretionary BA and outlays.
    - The losing mandatory account will not show an offsetting reduction.

- Permissive transfer authority (when transfers are permitted but not required)

    - The outlays that would result from such a transfer are estimated based on the best information available (primarily historical experience) and, where applicable, indications of original Executive or Congressional intent.

- Re-appropriations of expiring balances of BA

    - BA is scored as new BA in the fiscal year in which the balances become newly available.

- Rescissions and transfers of unobligated balances

    - Rescissions of unobligated balances are scored as reductions in BA and outlays in the year the money is rescinded.
    - Transfers of unobligated balances are scored as reductions in BA and outlays in the account from which the funds are transferred, and as increases in BA and outlays in the account to which the funds are transferred.
    - If the transactions result in a net negative BA amount in the source accounts, the BA will be projected at zero.

- Outlay estimates for both the transferring and receiving accounts will be based on the spending patterns appropriate to the respective accounts.

- Advance appropriations (when appropriation acts make BA available in a year after the budget year)

  - Advance appropriations of BA are scored as new BA in the fiscal year in which the funds become newly available for obligation, not the year in which the appropriations are enacted.

- Delay of obligations

  - If an appropriations act provides that a portion of the BA shall not be available for obligation until a future fiscal year, that portion shall be treated as an advance appropriation of BA.
  - If a law defers existing BA (or unobligated balances) from a year in which it was available for obligation to a year in which it was not available for obligation, that law shall be scored as a rescission in the current year and a re-appropriation in the year in which the obligational authority is extended.

- Contingent legislation (when the availability of an appropriation or authority to obligate is contingent upon some other act)

  - If the authority to obligate is contingent upon the enactment of a subsequent appropriation, new BA and outlays are scored with the subsequent appropriation.
  - If a discretionary appropriation is contingent upon the enactment of a subsequent authorization, new BA and outlays are scored with the appropriation.
  - If a discretionary appropriation is contingent on the fulfillment of some action by the Executive Branch or some other event normally estimated, new BA is scored with the appropriation and the outlays will be estimated based on the best information about when (or if) the contingency will be met.
  - If direct spending legislation is contingent on the fulfillment of some action by the Executive Branch or some other event normally estimated, new BA and outlays are scored based on the best information about when (or if) the contingency will be met.
  - Non-lawmaking contingencies within the control of the Congress are not scoreable events.

- Purchases, lease-purchases, capital leases, and operating leases are outlined in Table 5-1.

Table 5-1
Types of Asset Acquisition Arrangements and Budget Scoring

Type	Definition	BA Scoring	Outlay Scoring
Purchase	Government purchase of asset	• Year: when purchase authority is first made available • Amount: Government's estimated legal obligation	• Equal to estimated disbursements based on purchase arrangement • Total outlays equal total BA
Lease-purchase	Lease with asset ownership transferred to Government at or shortly after end of lease term.	• Year: When BA first available • Amount: Net present value of Government's total obligation.	• If Government assumes substantial risk (e.g., through guarantee of third party financing), outlays are spread over the acquisition period • If private sector retains risk, outlays are spread over lease period
Capital lease	Lease other than a lease-purchase that does not meet the criteria of an operating lease	• Same as lease-purchase	• If private sector retains substantial risk, outlays are spread over lease period. • Total outlays equal total BA

Operating lease	Lease meets these criteria:
	• General purpose asset; not built to Government specification
	• Private-sector market for asset
	• Ownership is not transferred to Government at or shortly after the end of the lease
	• No bargain-price purchase option in lease
	• Lease term does not exceed 75 percent of asset's economic lifetime
	• Present value of lease payments does not exceed 90 percent of asset's fair market value at start of lease
		• Year: When BA is first available
		• Amount:
		  – With no cancellation clause, amount is total under full lease term
		  – With cancellation clause, amount must cover lease payments the first year of the contract plus cancellation costs
		• For existing self-insuring funds, only BA for annual lease payment is scored
			• Same as capital lease

• Reclassification after an agreement

  – Except to the extent assumed in a budget agreement, a law that has the effect of altering the classification or scoring of spending and revenues (e.g., from discretionary to mandatory, special fund to revolving fund, on-budget to off-budget, revenue to offsetting receipt), will not be scored as reclassified for the purpose of enforcing a budget agreement.

- Scoring of receipt increases or direct spending reductions for additional administrative or program management expenses

  - No increase in receipts or decrease in direct spending will be scored as a result of provisions of a law that provides direct spending for administrative or program management activities.

- Asset sales

  - If the net financial cost to the Government of an asset sale is zero or negative (a savings), the amount scored is the estimated change in receipts and mandatory outlays in each fiscal year on a cash basis. If the cost to the Government is positive (a loss), the proceeds from the sale are not scored.
  - The net financial cost to the Federal Government of an asset sale shall be the net present value of the cash flows from:

    * The estimated proceeds from the asset sale;
    * The net effect on Federal revenues, if any, based on special tax treatments specified in the legislation;
    * The loss of future offsetting receipts that would otherwise be collected under continued Government ownership using baseline levels for the projection period and estimated levels thereafter; and
    * Changes in future spending, both discretionary and mandatory, from levels that would otherwise occur under continued Government ownership (using baseline levels for the projection period and at levels estimated to be necessary to operate and maintain the asset thereafter).

  - The discount rate used to estimate the net present value shall be the average interest rate on marketable Treasury securities of similar maturity to the expected remaining useful life of the asset for which the estimate is being made, plus two percentage points to reflect the economic effects of continued ownership by the Government.

- Indefinite borrowing authority and limits on outstanding debt

  - If legislation imposes or changes a limit on an outstanding debt for an account financed by indefinite BA in the form of borrowing authority, the legislation will be scored as changing BA only if and to the extent the imposition of a limit or the change in the existing limit alters the estimated amount of obligations that will be incurred.

Dynamic Scoring. When the CBO and the JCT provide estimates to Congress for any revenue impact changes from proposed legislation or tax cuts, it is typically assumed that the policy change will have little to no effect on the economy as a whole. This method for scoring bills is known as static scoring. It takes into account current and historic data, but does not forecast any future changes in the overall economy.

Dynamic Scoring attempts to predict the impact of fiscal policy changes on the economy and the reactions that may result from such a change. Proponents argue that dynamic scoring offers a more complete indication of possible economic growth or decline.

In a static world, the Government loses one dollar in revenue for every dollar it gives back to taxpayers in the form of a tax cut. Dynamic scoring would take into account any changes in overall economic conditions that could change the cost to the Government of a tax bill. Under dynamic scoring, revenue estimators would consider how a change in tax policy might affect compensation, prices, employment, and Gross Domestic Product (GDP). If any of these variables might be affected, the estimates would be adjusted for the expected revenue gain or loss to the Government.

The problem with assumptions is that different people will have different assumptions for forecasting the future. Although no-one can accurately predict what will happen in the future, dynamic scoring can be used as a tool for the Government to attempt to show the economic effects of proposed legislation.

Although dynamic scoring may provide new insights into Government tax and spending policies, there appears to be no reason to expect that either the Executive or Legislative Branches will change their reliance on static scoring in the near future.

Chapter 5: Overview of the Budget Process

Chapter 6

Key Players in the Budget Process

Several organizations in the Executive and Legislative Branches, in addition to the departments and agencies that prepare program and budget plans, play key roles in the budget process in terms of setting priorities, allocating funds, and determining revenue policies. This chapter describes those organizations and summarizes the tasks they perform in budget development and execution.

Executive Branch

- **The President**. The President sets the overall policy agenda and direction for the Executive Branch. Some policies flow from promises made during the Presidential campaign and others from application of the general policy principles to specific issues.

  With respect to the budget process, the President:

  – Is the final authority for decisions in the Executive Branch;
  – Makes decisions on issues concerning overall revenue policies, e.g., whether to cut or increase taxes, and overall spending, e.g., what are the spending priorities such as education or defense or support of urban areas;
  – Submits the Budget to Congress on the first Monday in February;
  – Negotiates key points with congressional leadership; and
  – Decides which legislative bills passed by Congress will be signed and which will be vetoed.

- **The President's Chief of Staff.** The Chief of Staff is the right hand of the President and is involved in all important matters involving the White House.

With respect to the budget process, the Chief of Staff:

- Previews White House staff presentations to the President on budget development;
- Works with the OMB Director and department heads to resolve politically sensitive budget issues; and
- Negotiates with Congress on specific issues and bills.

- **Budget Review Board (BRB).** This Board is a creation of President George W. Bush to review budget recommendations before they are submitted to the President for final approval. The Board, chaired by the Vice President, includes the Secretary of the Treasury, the Director of the Office of Management and Budget, the Chief of Staff to the President, and the Director of the National Economic Council.

With respect to the budget process, the BRB:

- Sets overall budget targets for the Administration under general guidance from the President; and
- Reviews agency appeals of OMB budget decisions.

- **Office of Management and Budget (OMB).** The Director of OMB is the principal policy advisor to the President on the budget and manages the budget process for the President. The leadership of OMB is composed of political appointees, but most of the staff members are career personnel. The budget staff is organized into Resource Management Offices (RMOs) charged with review and preparation of the Budget and implementation of management improvements for assigned areas of government. In addition, a Budget Review Division oversees the budget process and does central budget accounting. There currently are four RMOs: (1) National Security Programs; (2) Human Resource Programs; (3) Natural Resource Programs; and (4) General Government Programs. In addition, there is a Legislative Reference Office that clears legislation, and the three statutory offices — Office of Federal Procurement Policy, Office of Information and Regulatory Affairs, and the Office of Federal Financial Management.

With respect to the budget process and related matters, OMB:

- Sets the rules for preparation of departmental budgets and for budget execution reports (OMB Circular A-11);
- Provides budget targets to the departments and agencies consistent with guidance from the President;
- Reviews the budget requests of the departments and proposes alternative funding levels consistent with Presidential priorities;

- Works with the Council of Economic Advisors and Treasury to develop economic assumptions to be used in the President's Budget;
- Prepares the President's Budget document for submission to Congress in February and a Midsession Review document in July;
- Reviews and clears departmental congressional budget justification documents and testimony before they are provided to Congress;
- Negotiates with the committees of Congress over funding levels for appropriations bills;
- Prepares a Statement of Administration Policy containing the Administration's views on each bill being considered by Congress;
- Prepares an enrolled bill memo on each bill passed by Congress that provides the President with the views of the principal policy officials of the Administration regarding whether the bill should be signed or vetoed and what type if any signing statement should be issued;
- Clears all legislative proposals developed within the Administration and coordinates departmental responses to Congress on proposed legislation (OMB Circular A-19);
- Apportions funds made available in appropriations bills to the departments and agencies;
- Prepares special messages for the President to send Congress concerning proposed rescission and deferral of appropriated funds;
- Reviews and coordinates proposed regulations prepared by the departments and agencies; and
- Reviews and clears proposed forms for collection of information from the public.

- **National Economic Council (NEC).** The NEC, created by President Clinton, is responsible for advising the President on national and global economic matters. The NEC is a forum for discussing policy matters that affect the national economy, to include monitoring the strength of the U.S. and global economies.

  With respect to the budget process, NEC:

  - Coordinates the economic policy-making process with respect to domestic and international economic issues;
  - Makes certain the Budget reflects the President's economic policies;
  - Monitors implementation of the President's economic policy agenda; and
  - Negotiates with Congress on certain issues.

- **Council of Economic Advisors (CEA).** The CEA provides economic studies for the President and advises on the economic effects of potential policy decisions of the Government.

With respect to the budget process, CEA:

- Works with OMB and Treasury on economic assumptions to be used in the Budget;
- Prepares an economic report that accompanies the Budget describing the state of the economy and issues that deserve close watching;
- Appraises the various programs and activities of the Federal Government to determine their effectiveness; and
- Recommends reductions and priorities.

- **National Security Council, Domestic Policy Council, Council on Environmental Quality, Office of Science and Technology, Office of National Drug Control Policy, and other Presidential advisors.** Each of these groups is involved with development of Administration policy in a specific area and therefore concerned about how the Budget might affect those policies.

With respect to the budget process, these offices:

- Provide views to OMB and the President on departmental and agency budget requests;
- Provide a conduit for departments and agencies they work with to get their views on OMB proposals to the President; and
- Coordinate national securities spending across agencies and departments.

- **Office of Science and Technology.** This office is established in the Executive Branch. It coordinates counter terrorism budgets and activity throughout the Federal Government.

- **Department of the Treasury.** Treasury collects governmental receipts, manages governmental finances, and develops tax proposals.

With respect to the budget process, Treasury:

- Acts as the trustee directly and indirectly supporting, funding, and managing On and Off-Budget funds managed by the Treasury and other departments, agencies, and other Federal organizations;
- Works with OMB and CEA on economic assumptions for use in the Budget;
- Prepares revenue estimates for the Budget;
- Prepares documents describing the President's tax proposals; and
- Issues warrants to the departments and agencies identifying the specific amounts of money that can be withdrawn from the Treasury as a result of an appropriations act.

Legislative Branch

- **Congressional Leadership.** This includes the Speaker of the House, Minority Leader of the House, the Majority and Minority Leaders of the Senate, and other key leadership people.

  With respect to the budget process, the leadership:

  - Sets the agenda for each party within each house;
  - Rounds up votes to support positions during floor action;
  - Decides when legislative bills will be taken to the floor for full vote of the house; and
  - Negotiates with the President on key policy issues.

- **Budget Committees.** The committees in each house oversee the budget process in their respective houses.

  With respect to the budget process, these committees:

  - Receive views from other committees on what they think should be included in the Congressional Budget Resolution (CBR);
  - Prepare the CBR consistent with priorities of their individual houses;
  - Oversee the Congressional Budget Office; and
  - Assign revenue and spending targets to committees consistent with the CBR.

- **House Ways and Means and Senate Finance Committees.** These comittees are responsible for legislation affecting revenue and for the Social Security and Medicare programs.

  With respect to the budget process, these committees:

  - Draft legislation (revenue bills start in the House in accordance with the Constitution) consistent with overall revenue levels in the CBR;
  - Propose legislation affecting Social Security and Medicare programs; and
  - Propose legislation affecting governmental receipts.

- **Joint Committee on Taxation**. This committee is assigned the task of estimating the effects of all tax bills by preparing scorekeeping estimates.

- **House Committee on Rules.** This committee drafts a rule for each bill before it can go to the floor in the House of Representatives describing how floor debate will proceed. The rules cover the length of time for debate, amendments that will be considered to be in order, and other details.

- **Authorization Committees.** These committees review the policies of the departments and agencies over which they have jurisdiction. These include committees dealing with armed forces, foreign affairs, intelligence, science, transportation, the judiciary, agriculture, banking and housing, education and labor, veterans' affairs, and energy and commerce. Staff members are highly knowledgeable and often end up in policy positions in the departments.

  With respect to the budget process, these committees:

  - Draft legislation authorizing appropriations for programs in their areas; and
  - Draft legislation to revise permanent legislation to meet spending targets assigned to each committee in the CBR.

- **Appropriations Committees.** These committees are responsible for the annual appropriations bills. Each bill is prepared by a separate subcommittee. The staffs are very knowledgeable about departmental programs and often end up in political positions in the departments.

  With respect to the budget process, the appropriations committees:

  - Work closely with departments and agencies for which funding is provided in their bills;
  - Assign allocations to each subcommittee that in total are consistent with the targets in the budget resolution (302b allocations);
  - Draft appropriations bills consistent with subcommittee allocations;
  - Handle supplemental proposals as necessary; and
  - Take action on rescission messages from the President.

- **Government Reform (House) and Governmental Affairs (Senate) Committees**. These committees have jurisdiction over governmental operations including budget and accounting other than appropriations matters.

  With respect to the budget process, these committees:

  - Draft legislation, in coordination with other committees, on the budget process such as the Government Performance and Results Act, and the roles of institutions in the process.

- **Congressional Budget Office (CBO).** The CBO provides a variety of budget related services for the Congress including nonpartisan, objective analyses of key budgetary issues. The Director is appointed by the Speaker of the House and the President Pro Tempore of the Senate, after considering the recommendations from the two budget committees, to a term of four years. Either house may remove the Director by resolution. All other staff is appointed by the Director based on professional competence. CBO makes extensive use of outside professionally advisors to critique its work. Overall guidance comes from the budget committees.

With respect to the budget process, CBO:

- Prepares an annual economic and budget outlook report containing 10-year projections at the start of the year and an update at midyear;
- Provides an assessment of the President's Budget including the choice of economic assumptions, spendout rates (also known as outlay rates), and long term implications of policy choices for the appropriations committees;
- Provides a book of potential reductions to items in the President's Budget;
- Prepares a budget baseline based on current law for taxes and mandatory spending and inflation adjusted discretionary appropriations that is used by Congress during its budget deliberations;
- Prepares reports for authorizing committees on the cost of Federal mandates in reported bills;
- Provides budget analysis and cost reports on key policy issues;
- Provides advice as requested to committees on the potential costs of proposed programs;
- Provides an estimate of the cost of each bill before it goes to the floor of either house; and
- Monitors for Congress the status of spending bills.

- **Government Accountability Office (GAO).** GAO is the official auditor of the Government and provides a variety of services for the Congressional committees.

  With respect to the budget process, GAO:

  - Provides advice on proposed program budgets based on past results;
  - Provides advice on how management improvement can affect budget performance;
  - Provides Congress a report on OMB compliance with the sequestration process; and
  - Monitors Executive branch action on deferrals and rescissions.

- **Congressional Research Service (CRS).** The CRS, a component of the Library of Congress, provides Congress with confidential, nonpartisan research and analysis of major issues.

With respect to the budget process, the CRS:

- Prepares analyses for Members of Congress on major policy issues that may affect congressional action.

Independent Organizations

- **Board of Governors of the Federal Reserve System (FRB).** The FRB conducts the nation's monetary policy, regulates banking, maintains the stability of the financial system, and provides financial services.

  With respect to the budget process, the FRB:

    - Makes decisions on interest rates that affect Government borrowing costs; and
    - Provides advice to Congress about the effect on the economy of overall tax and spending levels.

Chapter 7

Formulation of the President's Budget

"[The President] shall from time to time give to the Congress Information of the State of the Union, and recommend to their Consideration such Measures as he shall judge necessary and expedient;"

Constitution, Article II, Section 3

By law, the President must submit a Budget to the Congress each year on or after the first Monday in January, but not later than the first Monday in February.[1] The President's Budget includes the following:

- A detailed plan for revenues and spending in the fiscal year that will start eight months later on October 1st (the "budget year") based on the President's priorities;
- Actual data on the most recently completed fiscal year, updated information on the current fiscal year, and planning estimates for four fiscal years following the budget year; and
- Any changes proposed to previously appropriated Budget Authority (BA).

The process for formulating the President's request receives less public exposure than the congressional process. Except for occasional White House announcements about areas targeted for budget increases, and leaks from agencies, contractors, and communities concerned about departmental and White House budget decisions, there is relatively little coverage in the mass media.

---

[1] 31 USC Sec. 1105, Preparation and submission of appropriations requests to the President.

All Federal departments and agencies and the Executive Office of the President are involved in the budget formulation process. The following agencies assist the President with the budget's formulation in the following ways:

- OMB manages the process for the President.
- The National Economic Council (NEC), created by President Clinton, oversees development of economic policies and provides a forum for cabinet members and White House officials to discuss program and policy priorities.
- The Council of Economic Advisers, OMB, and the Treasury Department jointly develop economic assumptions for the Budget. These assumptions cover inflation, real growth in the economy, interest, and unemployment.
- The Budget Review Board (BRB), created by President George W. Bush, reviews budget recommendations before they are submitted to the President for final approval. The Board, chaired by the Vice President, includes the Secretary of the Treasury, the Director of the Office of Management and Budget, the Chief of Staff to the President, and the Director of the National Economic Council.

History of the Executive Branch Budget Process

Prior to 1921, formulation of the budget and auditing responsibilities were assigned to a variety of Congressional committees. As the nation grew and the budget became more complex, this system proved inefficient primarily because there was no central body – other than the often politically charged Congress – responsible for reconciling all aspects of the budget. President Taft's administration (1909 – 1913) recognized this problem and proposed the adoption of a standardized annual budget system, but was unsuccessful due to resistance to change from Congress.

During World War I, when Federal expenditures skyrocketed, the need for a standard, central process was much more broadly recognized. Congress revisited former President Taft's proposal and passed a bill requiring the President to submit an annual Budget to Congress. President Wilson agreed with the concept, but vetoed the bill because it included a provision allowing the President to remove the Government's head auditor from office.

This concept was not implemented until after the war when President Harding, a Republican working with a Republican-controlled Congress, passed *The Budget and Accounting Act of 1921*, which included the provision opposed by Wilson. The Act did the following:

- Established the Bureau of the Budget, which was originally part of the Department of the Treasury, but was transferred to the Executive Office of the President in 1939 by President Roosevelt who wanted more control over departmental spending;
- Required the Bureau of the Budget to review all departmental budget requests to Congress;

- Required the President to submit a Budget proposal to Congress annually along with an assessment of the Nation's financial condition; and
- Established the General Accounting Office (GAO), which was to be overseen by the Comptroller General, a presidential appointee.

In 1948, as the Government focused on internal issues following World War II, the Bureau of the Budget, GAO, and Treasury collaborated to improve the efficiency and effectiveness of Government. The collaboration, known then as the "Joint Program," formed a charter that set the following mission that was later codified in *The Accounting and Procedures Act of 1950*:

> "... give the President better management in the executive branch, the Congress better information and bases for acting upon appropriations and other legislation, and the public a clearer picture of the financial condition and operations of the federal government."

Through the 1950s and '60s, various Presidential commissions recommended design changes to fortify the Bureau of the Budget's central leadership and address the problem of weighing sound budget decisions against tough management goals. This recommendation was finally implemented when proffered by the Ash Council, another Presidential commission, in 1970. The Bureau of the Budget was reorganized and renamed the Office of Management and Budget.

Today, OMB is charged by the President with "the development and implementation of budget, program, management, and regulatory policies."

Initial Work on Development of the Budget

Shortly after submitting the Budget for one fiscal year to Congress, work begins on the next fiscal year's Budget. Initial planning begins with the estimates for the outyears (years beyond the budget year) included in the Budget just submitted. OMB uses these figures in developing budget targets to be provided to the departments and agencies in the spring. (Figure 7-1)

Spring and Summer Policy and Program Reviews

Throughout the spring and summer, the departments and the Executive Office of the President conduct policy studies and program evaluations that can change the distribution of funds among departments and programs.

- For example, decisions flowing from a review directed by the Executive Office of the President on launch vehicles for space flight could affect funding proposals for the National Aeronautics and Space Administration (NASA) and the Department of Defense (DOD).

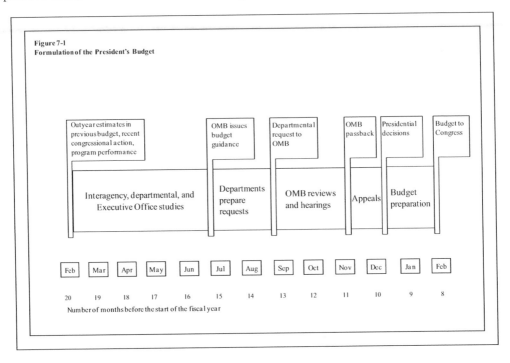

Figure 7-1
Formulation of the President's Budget

| Outyear estimates in previous budget, recent congressional action, program performance | | OMB issues budget guidance | Departmental request to OMB | OMB passback | Presidential decisions | Budget to Congress |

| Interagency, departmental, and Executive Office studies | Departments prepare requests | OMB reviews and hearings | Appeals | Budget preparation |

| Feb | Mar | Apr | May | Jun | Jul | Aug | Sep | Oct | Nov | Dec | Jan | Feb |

| 20 | 19 | 18 | 17 | 16 | 15 | 14 | 13 | 12 | 11 | 10 | 9 | 8 |

Number of months before the start of the fiscal year

- Departmental reviews can change the proposed allocation of funds among departmental programs.

Most departments have extensive internal review processes. The DOD has the most intensive process with a policy review and a detailed program review each year. DOD planning includes preparation of a detailed six-year plan that addresses the funding for every line item in the defense budget. Legislation creating the Department of Homeland Security requires the Department to develop long-term plans like those of DOD. Most other departments concentrate mainly on the next budget year.

OMB Guidance for Preparation of Departmental Budgets

In July, OMB issues guidance (OMB Circular A-11, Preparation, Submission, and Execution of the Budget) on budget concepts and rules that the departments must follow in preparing budget proposals. Although A-11 specifies the policies to be used in developing the departmental and agency budgets, exemptions may be requested.

The requirements of the Government Performance and Results Act (GPRA)[2] have been integrated into the Executive Branch budget process through Circular A-11. The Results Act has three essential components:

- **Strategic Plans.** Prepared by each department every three years, these provide a "big picture" plan of a department's mission, expected outcomes of programs, program performance goals, and management issues.

---

[2] Pub. L. 103-62, Aug. 3, 1993, the "Government Performance and Results Act of 1993."

- **Annual Performance Plans.**[3] Every year, each department and agency is required to prepare its own performance plan. OMB is also required to prepare a government-wide plan each year. The department/agency and OMB performance plans outline what is to be accomplished in the coming fiscal year at the proposed budget levels against the performance goals in the strategic plans.
- **Annual Performance Report.**[4] Prepared by the departments and agencies, these reports compare actual results to the measures in the Annual Performance Plan and identify any problems that kept the targets from being hit. This is accomplished through the Annual Performance and Accountability Reports issued by each department and agency in November after the end of the fiscal year. Eventually the performance results will be incorporated in all budget line items.

Beginning with the FY 2005 Budget, agencies have been required to submit performance budgets that include performance data with financial information and meet the GPRA requirement for an Annual Performance Plan. These performance budgets provide a detailed link between the general goals in the strategic plan and annual agency budgets and operations. The performance budget includes performance goals used to assess program performance, and other information needed to justify the agency budget request. Program costs are to reflect the full costs of programs including centrally funded administrative services and support.

Performance budgets require goals that are expressed in a quantifiable and measurable form. The guidance in OMB Circular A-11 requires that agencies link the proposed budget levels to expected results/outcomes. By identifying, tracking, and managing key performance indicators, agencies put themselves in position to create positive organizational transformation and create a Government that operates in a more business-like fashion.

Performance goals may be stated as "outcomes" or "outputs."

- **Outcomes.** These are the ultimate objectives of Government programs. This is the reason a program exists. To establish outcomes, there must be a clear definition of the expected result at the beginning of the program, e.g., deterrence of attack on the United States, completion of the census, development of a flu vaccine, etc.
- **Outputs.** An output measure presents the level of program activity or effort in a quantitative manner (e.g., number of pilots to be trained per year) or a qualitative manner (e.g., stratified levels of customer satisfaction). A reliance on output measures without linkage to strategic goals presents a risk that outcomes will not be achieved as anticipated in the performance budget.

OMB Circular A-11 specifies budget policies that the departments are to follow in developing their budget proposals, as follow:

---

[3] 31 USC Sec. 1115, Performance plans
[4] 31 USC Sec. 1116, Program performance reports

- **Advance appropriations.** Advance appropriations are not to be requested if the only purpose is to shift budget authority in the budget year to the following year.
- **Agency administrative actions.** Agencies must identify offsets when proposing administrative actions such as regulations, demonstrations, program notices, guidance to States or contractors, or other similar actions not required by law that would increase mandatory spending.
- **Environmental management.** Agencies should develop and implement management systems to integrate environmental accountability into agency day-to-day decision-making and long-term planning processes across all agency missions, activities, and functions.
- **Equal opportunity.** Program estimates should reflect programs to ensure or promote equal opportunity regardless of race, color, religion, national origin, sex, disability, or age.
- **Full funding.** Requests for acquisition of capital assets must propose full funding to cover the full costs of the project or a useful segment of the project. Specifically, requests for procurement programs must provide for full funding of the entire cost and requests for construction programs must provide for full funding of the complete cost of construction.
- **Government perquisites.** Estimates should reflect limited use of Government vehicles, Government aircraft, first class air travel, executive dining facilities, and conferences, in accordance with Presidential memoranda, dated February 10, 1993.
- **Multi-year appropriations.** Agencies should consider whether to request appropriations with multi-year availability, particularly for buildings, equipment, and other types of fixed capital assets, including major ADP and telecommunications systems, with long acquisition cycles.
- **Management improvement initiatives and policies.** Estimates should reflect actions to strengthen management and improve program performance in the following areas:

  - **Capital planning and investment control**. Estimates should reflect information technology (IT) investments that directly support agency strategic missions; employ an integrated planning, budgeting, and procurement process; are citizen-centered; and are consistent with the Clinger Cohen Act of 1996, the Paperwork Reduction Act, the Federal Acquisition Streamlining Act, and OMB Circular A–130, Management of Federal Information Resources.
  - **Electronic transactions and electronic recordkeeping**. Estimates should be based on E-Government projects managed through the agency's capital planning process and enterprise architecture.
  - **Security.** Estimates should reflect OMB security policies and National Institute of Standards and Technology (NIST) guidance.
  - **Privacy**. Estimates should include a description of the steps taken to ensure compliance with all OMB privacy policies.
  - **Improper Payments**. Estimates should reflect anticipated reductions in improper payments as reported in the Performance and Accountability Report.

- **Financial systems**. Estimates should reflect plans to achieve a single, agency-wide, integrated financial management system.
- **User charges.** User charges for programs must be reviewed at least once every two years and the results reported along with any resultant proposals in the Chief Financial Officers Annual Report.

Development of Department and Agency Budget Requests

Under law, the departments and agencies prepare budget requests in accordance with Presidential guidance.[5] In early September, the departments submit their detailed proposals to OMB.

- The proposals are to reflect the OMB guidance and the results of the spring and summer policy studies, congressional action on the last request, and actual program performance. The proposals are to include performance information on outcomes and output anticipated at the proposed budget levels. In addition, the departments and agencies are to submit PARTs that evaluate program management practices and results.
- Departmental requests often exceed the planning estimates issued by OMB.

A slightly different process is used for the Department of Defense. There are special procedures for a joint review of military department proposals by OMB and the Office of the Secretary of Defense (OSD). In contrast with other departments, the Secretary of Defense does not submit a budget request to OMB in September. Instead, the military departments and defense agencies submit their requests to both OMB and OSD in September for a joint review of the estimates. As part of the joint review process, OMB participates in all phases of DOD's planning, programming, budgeting, and execution system (PPBES), though the level of participation varies by Administration.

Revenue proposals are prepared by the Department of the Treasury, OMB, and the National Economic Council.

Writing Effective Budget Justification

Gaining support for new programs, expanding existing programs, or even maintaining current program levels will be increasingly difficult within the current fiscal situation. Success will require increased emphasis or program performance and the preparation of carefully crafted justification. Many people, some with little knowledge of the subject at issue, will have to be sufficiently impressed with the justification in order to gain the desired outcomes. These people range from other offices and superiors within the department, OMB and White House staff, members of congress and staff, program stakeholders, and the media.

In writing budget justification, three things are critical — style, substance, and spin.

---

[5] 31 USC Sec. 1108, Preparation and submission of appropriations requests to the President

Style means making the justification easy for the reader to understand. These are common-sense rules that should be followed for almost any type of professional writing. Among these are the following:

- **Short declaratory sentences**. Sentences should be clear to make certain the reader understands the proposal. Sentences should be limited to no more than three lines. Any sentence longer than that increases the chances of misinterpretation and confusion about the point being made.
- **Limit use of technical terms and jargon**. While such terms can have meaning to professionals working in the subject matter under consideration, many, if not most, of the readers who need to be reached and influenced often lack that professional knowledge. Too much use of technical language can irritate the reader as well as add confusion to the issue. Almost all issues can be explained in common words and reducing them to the common words may actually improve understanding of the project under consideration.
- **Avoid meaningless words.** Adverbs and adjectives should be used sparingly. Although there may be a temptation to describe expected results as a "great" improvement or "very good," such words lack meaning. Unless a scale is provided to explain how much improvement is "great" compared to "outstanding" or "good," the word is meaningless and tends to make the reader think it was used to inflate the value of the project.

Substance refers to the details of the budget proposal. In developing a proposal for a new program, the following points should be addressed.

- **Problem to be solved.** State precisely what will be done. There should be no confusion over what is being discussed and what is being proposed. The strongest case can be made by stating the problem or opportunity, the magnitude of the problem or opportunity, and how the proposal will help resolve the issue. This is best done in terms of a measurable outcome. Expected performance levels are useful.
- **How the U.S. will be better.** Show how the program will benefit national objectives. This can include meeting the objective faster, more efficiently, or at a higher level of achievement.
- **Uniqueness**. State how the program will make or is making a unique contribution to solving a problem that would not be achieved otherwise.
- **Duration.** The duration of a new program or increased level of effort should be made clear. This would include stating whether the increased funding is for a one-time effort or a continuing program. If a continuing program, some indication of future costs would be useful. Projected progress by year toward obtaining the desired outcome should be included.
- **Stewardship.** If supporting an existing program, it would be helpful to show that the program is being managed well by using PART evaluations and other independent assessments.

- **Other participants**. Identify other agencies, foreign governments, state or local governments, or the private sector that will be participants in the program.
- **Cost.** State the budget year cost and include a projection of future resource demands to carry out the program.
- **Financing.** If the program is new, state whether it is to be financed with appropriations, user fees, tax credits, or to be carried out through regulation.
- **Program risk.** Be upfront about program risks. If the program obtains funding and then falters, OMB and Congress will lose confidence in the department with potentially negative effects on other departmental initiatives.
- **Legal basis.** The justification should emphasize the legal basis for program. This would include a treaty obligation or legislation directing a program for a specific purpose.

Spin is the way the proposal is presented to convince the decision-makers and others as to why they should want to support and push the program.

- **Priorities.** Tie the program to Presidential priorities and the goals and objectives in the department's strategic plan. A program manager has to get the program through the departmental budget process before it goes to the OMB and then to Congress. The connection to departmental priorities is essential to get through the important first step of the process. A successful proposal will be very clear about the connection and why the departmental secretary or agency director would want to approve and support the proposal. For OMB approval, the connection to Presidential priorities is essential. In the current environment, for example, showing a direct connection to improving homeland security or energy independence would be helpful. For dealing with the Congress, it should provide a defense against the claims that are likely to be raised as a result of partisan politics.
- **Descriptors.** In that the people who make or influence the key decisions are busy, the proposal has to be stated in a simple, concise manner. "Buzzwords" or shorthand ways to describe the program often can be useful if the program is a major initiative and likely to receive media coverage. Examples of such descriptions would include the following, "War-on-Terror," "death tax," and "terrorist surveillance program." If the proponents do not develop appropriate "buzzwords," program opponents will develop ones to disparage the program.
- **Stakeholders**. The likely views of stakeholders should be understood. Such stakeholders include the program beneficiaries, the service providers, and the bill payers (taxpayers). Formulation of the President's Budget will be focused on the Administration's program priorities. Congressional review, however, will give weight to stakeholder considerations. While stakeholder views should not drive Administration recommendations, agency and Administration leaders should be aware of the potential views in order to respond to the issues that might be raised. Data that may help get the stakeholders to support the proposal should be emphasized in testimony and in the President's Budget documents.

OMB and White House Review of Departmental Requests

During September and October, OMB staff review the requests.

- OMB staff holds hearings with departmental representatives to review the consistency of the request with presidential policy and Federal responsibilities, program performance, and the validity of the pricing and scheduling assumptions.
- OMB and departmental policy officials discuss Presidential and departmental priorities.

In late October and early November, the OMB Director reviews the requests.

- OMB staff present issue papers that analyze the departments' requests, discuss program performance, provide options to the requests, and comment on likely congressional and public reaction. Budget tables show the possible distribution of funds among departments and budget functions.
- Policy officials in OMB, the NEC, and other parts of the Executive Office of the Presidents provide their views on program priorities and trade-offs among departments and functions.

In late November, the Director "passes back" decisions to the departments on what the Budget will include. These include the overall budget level (BA and outlays) and budget and policy guidance for specific programs, where appropriate.

Departmental Appeals of OMB Passbacks

The departments generally appeal OMB passback decisions; both the specific program guidance and the overall budget level.

In late November and early December, departmental appeals of OMB passback decisions are resolved.

- OMB and the department will attempt to reach agreement.
- Major issues that the department and OMB cannot resolve are forwarded to the President or a board established by the President for resolution. In the Bush Administration, a Budget Review Board (BRB) composed of the Vice President, the Secretary of the Treasury, the Director of OMB, the Chief of Staff, and the National Economic Council Director review the appeals and attempt to resolve differences between the departments and OMB.
- The departments can appeal decisions of the BRB to the President.
- The President will make final decisions on the open issues before the end of December after hearing the departmental and OMB cases and receiving White House staff's views.

Preparing Budget Documents for Submission to the Congress

During January, OMB and the departments reconcile the numbers and prepare the final Budget documents.

In February, the President submits the Budget to Congress.

- The documentation includes the Budget message of the President, a description of the President's priority programs, and supporting information.
- The *Budget Appendix*, a book comparable in size to the telephone book of a large metropolitan area, includes details on every account in the Budget. Currently, there are more than 2,200 accounts in the Budget.
- The departments provide detailed justification data to the relevant congressional committees for each program. Before they are sent to Congress, congressional budget justification documents prepared by the departments must be cleared by OMB to ensure consistency with Presidential policy.

Mid-year Update of Budget Estimates

Before July 16th each year, the President must submit to Congress an update of the Budget estimates, the "mid-session review."[6] This document shows the budgetary effect of laws enacted since the Budget was submitted, changes to economic assumptions, and changes proposed by the President.

Budgeting During the Transition from one Administration to Another

The Process for formulation of the President's Budget is very different and in fact, shortened after an election year. The election year process formally commences post election. Informally, many of the most significant budget issues are discussed and decided without the assistance of executive budget professionals during the campaign. Much of the expertise required to put together the candidates' budget proposal comes from the candidates' Congressional allies and industry/non-profit advocates for specific programs.

Notwithstanding the new Administration's policy priorities, the incoming president's budget transmitted to Congress does not impact 90 to 95 percent of the overall Federal budget.

As discussed earlier, outgoing presidents are less insistent about preparation of a comprehensive Federal budget. The outgoing administration is more committed to maintaining their fiscal and economic policy for legacy purposes. They also target issues to keep their base support for their political party.

---

[6] 31 USC Sec. 1106, Supplemental budget estimates and changes, subsection (b).

Content & Role of Transition Budget Books. The budget process during presidential transition begins with the preparation of Department and Agency transition budget books.

The transition budget books provide a brief summary of base programs and different budget policy scenarios, including:

- Baseline projections consistent with Office of Management and Budget (OMB) and Congressional Budget Office (CBO) guidelines;
- Full funding estimates for current programs and policies;
- Unfunded requirements; and
- New initiatives.

Other budget materials include issue papers, which analyze the major budget policy issues, as well as increases, decreases or new incentives driven by the winning campaign not included in the previous president's budget.

All of these things have a bearing on near-term budget execution decisions regarding procurements, contracts, loan guarantees, etc., to be issued within the 3 to 6 months of assuming office.

Review & Decision-Making Process. The decision-making process follows:

- The incoming transition team for each department or agency identifies changes they would like to see made to the budget that was formulated under the outgoing president;
- Each department or agency prepares budget proposals and supporting justifications, which are submitted to OMB for review;
- OMB career staff review the proposals and prepare the Director's Review Book, inclusive of issue papers;
- OMB staff also identify and prepare decision papers based upon guidance from the incoming OMB transition team;
- The modifications are decided by OMB's new political management; and finally
- OMB passes back decisions associated with the department's or agency's budget change request.

Recent Budget Transition Approaches.

- <u>**Gerald R. Ford to Jimmy Carter.**</u> President Ford prepared a full-blown budget. The Ford strategy was to leave behind a very detailed budget blueprint as a benchmark to evaluate the Carter Administration. The Ford budget process tied up the resources of the career bureaucracy until the late stages of the transition. The Carter Administration subsequently submitted a selected list of budget amendments to Congress in late spring 1977. The first full Carter Budget did not take place until 1978.

- **Jimmy Carter to Ronald W. Reagan.** President Carter prepared a detailed budget blueprint. The Reagan transition team proactively sought to quickly reverse the Carter budget. The Reagan transition team informally worked with the OMB career staff to identify issues, prepare issue papers, and develop recommendations for changes during the transition process—and they did this in parallel with the formulation of the Carter budget. President Reagan had campaigned on three main issues: tax cuts, defense build-up, and deficit reduction. President Reagan submitted a revised budget plan to Congress within a month of his inauguration. The budget was primarily a shell to support the DOD budget build-up and the proposed reduction in marginal tax rates. The Reagan budget contained the "major asterisk"—a plug made to account for unspecified future budget cuts.

- **Ronald W. Reagan to George H.W. Bush.** President Reagan prepared a detailed budget blueprint. President-elect Bush decided to defer to President Reagan on the outgoing budget. The Bush transition team identified a discrete set of budget issues to review. The Reagan transition team also closely managed the flow of information to the Bush transition team. The Bush transition team proposed selected amendments to the Reagan budget. There were no major policy differences between the outgoing Reagan budget and the Bush budget.

- **George H.W. Bush to Bill Clinton.** President Bush started the process of not submitting a detailed budget. President Bush prepared a general budget baseline projection. The outgoing budget was a "policy wonk" document; it discussed alternative policy scenarios for spending policies. The Clinton transition team was faced with the challenge of preparing a full-blown budget from scratch. Clinton campaigned around several issues—economic stimulus, tax fairness, and defense conversion. The Clinton budget was submitted to Congress in two stages—an initial stage in which the Administration selectively highlighted initiatives, followed by the formulation of a more detailed budget. On February 17, 1993, the initial top-level economic plan and budget was submitted to Congress. On April 8, 1993, the detailed Clinton budget was submitted to Congress.

- **Bill Clinton to George W. Bush.** President Clinton issued a general budget projection in January 2001. The budget document was more backward-looking than forward-looking; it chronicled the achievements of the Clinton/Gore Administration. The Bush transition team worked to identify selective increases or cuts and imposed a freeze on the rest of the budget. Bush inherited a large budget surplus and campaigned on the issue of tax cuts. The Bush strategy was to deliberately downplay the budget in order to focus Congress' attention on tax cuts. On February 28, 2001, President Bush submitted a high-level budget to Congress, along with his tax cut plan. On April 7, 2001, President Bush submitted a detailed budget proposal to Congress.

- **George W. Bush to Barack Obama.** President Bush similarly decided to prepare a budget baseline projection. Prior to submission of a budget, President Obama submitted a request to Congress in January 2009 for an economic stimulus package of Government spending to reignite the economy that was in deep recession and to make good on campaign promises. A budget outline, '*A New Era of Responsibility: Renewing America's Promise*' on February 26, 2009 that described the major policy initiatives including energy advancement, education increases, and science funding. Full documentation for the budget was issued in May.

Chapter 8

Congressional Budgetary Processes

"No Money shall be drawn from the Treasury, but
In Consequence of Appropriations made by Law..."

Constitution, Article 1, Section 9, Paragraph 7.

"All Bills for raising Revenues shall originate in the
House of Representatives; but the Senate may propose
Or concur with Amendments as on other Bills."

Constitution, Article 1, Section 7, Paragraph 1.

The congressional process has four main elements:

1. Development of a Concurrent Budget Resolution (CBR);
2. Reconciliation of permanent law to the requirements of the CBR;
3. Authorization of new and annual programs; and
4. Appropriation of funds for annual programs.

In contrast to the closed process for formulating the President's Budget, the congressional process is open except for some committee hearings on national security issues and bill markup sessions.

Citizens and organizations interested in particular legislation can insert themselves into the congressional process. They can:

- Meet with their Representatives and Senators;
- Request time to appear in hearings before the committees and subcommittees; and
- Recommend actions and propose language for inclusion in bills.

The President, White House staff, and the rest of the Executive Branch follow each step of the congressional process very closely. The end results of these processes are bills that the President must approve or veto. The Administration informs Congress of its views on each bill through a Statement of Administration Policy (SAP), prepared by the Office of Management and Budget (OMB) and coordinated with all departments and agencies affected by the bill. The SAP states whether the Administration supports the bill, recommends changes to the bill as written, or recommends a veto.

The departments and agencies devote considerable time and effort to the committees.

- They ensure that the members of the authorization and appropriations committees understand their priorities and problems.
- Policy officials and staff testify before the committees that have roles in the congressional budget process. All written testimony provided to Congress is first cleared by OMB to ensure that it is consistent with the President's Budget and policies.

The committees work more closely with the departments and agencies than with the White House.

- Committees tend to be protective of their client agencies.
- Issues on which the departments did not prevail during the development of the President's Budget often resurface in Congress.

Committee staff members play key roles in congressional action.

- Departmental budgets contain so many line items that it is almost impossible for a Representative or Senator to understand all the details. Committee staffs master those details.
- Committee staffs write the committee reports accompanying each bill that explain the committees' actions and provide direction to the various departments and agencies. Although the direction found in "report language" is not legally binding, departments and agencies customarily follow it as though it were.

The Congressional Budget Office (CBO) supports the congressional budget process.

- CBO prepares periodic reports, special analyses, a book of possible budget reductions, and budget baseline estimates for congressional action.
- CBO publishes a review of the President's Budget shortly after it is submitted to Congress that includes a repricing of the Budget using CBO, rather than OMB, economic and spending rate assumptions.
- Congressional committees use CBO-developed economic assumptions and outlay rates to evaluate the effect of alternative budget proposals.
- CBO provides Congress with estimates of the budgetary effect of each bill.[1]

Congress has many opportunities to address specific programs. For each bill (authorization and appropriations), these opportunities present themselves in:

- House and Senate subcommittee markups of the bill;
- Full committee markup of the bill in the House and Senate;
- Floor action on the bill in each house; and
- Conference committee bill actions. (These committees can take actions not included in either house's bill.)

An important step in the House that is not applicable to the Senate is the rule for floor debate. Before a bill is taken to the House floor, a rule is created and approved by the Rules Committee and passed by the House which states the time for debate, the amendments that will be considered, and the order of the amendments.

Prior to 1974, the Congressional budgeting process was fragmented and complicated. Because there was no process for Congress to establish its own spending and revenue priorities, it tended to respond to the President's Budget in piece-meal fashion. Congress would take up appropriations for each area separately; i.e., it might pass a defense appropriation bill, then a transportation bill, then a foreign aid appropriation bill without an overall plan for meeting any specific spending or revenue targets. Additionally, the lack of a formal congressional process led to increasing Executive influence on the Federal Budget. President Nixon's impoundment of public works funds appropriated by Congress was a component of the impetus for reform.

In response to these problems, Congress passed the Congressional Budget and Impoundment Control Act of 1974. The Act was designed to coordinate decisions on sources and levels of revenues and on spending priorities and levels of expenditures. The main features of the Act were:

- Each year, Congress would adopt a concurrent resolution imposing overall constraints on revenues and spending as well as distributing the overall con-

---

[1] 2 USC Sec. 602, Duties and functions

straint on spending among the various congressional committees for them to apply to their respective programs and activities;

- Budget committees were created in the House and the Senate to develop the concurrent resolution;
- The Congressional Budget Office (CBO) was established to provide independent budget information and analysis to Congress;
- A timetable was established for congressional action on the budget; and
- Procedures were adopted that denied the President the ability to impound funds without congressional agreement.

Figure 8-1 shows the steps in the congressional process and the approximate timing.

Concurrent Budget Resolution

The first step in the congressional process is the preparation of a Concurrent Budget Resolution (CBR). The CBR states the budget priorities of Congress for the next five fiscal years. For example, it will state whether Congress wants to reduce or increase taxes, reduce or increase defense or domestic spending, or adjust entitlement programs.

The CBR includes budget aggregates, functional allocations of spending, and reconciliation instructions.[2]

- Aggregates include total revenues, total new budget authority, total outlays, the surplus or deficit, the debt limit, total new direct loan obligations, and new primary loan guarantee commitments.
- Functional allocations show total spending, both mandatory and discretionary, by budget function.
- A section 302 allocation is provided to the appropriations committees stating the maximum amount that may be appropriated.
- Reconciliation directives instruct the authorizing and finance committees on the dollar amount of revenue or spending changes they must achieve by revising permanent laws concerning revenue and spending.

Major steps in developing the CBR include the following:

- In mid-March, six weeks after the submittal of the President's Budget, each congressional committee provides funding and revenue recommendations for the programs under its jurisdiction to the budget committee of the relevant house;
- The House and Senate Budget Committees develop resolutions for their respective chambers;

---

[2] 2 USC Sec. 632, Annual adoption of concurrent resolution on the budget

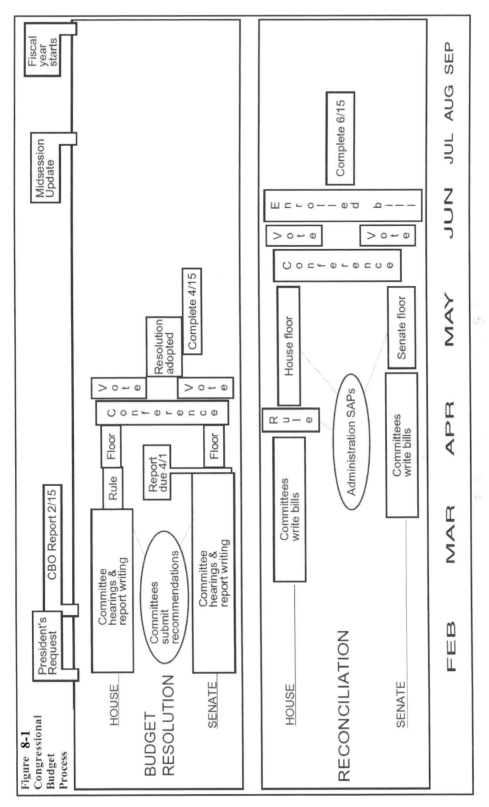

Figure **8-1**
Congressional
Budget
Process

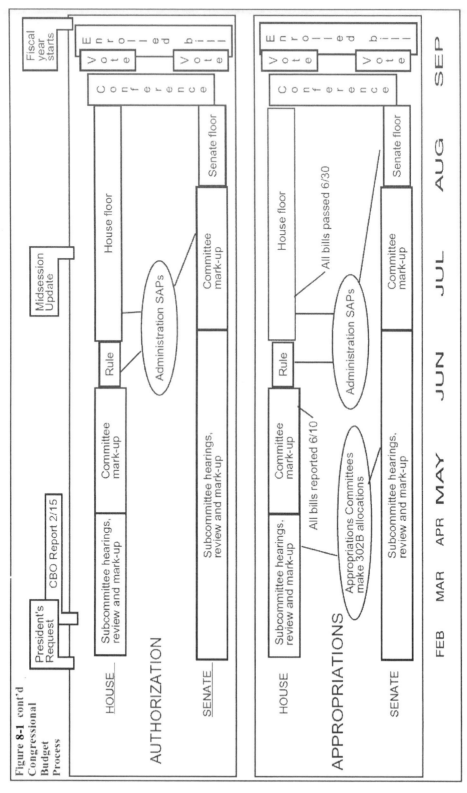

Figure 8-1 cont'd
**Congressional
Budget
Process**

- Budget committee reports specify the programmatic assumptions used in developing the amounts for each budget function;
- The Senate Budget Committee is obligated by law to report to the Senate by April 1st;
- Each chamber passes a resolution;
- A joint House-Senate Conference resolves differences between the two resolutions and develops a consensus position;
- Each chamber votes for or against the Conference position; and
- Congress, by law, must adopt a resolution by April 15th.[3]

After the resolution is adopted, the total budget authority and outlays specified therein are allocated to the House and Senate committees with jurisdiction for the particular subject matter.

- Discretionary spending is under the jurisdiction of the appropriations committees.
- Amounts proposed by the committees may not exceed the amounts in the resolution.

The CBR is not a law and does not require Presidential approval. Nevertheless, Congress often attempts to obtain Presidential agreement because the allocations included in the CBR set the overall funding levels that become the basis for appropriations bills sent to the President for approval. In several years, the Congress has been unable to adopt a budget resolution. In those cases, the spending and revenue levels approved for that fiscal year in the previous CBR become the targets.

Reconciliation

Authorization and finance committees customarily issue directives to legislate policy changes in mandatory spending or revenue programs to achieve CBR targets. This process, created in a budget resolution in 1974, is called reconciliation.[4]

- The CBR specifies the dollar amount of change that each committee must achieve — Section 302(a) allocations in accordance with the Congressional Budget Act.
- Each committee has discretion to determine which laws and programs to change to achieve the required levels.[5]

---

[3] 2 USC Sec. 631, Timetable

[4] The Budget Reconciliation Process at http://www.rules.house.gov/archives/bud_rec_proc.htm. Parliamentary Outreach Program. U.S. House of Representatives, Committee on Rules, Majority Office.

[5] 2 USC Sec. 641, Reconciliation

Reconciliation action can take any of the following forms:

- An increase or reduction in tax levels;
- A change in the benefits or eligibility requirements for entitlement programs;
- A requirement that Government agencies charge fees; or
- A change in budget laws.

Congress often enacts a single Omnibus Budget Reconciliation Act (OBRA) that includes all the legislation necessary to carry out all the reconciliation directives with respect to spending in the CBR. Tax matters typically are contained in separate legislation. As required by the Constitution, tax legislation starts in the House.

Action on reconciliation is to be completed by June 15th. Like other congressional deadlines on budget matters, the reconciliation date is seldom met.

- Reconciliation issues address tax and entitlement programs, which often are quite controversial and involve considerable give-and-take between Congress and the President. In some cases, e.g., FY 1996 and FY 1997, Congress never finished reconciliation due to differences with the President over Medicare and other politically sensitive issues.

Program Authorization

Authorization acts are derived from the legislative practice of distinguishing between the laws enacted to set Federal policies and the laws that fund them. Authorization laws establish, continue, and modify Federal programs. With respect to funding, authorizations take two forms:

- Some authorize programs and limits on the amounts of funding that can be made available in appropriations bills.

  - These may be annual authorizations or multiyear authorizations.
  - When an authorization expires, Congress may extend the life of the program through reauthorization or extend a program by simply providing new appropriations. Appropriations made available after an authorization has expired are considered "unauthorized" appropriations. Although the House and Senate each have laws precluding appropriations for a program that has not been authorized, if a point of order is not raised in either the House or the Senate, the appropriation may proceed through the legislative process

- Other authorizations, known as mandatory spending or direct spending programs, set policy and make funds available without further appropriations action. Mandatory spending includes funding for most major entitlement programs.

- These authorizations may provide specific dollar amounts (definite authorizations) or "such sums as are necessary" (indefinite authorizations).
- More than half of all Federal spending is for programs for which the appropriations are provided for in the authorization legislation.
- These laws typically provide permanent authorization, though some, such as the Food Stamp program and income support programs, require periodic renewal.
- Most entitlement spending is provided under laws that provide benefits to all eligible participants. Laws providing for an entitlement usually contain formulas or criteria that specify who is eligible. Unless the law is changed, these individuals retain a right to the benefits, regardless of the budget situation.
- Although some entitlements are funded in annual appropriation acts, the amounts provided are controlled by the authorization law. Even though the funding is included in an appropriations bill, it is still considered mandatory spending. The appropriations bill simply liquidates the obligation by appropriating sums necessary to cover the cost of the program. In the appropriations process, Congress does not have the discretion to change the amount to be spent.

Although the authorization of an appropriation typically precedes the enactment of the appropriation, this is not always the case. When authorization is delayed, Congress may enact an appropriation that contains its own "authorization."

An authorization may originate in either chamber, though it typically starts in the House of Representatives.

In addition to providing authority for an appropriation, an authorization may also include:

- Limits on the amount that can be appropriated for a program;
- Limits on the types of costs that can be incurred; and
- Other direction affecting program management and program content.

Some programs require annual authorization, other programs receive authorization for a specified number of years, and still others are authorized for an indefinite time period.

- The military programs of the Department of Defense (DoD) are an example of programs that require annual authorization. Each year, Congress authorizes all DoD programs, addressing every line item in the appropriations bill.

- Funding for regulatory agencies, by contrast, is usually authorized for a specified number of years.
- Funding for Social Security, Medicare, and retirement benefits for Federal Government employees is provided in authorizing legislation for an indefinite number of years and is not part of the annual appropriations process. ⸝

Authorization bills are under the jurisdiction of committees other than the House and Senate Appropriations Committees. A summary of the committees responsible for authorizations, by topic, is in Table 8-1.

PAYGO Restrictions on Mandatory Spending and Revenue Legislation

PAYGO (or pay-as-you-go) rule requires that new mandatory spending or tax changes must not add to the Federal deficit, that is they must be "budget neutral." The goal is to require Congress to prioritize expenses and exercise fiscal restraint.

Mandatory (or direct spending) generally is provided in substantive legislation under the jurisdiction of the legislative committees and is used principally to fund entitlement programs — such as Social Security, Medicare, Medicaid, Federal employee and military retirement, and unemployment compensation. This does not affect discretionary spending that is provided in the annual appropriations.

If revenue is to be reduced through a reduction in tax rates, for example, the effect on the deficit must be offset either through increased revenues elsewhere or spending reductions of the same amount.

The rule applies to any bill or joint resolution that includes one or more provisions affecting direct spending or revenues.

PAYGO provisions have been enacted into law three times:

- **The Budget Enforcement Act of 1990 (BEA).** This Act required all increases in direct spending or revenue decreases to be offset by other spending decreases or revenue increases. It was hoped that this would control increases in deficit spending. Legislation designated as "emergency" was exempt. If OMB determined the requirements had not been met, the President was to sequester funds from the programs subject to sequester to make up the difference. This PAYGO law expired in 2002 with the expiration of the Budget Enforcement Act.

- **The Restoring Fiscal Discipline Act of 2007.** This Act made it out of order in the Senate to consider any direct spending or revenue legislation that would increase or cause an on-budget deficit during certain specified time periods.

- **Statutory Pay-As-You-Go Act of 2010.** This bill reinstated PAYGO rules similar to those in the BEA. This rule required any increased mandatory spending or revenue reduction legislation be deficit neutral before approved by Congress. An exception is made for "emergency" legislation, though any Senator may object to the "emergency" classification; a three-fifths vote is required to counter the objection. Congress can suspend these rules if three-fifths of the members vote to do so.

The 2010 Act requires the chairs of the Budget Committees to request from the Director of the CBO an estimate of the budgetary effects of a PAYGO Act before a vote is taken on the legislation in either chamber. If CBO determines the PAYGO requirement is met, the legislation is cleared for a vote.

OMB is required to maintain and make publicly available a continuously updated PAYGO scorecard. OMB also is designated to make an annual report public, including an up-to-date document containing the PAYGO scorecard, within 14 business days of the end of a congressional session. If report shows a debit on either PAYGO scorecard for the budget year, the President is obligated to sequester funds from the non-exempt accounts to make up the difference. The 2010 Act also exempted almost all mandatory programs exempt from sequestration.

Earmarks

Appropriations bills provide the budgetary resources for the majority of Federal programs. These bills often contain funds added by the Congress for projects of local interest to a Representative or Senator. These special interest projects, called earmarks, have become an issue between the Congress and the President.

Last year, the President made it clear he opposed most types of earmarks. In response, the earmarks dropped to approximately $15.6 billion in 2010 from the level of $19.9 billion in 2009.

One of the main challenges with earmarks in appropriations bills is there is not a clear consensus definition of the term.

According to OMB, earmarks are funds provided by the Congress for projects or programs where the congressional direction (in bill or report language) circumvents the merit-based or competitive allocation process, or specifies the location or recipient. Congress includes earmarks in appropriation bills and in authorization bills.

The Congressional Research Service (CRS) notes that earmarks are often contained only in reports issued by House and Senate Appropriations Committees rather than in the actual legislation. For some bills, an earmark may refer to funds set aside within an account for a specified program, project, activity, institution, or location. In others, the application may reflect a more narrow set of directives to fund individual projects, locations, or institutions.

Citizens against Government Waste (CAGW) defines earmarks as line-items in an appropriations bill that designates tax dollars for a specific purpose in circumvention of established budgetary procedures. CAGW has seven sets of criteria for earmarks:

- Not specifically authorized;
- Not competitively awarded;
- Not requested by the President;
- Greatly exceeds the President's budget request or the previous year's funding;
- Not the subject of congressional hearings; and
- Serves only a local or special interest.

Another characteristic of earmarks, generally used in foreign operations appropriations is that they are sometimes defined as either "hard" or "soft." A hard earmark is defined as an earmark where the Administration is required to spend a certain amount on a certain activity, organizational or country program and will use wording such as allocate, direct or shall in the text. A soft earmark will use wording such as recommend, endorse, urge or should in the text. Soft earmarks generally seek adaptations of Congressional targets and are orchestrated by executive agencies.

Earmarks are not a new issue. The first recognized use of earmarking was the Bonus Bill of 1817, introduced by John Calhoun to provide United States highways linking the East and South to the West using an "earnings bonus" from the Second Bank of the United States. This was the first instance of directing Federal money to a specific local project. It was a part of the American System proposed by Henry Clay, a colleague of Calhoun. Calhoun argued for it using the general welfare and post roads clauses in the Constitution. Since then, earmarks have become commonplace.

In 2006, the U.S. House of Representatives passed H.R. 4975, the Lobbying Transparency and Accountability Act. The bill made it inappropriate to consider appropriations measures containing earmarks if the legislation, its accompanying reports, or managers' joint explanatory statements did not list such earmarks or name the requesting Members.

Speaker of the House Dennis Hastert (R-IL) and House Majority Leader John A. Boehner (R-OH) agreed, as a condition for support of the bill by House Appropriations Chairman Jerry Lewis (R-CA), that the earmark disclosure provisions would also be applied to authorization and tax legislation and not just to appropriations.

In March of 2010, the Democratic Party called on the House to completely ban earmarks for private for-profit companies. However, this means that earmarks can still be

Table 8-1
Policy Areas and Committee Jurisdiction

Policy area	House Committee	Senate Committee
Agriculture, nutrition, Food Stamps, forestry, crop insurance, farm credit, rural electrification & development	Agriculture	Agriculture
Banks and banking, deposit insurance, Defense Production Act, economic stabilization, aid to commerce and industry (except transportation), money and credit, public and private housing, securities and exchanges, urban development	Financial Services	Banking, Housing, and Urban Affairs
Civil aviation, navigation, highway safety, Coast Guard, inland waterways, Merchant Marine (except national security aspects), railroads, water transportation	Transportation and Infrastructure	Commerce, Science, and Transportation
Communications regulation	Energy and Commerce	Commerce, Science, and Transportation
Education and labor generally, child labor, wages and hours of labor, miners welfare	Education and Labor	Health, Education, Labor and Pensions
Energy policy	Energy and Commerce	Energy and Natural Resources
Energy R&D	Science	Energy and Natural Resources
Environmental R&D	Science	Environment and Public Works
Export controls	Foreign Affairs	Banking, Housing, and Urban Affairs
Fisheries and wildlife	Natural Resources	Environment and Public Works
Food programs for school children	Education and Labor	Agriculture
Foreign relations, foreign loans, international conferences and congresses, foreign assistance, United Nations	Foreign Affairs	Foreign Relations
Government operations, accounting, Federal civil service, postal service, public information and the National Archives	Oversight and Government Reform	Homeland Security and Governmental Affairs
Overall homeland security and Department of Homeland Security activities in border and port security, customs, management of homeland security information, domestic terrorism response preparedness, R&D and transportation security	Homeland Security	Homeland Security and Governmental Affairs
Immigration and naturalization, claims against the United States, national penitentiaries, patents, copyright, and trademarks	Judiciary	Judiciary
Intelligence	Intelligence	Intelligence
Irrigation and reclamation, public lands, mineral interests	Natural Resources	Energy and Natural Resources
Marine affairs, coastal zone management, and oceanography	Natural Resources	Commerce, Science, and Transportation

Table 8-1, continued
Policy Areas and Committee Jurisdiction

Policy area	House Committee	Senate Committee
National Aeronautics and Space Administration, National Institute of Standards and Technology, National Science Foundation, National Weather Service, scientific R&D, marine research	Science	Commerce, Science, and Transportation
National security including Department of Defense military functions, Merchant Marine (national security aspects), military application of nuclear energy, selective service, strategic and critical materials	Armed Services	Armed Services
Native Americans generally	Natural Resources	Indian Affairs
Nuclear energy industry regulation	Energy and Commerce	Environment and Public Works
Public health and biomedical research and development	Energy and Commerce	Health, Education, Labor and Pensions
Railroad retirement	Transportation and Infrastructure	Health, Education, Labor and Pensions
Revenue measures, debt, Social Security, Medicare, unemployment insurance	Ways and Means	Finance
Road construction/maintenance, flood control, improvement of rivers and harbors, public buildings, and public works (bridges and dams except international)	Transportation and Infrastructure	Agriculture
Small business	Small Business	Small Business
Veterans affairs	Veterans Affairs	Veterans Affairs
Water and power	Transportation and Infrastructure	Energy and Natural Resources

passed to aid other pet projects including non-profits and municipalities in their congressional districts.

Soon after, House Republicans announced their entire 178-member conference would not seek any earmarks this year, denouncing all of the line-item expenditures as wasteful and corrupting; calling the earmark process "a symbol of a broken Washington." House Minority Leader John Boehner (R-Ohio) said the Republican gambit was a key step in demonstrating fiscal restraint, even if the move doesn't lead to an actual reduction in Federal spending. He went on to say the following:

> "Republicans took an important step toward showing the American people we're serious about reform by adopting an immediate, unilateral ban on all earmarks. But the more difficult battle lies ahead, and that's stopping the spending spree in Washington that is saddling our children and grandchildren with trillions of dollars in debt,"

At the time of writing, the Senate had not yet determined whether it would follow the initiative set by the House.

Appropriations

The Appropriations Committee in each chamber allocates the discretionary amounts approved in the CBR among its subcommittees. These allocations, referred to as 302(b) allocations (in reference to 302(b) of the Congressional Budget Act), provide linkage between the CBR and the funds in the annual appropriations bills. Although the budget resolution includes "appropriate" levels of discretionary spending by budget function, the appropriations committees are not required to follow that guidance. The operative direction in the resolution is only the total funding allocated to the committee.

As previously stated, Congress usually authorizes a program before it appropriates funds. In the absence of an authorization, however, inclusion of funds for a program in an appropriations bill generally provides congressional approval, unless there is a law specifically prohibiting the expenditure.

A separate subcommittee is responsible for each of the annual appropriations bills. Jurisdiction of the various subcommittees is shown in Table 8-2.

Appropriations bills are initiated in the House.

- The subcommittees hold hearings with witnesses from the departments and outside groups, review detailed budget justification materials prepared by the departments and agencies, and draft bills.
- The full Appropriations Committee then reviews and passes the bill, often with amendments. This step is referred to as full-committee markup.
- By law, the House may not begin to consider appropriations bills until May 15th in order to provide time for the passage of a budget resolution.
- All appropriations bills are to be reported by the House Appropriations Committee by June 10th.[6]
- After passage by the House, often with amendments, the bill is forwarded to the Senate for action.
- By June 30th, House action on all appropriations bills is to be completed.

Senate committees conduct their own hearings, receive appeals to House bills from the Administration, and prepare draft bills in anticipation of the House bill.

Often, the appropriations bills are not completed by the start of the fiscal year. In such cases, Congress prepares a joint continuing resolution to provide appropriations for the affected agencies or departments to continue operations at some specified level up to

---

[6] 2 USC Sec. 638, House committee action on all appropriation bills to be completed by June 10

a specific date or until their regular appropriations are enacted. Like regular appropriations bills, continuing resolutions (CRs) must be presented to the President for approval or veto.

Ensuring Consistency between Appropriations, Reconciliation, and Revenue Bills and the Budget Resolution

Since 1990, Congress has developed rules designed to instill discipline in its budget deliberations. Actions that could affect the budget or achievement of the budget resolution are prohibited and are subject to being ruled out of order. In the House, a waiver to the prohibition is handled by a "special rule" reported by the Rules Committee. All House special rules require a simple majority for passage. The Senate has tougher rules in that some prohibitions require a three-fifths vote of the Senate to override.

- Prohibitions that require a three-fifths vote of the Senate to override include the following:

  - Consideration of an annual appropriations bill before the Appropriations Committee has made its spending subdivisions (302(b) allocations);
  - Legislation that would cause total spending to exceed or revenues to fall below the aggregate spending or revenue levels for the budget year or for the total of the five years covered by the CBR;
  - Legislation that exceeds a spending allocation or subdivision made under the CBR for the first budget year or for the total of all fiscal years for which spending allocations or subdivisions are made;
  - An amendment to a reconciliation bill that is not deficit-neutral;
  - Reconciliation legislation that includes changes in Social Security;
  - Direct spending or revenue legislation that increases the deficit during the period of the most recently adopted CBR and the following five years; and
  - Non-germane amendments to resolution or reconciliation legislation (Byrd Rule).

- House and Senate prohibitions that require a simple majority in both houses to override include the following:

  - Legislation providing new contract, borrowing, or credit authority that exceeds the amounts in appropriations acts; and
  - Spending, revenue, or debt-limit legislation for a fiscal year before a CBR for that year (or, in the Senate, a resolution covering that year) has been adopted.

Presidential Action on Bills

When Congress finishes action on a bill, it is presented to the President to approve or veto.

A bill is enacted (approved) when:

- The President has signed it; or
- It has sat on the President's desk for 10 days while Congress is in session.

Most bills that become law are signed by the President. Some become law without signature when the President disagrees with some feature of a bill but nevertheless strongly wants other provisions that are included in the bill.

A bill is vetoed when the President:

- Returns it unsigned within 10 days to Congress; or
- Holds it, if Congress adjourns within 10 days.

If a bill is vetoed, Congress can:

- Override the veto by a two-thirds vote in each house;
- Rewrite the bill to make it acceptable to the President; or
- Give up on the action.

Table 8-2
Jurisdiction of Appropriations Subcommittees

Subcommittee	Jurisdiction
Agriculture, Rural Development, Food and Drug Administration, and Related Agencies	• Department of Agriculture (Except Forest Service) • Farm Credit Administration • Farm Credit System Financial Assistance Corporation • Commodity Futures Trading Commission • Food and Drug Administration (HHS)

Commerce, Justice, Science, and Related Agencies	• Department of Commerce
	• Department of Justice
	• National Aeronautics and Space Administration
	• National Science Foundation
	• Related Agencies
	  – Antitrust Modernization Commission
	  – Commission on Civil Rights
	  – Equal Employment Opportunity Commission
	  – International Trade Commission
	  – Legal Services Corporation
	  – Marine Mammal Commission
	  – National Intellectual Property Law Enforcement Coordination Council
	  – National Veterans Business Development Corporation
	  – Office of Science and Technology Policy
	  – Office of the United States Trade Representative
	  – State Justice Institute

Defense	• Department of Defense - Military • Departments of Army, Navy (including Marine Corps), Air Force, Office of Secretary of Defense, and Defense Agencies (Except Department of Defense-related accounts and programs under the Subcommittee on Military Construction and Veterans Affairs and the Office of the Assistant Secretary of the Army (Civil Works)) • Central Intelligence Agency • Intelligence Community Staff

Energy and Water Development	• Department of Energy
	• Department of Defense-Civil; Department of the Army; Corps of Engineers-Civil
	• Department of the Interior; Bureau of Reclamation; Central Utah Project
	• Related Agencies
	  – Appalachian Regional Commission
	  – Defense Nuclear Facilities Safety Board
	  – Delta Regional Authority
	  – Denali Commission
	  – Nuclear Regulatory Commission
	  – Nuclear Waste Technical Review Board
	  – Tennessee Valley Authority

Financial Services	• Department of the Treasury
	• District of Columbia
	• The Judiciary
	• Executive Office of the President
	  – Compensation of the President
	  – Council of Economic Advisers
	  – Executive Residence at the White House
	  – Federal Drug Control Programs
	  – High Intensity Drug Trafficking Areas Program

Table 8-2 (cont.)
Jurisdiction of Appropriations Subcommittees

Subcommittee	Jurisdiction
Financial Services (cont.)	– National Security Council – Office of Administration – Office of Management and Budget – Office of National Drug Control Policy – Office of Policy Development – Official Residence of the Vice President – Special Assistance to the President Unanticipated Needs – White House Office – White House Repair and Restoration – Independent Agencies – Consumer Product Safety Commission – Election Assistance Commission – Federal Communications Commission – Federal Deposit Insurance Corporation, Office of Inspector General – Federal Election Commission – Federal Labor Relations Authority – Federal Trade Commission – General Services Administration – Merit Systems Protection Board – Morris K. Udall Scholarship and Excellence in National Environmental Policy Foundation – National Archives and Records Administration – National Historical Publications and Records Commission – Office of Government Ethics – Office of Personnel Management and Related Trust Funds – Office of Special Counsel – Securities and Exchange Commission – Selective Service System – Small Business Administration – United States Postal Service, Payment to the Postal Service Fund – United States Tax Court General Provisions, Governmentwide
Homeland Security	• Department of Homeland Security

Interior, Environment, and Related Agencies	• Department of the Interior (Except Bureau of Reclamation and Central Utah Project)
	• Environmental Protection Agency
	• Other Agencies
	  – Advisory Council on Historic Preservation
	  – Agency for Toxic Substances and Disease Registry (HHS)
	  – Chemical Safety and Hazard Investigation Board
	  – Commission of Fine Arts
	  – Council on Environmental Quality and Office of Environmental Quality
	  – Forest Service (USDA)
	  – Indian Health Service
	  – Institute of American
	  – Indian and Alaska Native Culture and Arts Development
	  – John F. Kennedy Center for the Performing Arts
	  – National Capital Planning Commission

Table 8-2 (cont.) Jurisdiction of Appropriations Subcommittees	
Subcommittee	Jurisdiction
Interior, Environment, and Related Agencies(cont.)	– National Foundation on the Arts and the Humanities (Except Institute of Museum and Library Services) – National Gallery of Art – National Institute of Environmental Health Sciences (HHS, formerly EPA/Superfund) – Office of Navajo and Hopi Indian Relocation – Presidio Trust – Smithsonian Institution – United States Holocaust – Memorial Museum – White House Commission on the National Moment of Remembrance – Woodrow Wilson International Center for Scholars

Labor, Health and Human Services, Education, and Related Agencies	• Department of Education
	• Department of Health and Human Services (Except Agency for Toxic Substances and Disease Registry; Food and Drug Administration; Indian Health Services and Facilities; and National Institute of Environmental Sciences (formerly EPA/Superfund))
	• Department of Labor
	• Related Agencies
	  – Committee for Purchase From People Who Are Blind or Severely Disabled
	  – Corporation for National and Community Service
	  – Corporation for Public Broadcasting
	  – Federal Mediation and Conciliation Service
	  – Federal Mine Safety and Health Review Commission
	  – Institute of Museum and Library Services
	  – Medicare Payment Advisory Commission
	  – National Commission on Libraries and Information Science
	  – National Council on Disability
	  – National Education Goals Panel
	  – National Labor Relations Board
	  – National Mediation Board
	  – Occupational Safety and Health Review Commission
	  – Railroad Retirement Board
	  – Social Security Administration

Legislative Branch	• House of Representatives • Joint Items • Architect of the Capitol (Except Senate Items) • Botanic Garden • Capitol Police • Capitol Visitors Center • Congressional Budget Office • Government Accountability Office • Government Printing Office • John C. Stennis Center • Library of Congress • Office of Compliance • Open World Leadership Center • United States Capitol Preservation Commission

Table 8-2 (cont.)
Jurisdiction of Appropriations Subcommittees

Subcommittee	Jurisdiction

Military Construction, Veterans Affairs, and Related Agencies	• Department of Defense; Military Construction, Army, Navy (including Marine Corps), Air Force, Defense-Wide, and Guard and Reserve Forces Chemical Demilitarization Construction, Defense -Wide Military Family Housing Construction and Operation and Maintenance, Army, Navy (including Marine Corps), Air Force, and Defense-Wide Family Housing Improvement Fund, Military Unaccompanied Housing Improvement Fund Homeowners Assistance Fund, Base Realignment and Closure Accounts NATO Security Investment Program
	• Department of Veterans Affairs
	• Related Agencies
	  – American Battle Monuments Commission
	  – Armed Forces Retirement Home
	  – Department of Defense, Civil, Cemeterial Expenses, Army U.S. Court of Appeals for Veterans Claims

State, Foreign Operations, and Related Programs	Agency for International Development
	• Department of Defense
	  – Foreign Military Financing Program
	  – International Military Education and Training
	• Department of State
	• Department of the Treasury
	  – Debt Restructuring
	  – International Affairs Technical Assistance
	  – International Monetary Fund
	  – Multilateral Development Banks
	• Export-Import Bank
	• Millennium Challenge Corporation
	• Overseas Private Investment Corporation
	• Peace Corps
	• Trade and Development Agency
	• Related Agencies
	  – African Development Foundation
	  – Broadcasting Board of Governors
	  – Commission for the Preservation of America's Heritage Abroad
	  – Commission on International Religious Freedom
	  – Commission on Security and Cooperation in Europe
	• Congressional-Executive
	  – Commission on the People's Republic of China
	  – HELP Commission
	  – Inter-American Foundation
	  – United States-China Economic and Security Review Commission
	  – United States Institute of Peace

Transportation, Housing and Urban Development, and Related Agencies	• Department of Housing and Urban Development
	• Department of Transportation
	• Related Agencies
	  – Architectural and Transportation Barriers Compliance Board
	  – Federal Maritime Commission
	  – National Transportation Safety Board
	  – Neighborhood Reinvestment Corporation
	  – United States Interagency Council on Homelessness
	  – Washington Metropolitan Area Transit Authority

Chapter 8: Congressional Budgetary Processes

Chapter 9

Budgetary Gimmicks

Since the mid-1980's, a variety of techniques have been used to make spending in the President's Budget and in appropriations bills appear smaller than it actually is. Most of the gimmicks are to limit the estimates of spending from discretionary appropriations in the budget year. Other gimmicks reduce the estimates of future deficits.

The Gramm-Rudman-Hollings act of 1985, which placed a limit on the estimated deficit, created an incentive for reducing the estimated outlays in the budget year to as small a number as possible. Similarly, the annual Congressional Budget Resolutions and past budget enforcement acts created incentives to hold down annual appropriations (discretionary budget authority) as well as the estimated outlays. Since the controls apply to estimated outlays as opposed to actual outlays, there is no penalty if the estimates prove to be off the mark.

In response to these controls, both the Executive Branch and the Congress resorted to a variety of actions to stay within the budgetary limits while at the same time providing funds for desired programs. While these actions might be viewed as "gimmicks" to disguise the true cost of Government programs, their proponents consider them prudent measures used to stay within the law. When these measures failed to produce the desired results, the budget caps were changed late in the annual budget process to avoid a Government shutdown.

In this chapter, the term "gimmicks" applies to actions which run counter to normal budgetary conventions to reduce appropriations and estimated spending without affecting the level of Government programs and services. These actions include changing the law to delay payments and directing the budgetary scorekeepers on the estimates to be used for scoring legislation. Such gimmicks, however, do not include actions by the Congress to use the economic assumptions in the President's Budget to evaluate annual appropriations rather than the economic assumptions developed by the

Congressional Budget Office (CBO). These actions are matters of judgment and within the confines of normal budgetary conventions.

Some of the actions that have been taken in past President's Budgets to stay within the spending limits merely divert the problem to Congress. These include significantly underestimating outlays by using spend-out rates that are different from past experience.

The CBO produces reports that provide independent estimates of the spending plans in the President's Budget and identifies for the Congress any suspicious numbers. The CBO also estimates the cost of legislation proposed by Committees before the legislation goes to the floor of Congress for debate. The Budget Committees, however, can direct the CBO to score a bill using different numbers and assumptions than those resulting from the CBO's internal analysis. This directed scorekeeping is one way Congress can get around troublesome budget issues.

The use of unconventional means to disguise the true size of Government spending reached a peak in 2000. For FY 2000, the budget limits set in 1997 proved to be too small to permit the Congress and the Administration to produce politically acceptable budgets, especially with the unexpected surge in surplus funds.

Examples of Gimmicks

The following paragraphs describe some of the techniques used to reduce the "on paper" budgetary cost of Government programs without significantly affecting the programs.

- **Delay pay dates.** One of the simplest methods to reduce outlays in a given year is the same as that which most Americans employ to stay within their family budgets: delay payment to a later period. Moving the pay date for Federal civilian or military personnel from the last day in a month to the first day of the next month moves an outlay from one fiscal year to the next when the action is first taken.

  Examples include:

  – In 1986, the military pay date was changed from September 30 to October 1 effectively reducing estimated outlays in 1986 by nearly $2 billion.
  – In 2000, Congress delayed the last pay day for civilians and military personnel in FY 2000 to the first day of FY 2001 and claimed a savings of $4.3 billion. Because October 1st fell on a Sunday, the military normally would have been paid on Friday. By delaying the payment to no earlier than Sunday, the Congress was able to take credit a second time for delaying military pay.

- **Delay bill payment.** Like slipping a pay date, paying bills that come due late in the fiscal year can be delayed until the start of the next fiscal year. For Congress to take credit for this, the delay must be mandated in legislation to get around the Prompt Payment Act.

  An example of this is the FY 2000 Defense Appropriations Act that required the Department of Defense to do the following:

  – Extend the payment dates for progress payments made to contractors by five days; and
  – Change prompt payment procedures, in the last month of the fiscal year, to require that payments be made no earlier than one day before the date on which the payment is due.

- **"Lowball" estimated outlays.** The Administration and Congress have, at times, used outlay or spending rates that are inconsistent with historical experience. Ostensibly, it can be argued that the lower rates are plausible given the uncertainty of the estimating process. However, greatly underestimating spending can result in estimated outlays that are lower than plausible.

  An example is:

  – In evaluating the President's Budget for FY 2000, the CBO concluded that the estimated outlays for the Department of Defense were understated by $10 billion based on historical spending patterns. Because the difference was too great for Congress to correct and stay within the budget ceilings, the Budget Committees directed CBO to use the Administration's estimates. Although the Appropriations Committees can often make program adjustments that reduce estimated outlays by $2 or $3 billion, a $10 billion adjustment exceeded what was realistically "doable". As evidence that the estimate was understated, the Administration increased the estimated defense outlays for FY 2000 in the following year's Budget.

- **Incrementally and advance fund programs.** For the most part, investment programs in the Budget are fully funded. This means that sufficient budget authority is proposed in the Budget to fund the life of a multi-year project in one year rather than funding it one year at a time to cover just the work done that year. For example, in constructing a major building, the full budget authority would be requested and appropriated in one year even though construction could last three years. Incremental funding, on the other hand, would require appropriations to be requested in each of the three years the building was being constructed. Within a limited level of budget authority, incremental funding allows more projects to get started in the current budget year than would be possible under full funding. The downside is that incremental funding generally requires appropriations in future years to complete the project and actual outlays would not change.

One way to incrementally fund a program and to avoid the need for appropriations action in future years is an advance appropriation. In this case, an annual appropriations act includes appropriations that become available in later years, thus fully funding the program within a single appropriations act. The budget authority is recorded in the year the funds become available, not in the year enacted. Advance appropriations have been used to shift budget authority from one year to the next and in the process make funds available for other programs in the budget year.

- **Project user fees, asset sales, and spectrum auctions**. Increases in receipts, such as user fees and asset sales, are often proposed in the President's Budget as a way to finance additional spending. Opponents of the proposed receipts and fees may view them as gimmicks. Their advocates, however, see them as analytically sound ways to pay for additional programs. Nevertheless, fees and asset sales can become major issues in the Congress when writing appropriations bills after hearing constituent concerns.

    - **User fees.** Often, the political feasibility of a user fee is not of major consequence in development of the President's Budget. The Administration may conclude a new or expanded user fee is a good idea and propose it in the Budget. For example, proposing a fee saves money in the Budget and makes sense when the benefit of a program applies to only a few people who have the resources to cover the fee cost. Estimated receipts from fees proposed in the Budget are generally lower than the actual result.
    - **Spectrum auction receipts.** Spectrum auction receipts are subject to many influences including an incentive to overstate them in the Budget. Generally, the actual receipts are short of the estimate.
    - **Asset sales**. Sales of assets can be proposed as a way to hold down funding. For several years, several Administrations proposed to sell the Naval Petroleum Reserves and claimed the receipts in the Budget.

- **Delay obligations.** Appropriations acts sometimes specify that some of the funds provided for certain programs cannot be obligated before the last month of the fiscal year leading to lower estimated outlays than would otherwise occur.

    An example is:

    - The FY 2000 appropriations act for the Department of Health and Human Services delayed the availability of almost $5 billion until September 29th of the fiscal year. While it did not affect the budget authority in the bill, it pushed outlays from 2000 to 2001.

- **Use emergency appropriations authority.** The Budget Enforcement Act (BEA) of 1990 provided for emergency appropriations outside the limits set in law on discretionary budget authority and outlays. The only criterion was that the Congress and the President both declare an appropriation to be an emergency.

Many of the appropriations deemed to be emergencies have truly been for unplanned and unforeseen activities such as Desert Storm, which began as the 1990 Act was being written, other military operations, assistance for recovery from disasters, and of course, the September 11th terrorist attacks. Many other emergency appropriations do not appear to have any characteristics that would qualify them for the emergency label other than the political emergency that might occur if the programs do not get funded.

Examples include the following:

  - In 2000, Congress deemed $4.5 billion appropriated for the decennial census to be an emergency, though the census could hardly be considered to be unforeseen on unplanned since it is one of the few requirements of Government spelled out in the Constitution.
  - With the large emergency supplemental appropriations in recent years for the war-on-terror, the Congress has been reducing the base program for operations and maintenance and making up for it in the supplementals. The savings from the cuts to the base program have been used to fund earmarked programs in procurement and research, development, test, and valuation.

- **Propose rescissions.** A rescission is the elimination of budget authority previously provided in an appropriations act. In the year in which the rescission occurs, budget authority is reduced by the amount of the rescission and outlays are reduced by the amount of the estimated outlays that would have occurred in that year. The President's Budget sometimes includes rescissions as a way to reduce the authority and outlays in the budget year.

An example is:

  - The 2000 Defense budget included a rescission of $1.65 billion with an outlay savings of $0.9 billion in 2000. There was no detail on what would be rescinded; rather the Secretary of Defense would decide what to rescind. Blanket authority of that magnitude has to be considered a gimmick because the Administration knows that the Congress will not accept such open-ended authority.

Other Budgetary Actions that may Appear to be Gimmicks

There are other items in the budget and enacted legislation that some observers might consider to be budgetary gimmicks. They include sunset dates on tax reductions, leasing programs, and proposing budget cuts that Congress routinely rejects, and ignoring the future year costs of programs that both the Administration and the Congress support.

Sunset dates. Tax cuts with sunset dates makes the revenue reductions seem smaller than if they were enacted on a permanent basis. Congress did this in the Economic Growth and Tax Relief Reconciliation Act of 2001 and the Jobs and Growth Tax Relief Reconciliation Act (enacted in 2003) even though there was no indication that they intended to see the tax cuts actually end. As a result of this, President Bush's Budgets for FY 2005 through FY 2009 have all included proposals to make many of the tax cuts permanent. As an extension of this, the President's Budget proposes that the baseline budget projections used by Congress be changed to assume that the 2001 and 2003 tax cuts were intended to be permanent. Under this proposal, extension of the tax cuts costing $1.6 trillion through 2018 would be scored as having no cost.

Leasing. Leasing programs spread the budget authority for obtaining the use of an asset over the period of the lease as opposed to full funding the cost upfront if the asset were to be purchased by the Government. Detailed budget scoring rules have been adopted to take away the incentive to use amortization as a way around discretionary budget limits. Nevertheless, there have been efforts to amortize assets in order to avoid the upfront acquisition costs.

Annual rather than permanent fixes to tax and spending issues. The Alternative Minimum Tax (AMT) was designed to keep a small number of high-income people from avoiding the payment of any income tax. Because the income level to which the AMT applies was not indexed for inflation, this tax now affects millions of taxpayers — an unintended result. Rather than proposing a permanent fix to this problem, the FY 2008 and FY 2009 Budgets, for example, proposed relief only in the budget year. This results in the projection of receipts in subsequent years being higher than they would be if a permanent fix of the AMT issue were to be proposed. According to the CBO, extending relief or eliminating the tax would reduce receipts and increase the deficit by between $40 billion and $100 billion per year. A similar move has been made for a mandated cut in Medicare payments to doctors. The Congress has been postponing the start date annually but assuming in budget projections that the cut would occur in future years. The President's FY 2011 Budget includes the costs of these in the projections for future years.

Start collecting taxes to pay for new programs before the spending commences. The health reform bills being considered by the Congress start tax collections in 2011 but do not start the new benefits until 2013. This action permits program costs to be fully offset by new revenues.

Chapter 10

Budget Execution

Budget execution is what happens after an appropriations bill becomes law.

Before any appropriated funds can be used, they must be apportioned by the President to the organizational unit that will carry out or execute the program.[1]

Most of the funds will be spent as provided for in the appropriations and authorization acts. Sometimes, however, changes are desired to the budget authority (BA) provided in an act.

- The President may not want to spend the money for a specified program;
- The full amount of available funding may not be needed;
- It may not be feasible to use the funds immediately or even during the period of availability due to program delays; and
- A new requirement may develop, often of an emergency nature, which requires funding not provided for in the act.

Depending on the situation, the President can delay use of the funds or ask the Congress to rescind the budget authority. A rescission is the withdrawal of budget authority in an appropriation or rescission act.

In order to respond to new requirements that arise during the year, most departments have the authority to reprogram BA among programs within an account and to transfer BA from one account to another after informing their Congressional appropriations subcommittees.

---

[1] 31 USC Sec. 1513, Officials controlling apportionments, subsection (b)

Apportioning Appropriated Funds

Under current law, departments cannot obligate appropriated funds until they have been released by the President. The process for releasing funds is called apportionment. OMB has been delegated the authority to apportion funds.

Agencies submit apportionment requests to OMB for each budget account by August 21st, or within 10 calendar days after the approval of the appropriation, whichever is later. This is done on a standard form used by all departments and agencies, *"SF 132 APPORTIONMENT AND REAPPORTIONMENT SCHEDULE."*

OMB approves or modifies the apportionment specifying the amount of funds agencies may use by time period, program, project, or activity. Funds are generally apportioned for each quarter of the fiscal year to reduce the chances of a funding shortage in an account before the end of the year.

An initial apportionment for an appropriation must occur by the later of:

- 20 days before the beginning of the fiscal year; or
- 30 days after enactment of the appropriation.

Revisions to apportionments and reapportionments may be made whenever necessary.

In addition to OMB's apportionment action, the Department of the Treasury must issue a warrant certifying the amount of funds that can be withdrawn from the Treasury. This is based on both the language of the bill and the OMB apportionment.

Funds not released for obligation are termed "reserves" and must be reported to Congress.[2]

Funds not required to carry out the objectives of the appropriation are to be recommended for rescission by the President.

Deferring the Apportionment of Appropriated Funds

Deferral of funds includes:

- Withholding BA during the apportionment process;
- Delaying obligations; or
- Taking other action that precludes obligation during the period of funding availability.

---

[2] 31 USC Sec. 1512, Apportionment and reserves, subsection c.

Deferrals are permissible only under the following circumstances:

- To provide for contingencies;
- To achieve savings made possible as a result of changes in requirements or efficiency of operations; or
- As specifically provided by law.

The President must send Congress a special message whenever BA provided for a specific purpose or project is deferred.[3]

- The special message specifies the amount, account, department, project, length of deferral, reason, legal authority, budgetary effect, and any other relevant information.
- The deferral message may include one or more deferrals.

The Congress is not required to take any particular action in response to a deferral message.

Requesting Congress to Rescind Appropriated Funds

The President must send the Congress a special message to rescind budget authority.[4]

- A special message is required to reduce existing authority or if BA provided for one year is to be held in reserve for the whole year.
- The special message specifies the amount, account, department, project, reason, budgetary effect, and any other relevant information.

For the rescission to occur, the Congress must pass a rescission bill.

- The bill can only rescind, in whole or in part, BA proposed for rescission in the special message from the President.
- The bill must be passed before the end of 45 calendar days of continuous session after the President submits the rescission proposal.

If the Congress does not pass a rescission bill within the allotted time, the BA proposed for rescission must be made available for obligation.

Funds made available for obligation due to lack of a rescission bill may not be proposed again for rescission by the President.

Congress can initiate action on rescissions independently of the President. This is normally done in appropriations bills.

---

[3] 2 USC Sec. 684, Proposed deferrals of budget authority.
[4] 2 USC Sec. 683, Rescission of budget authority.

Procedures for Rescissions and Deferrals

The law contains detailed procedures for handling rescissions and deferrals.[5]

Each special message on deferrals and rescissions is transmitted to the House, the Senate, and the Comptroller General (the head of the Government Accountability Office) on the same day.

The Comptroller General provides Congress with an analysis of the facts.

If BA is reserved or deferred and the President has not transmitted a special message, the Comptroller General must report that fact to the Congress. This report has the same effect as a special message from the President.

By the 10th of each month, the President must send Congress a report listing all BA proposed for rescission, reservation, or deferral during that fiscal year.

If BA is not made available as required, the Comptroller General is to bring a civil action in the United States District Court for the District of Columbia.

- The Comptroller General must provide Congress an explanatory statement and wait for 25 calendar days of continuous session before taking legal action.
- The court is empowered to take action to make the BA available.

Responding to New Program Needs that Arise During Budget Execution

In order to be able to respond to new and changing requirements, most departments are provided some flexibility in law to move funds within accounts and among accounts.

- A reprogramming is the shifting of budgetary resources within an account.
- A transfer is the shifting of budgetary resource between accounts.

The rules for reprogramming and transfer of the funds provided by a specific appropriations act are determined by the responsible subcommittees of the House and Senate appropriations committees. Generally, the rules vary for each subcommittee.

Reprogramming usually requires advance notification to the appropriations committees. Although the notification process is sometimes prescribed in authorizing or appropriations laws, it often is non-statutory and based on instructions in committee reports or correspondence. For example, the conference report accompanying the FY 2004 Department of the Interior appropriations bill contained detailed guidance for

---

[5] Title 2 U.S.C. Chapter 17B, Impoundment Control

reprogramming funds within the Department's accounts. Guidance for the Department of Homeland Security was included in the 2004 and 2005 appropriations acts and therefore has the force of law.

Transfer rules tend to be more formal than reprogramming since they involve the movement of funds between accounts for which specific appropriations were made in law. While approval of the Congress is not legally required under the Supreme Court's *Chadha*[6] decision, departments generally respect the views of the committees, which can take away the reprogramming authority if they believe the departments are misusing it or using it in a way to thwart the will of Congress.

For most departments and agencies, transfer authority is limited to a percentage (e.g., three to ten percent) of the funds available in an appropriations account with advance notification to the Appropriations Committee. An illustration of the language to control the transfer of funds in an appropriations act is contained in Section 503 of the Department of Homeland Security appropriations act for FY2006:

> "(c) Not to exceed 5 percent of any appropriation made available for the current fiscal year for the Department of Homeland Security by this Act or provided by previous appropriations Acts may be transferred between such appropriations, but no such appropriations, except as otherwise specifically provided, shall be increased by more than 10 percent by such transfers: *Provided,* That any transfer under this section shall be treated as a reprogramming of funds under subsection (b) of this section and shall not be available for obligation unless the Committees on Appropriations of the Senate and the House of Representatives are notified 15 days in advance of such transfer."

In contrast, transfer authority specified in the Defense Appropriations Act is a dollar amount, typically in the range of about 0.8 percent of the total budget authority provided in the Act.

Using Appropriated Funds before they Lapse

Appropriated funds must be obligated within a certain period or they lapse and become unavailable. Unless specifically made available for a longer period, the appropriation is an annual account for which the obligation period expires after one year. Appropriations can also be made for multiple years or for an indefinite period (no-year appropriation).

---

[6] INS v. Chadha, 462 U. S. 919 (1983)

After the period of availability for obligation has ended, obligations may be incurred in an account to cover amounts required for contract changes.[7] The term "contract change" means a change to a contract that requires the contractor to perform additional work; it does not include adjustments to pay claims or increases under an escalation clause.

- If a contract change exceeds $4 million but is less than $25 million, the obligation may be made if it is approved by the head of the agency or by an officer within the office of the head of the agency who has been delegated approval authority.
- If the contract change exceeds $25 million, the obligation may not be made until 30 days after the head of the agency submits to the appropriate authorizing and appropriations committees a notice of intent and a description of the legal basis and policy reasons for the proposed obligation.

Five years after the period of availability of a fixed appropriation account ends, the account is closed and any remaining balances (whether obligated or unobligated) in the account are cancelled and not available for obligation or expenditure.[8] Collections authorized or required to be credited to an appropriation account, but not received before the account is closed, are deposited in a miscellaneous receipts account in the Treasury.

The life cycle of an appropriation account is summarized in Table 10-1.

Paying for Claims Against the Government

When the Government is sued and loses the case, the settlement is paid from the Judgment Fund (a mandatory account) in the Department of the Treasury.[9] If the issue was a contract dispute, the department/agency that awarded the contract must reimburse the Judgment Fund.[10]

If the Government wins a case concerning a contract dispute and the contractor must pay the Government, the money is returned to the account from which the contract was awarded unless that account is closed. If the account is closed, the payment goes into a miscellaneous receipt account in the Treasury.[11]

---

[7] 31 USC Sec. 1553, Availability of appropriation accounts to pay obligations
[8] 31 USC Sec. 1552, Procedure for appropriation accounts available for definite periods
[9] 31 USC Sec. 1304, Judgments, awards, and compromise settlements
[10] 41 USC Sec. 612, Payment of claims
[11] 31 USC Sec. 3562, Disposition of recovered funds

Table 10-1
Life Cycle of Annual and Multi-year Appropriation Accounts

Status of appropriation account (period)	Length of period	Actions than can be taken during period		
		Incur new obligations	Adjust obligations	Liquidate obligations
Available	One year unless law specifies a longer period	Yes Funds available for valid obligations	Yes Amounts obligated for contracts incurred in this period can be adjusted	Yes • Obligations incurred in this period can be liquidated • Up to 1% of appropriation can be used to liquidate obligations incurred from appropriations that are now closed
Expired	Begins when available period ends and lasts for five fiscal years unless law specifies otherwise	No	Yes Contracts awarded during available period can be adjusted: • Over $4m requires agency head approval • Over $25m after 30 days notification of authorization and appropriations committees	Yes Obligations incurred during available period can be liquidated
Closed	Begins when expired period ends	No	No	No Obligations incurred during available period that come due must be paid from an appropriation that is still available

Monitoring Budget Execution

The departments and agencies are required to report on their actual financial transactions at least quarterly. They do this on a standard form, *"SF 133 REPORT ON BUD-GET EXECUTION AND BUDGETARY RESOURCES,"* which shows the status of funds available, obligations, and outlays. The categories of programs, projects, and activities are the same as those for which funds were apportioned on the *"SF 132 APPORTIONMENT AND REAPPORTIONMENT SCHEDULE."* At the end of the fiscal year, each department reports on its overall financial results and performance for the year in an annual Performance and Accountability Report.

The Financial Management Service (FMS) within the Department of the Treasury provides government-wide accounting and reporting. FMS publishes government-wide financial information in several reports: the Daily Treasury Statement; the Monthly Treasury Statement; the Treasury Bulletin; the Combined Statement of Receipts, Outlays and Balances of the United States Government; and an annual Financial Report of the U.S. Government. FMS gathers financial information from the departments through FACTS II (Federal Agencies' Centralized Trial-balance System II). This system allows the electronic submission of data by the departments and agencies that fulfill FMS information needs.

Departments can obtain detailed guidance on the intricacies of appropriations law from the "Red Book: Principles of Federal Appropriations Law," published by the GAO. It includes court decisions and GAO interpretations of the law.

Additional details on financial reporting and management are contained in Chapter 11.

Prohibited Actions

For employees in the Executive Branch, obligations or expenditures in excess of an apportionment are prohibited. If the limit is exceeded, all relevant facts and a statement of actions taken must be reported immediately to the President and Congress and a copy transmitted to the Comptroller General on the same date.[12] The person who took the prohibited action is subject to administrative discipline including, when circumstances warrant, suspension from duty without pay or removal from office.[13] If the person knowingly and willfully violated the law, they shall be fined not more than $5,000, imprisoned for not more than 2 years, or both.[14]

Auditing Agency Operations

Agency operations are evaluated by the Government Accountability Office (GAO) and the agency Inspectors General.

---

[12] 31 USC Sec. 1517, Prohibited obligations and expenditures
[13] 31 USC Sec. 1518, Adverse personnel actions
[14] 31 USC Sec. 1519, Criminal penalty

GAO is the audit, evaluation, and investigative arm of Congress. It examines the use of public funds, evaluates Federal programs and activities, and provides analyses, options, recommendations, and other assistance to help the Congress make oversight, policy, and funding decisions. With respect to financial management, the key tasks of the GAO are to:

- Perform program audits and evaluations;
- Develop standards for audits of organizations and programs; and
- Interpret laws governing expenditure of public funds.

Each department and major agency has an Inspector General (IG), appointed by the President with Senate confirmation, who reports directly to the department head or deputy. The IG can be removed only by the President who must report the reason for removal to Congress. Tasks assigned to the IG are:

- Conduct and supervise audits and investigations of programs and operations;
- Recommend policies to promote economy and efficiency;
- Recommend policies to prevent and detect fraud and abuse;
- Keep the department head and Congress informed of findings, including semi-annual reports that summarize IG findings and corrective actions taken by the department; and
- Report to the Attorney General likely violations of Federal criminal law.

Chapter 11
Federal Financial Management Systems

Financial management systems track the status of appropriated funds. Reports from the systems are used to formulate policy, plan actions, and evaluate performance. Sound processes for preparing and auditing financial reports are essential for the economical, efficient, and effective management of programs, as well as for public accountability.

Many reforms have been made to the Government's rules, processes, and procedures for managing financial activities and monitoring and evaluating systems and programs, including the Chief Financial Officers Act of 1990 (CFO Act).

In 2001, President Bush recognized that the Government's financial systems were less than adequate. Accordingly, he made improved financial management one of the five Government-wide initiatives within his Management Agenda, citing the following problems:

- Federal agencies recently identified $20.7 billion in erroneous benefit and assistance payments associated with just 13 programs. That amount represents more than the total annual expenditures of seven states.[1]
- A clean financial audit is a basic prescription for any well managed organization, yet the Federal government has failed all four audits since 1997. Moreover, most Federal agencies that obtain clean audits only do so after making extraordinary, labor-intensive assaults on financial records.[2]
- Without accurate and timely financial information, it is not possible to accomplish the President's agenda to secure the best performance and highest measure of accountability for the American people.[3]

---

[1] United States. Executive Office of the President, Office of Management and Budget. The President's Management Agenda: Fiscal Year 2002. Washington: Government Printing Office, 2001. http://www.whitehouse.gov/omb/budget/fy2002/mgmt.Pdf
[2] Ibid.
[3] Ibid.

President Bush directed that the following steps be taken to fix the financial systems:

- Determine the extent of erroneous payments and then set goals for reducing such payments;
- Improve the timeliness of financial reports by re-engineering reporting processes, instituting quarterly financial statements; accelerating end-of-year reporting; and measuring systems compliance with agencies' ability to meet requirements set by the Office of Management and Budget (OMB) and the Department of the Treasury (Treasury);
- Enhance the usefulness of reports by requiring comparative financial reporting, reporting specific financial performance measurements and integrating financial and performance information;
- Ensure reliability by obtaining and sustaining clean audit opinions for components of agencies and the Government as a whole; and,
- Change the budget process to allow the Government to better measure the real cost and performance of programs.

Since then, the Government's financial community, as a whole, has focused on improving Federal financial management systems.

This chapter reviews the initiative's progress and the Government's structure for financial management.

Progress in Improving Financial Management

Performance and Accountability Reports. In accordance with the CFO Act, each Federal department and agency must prepare an annual Performance and Accountability Report (PAR) that shows financial activity, performance information, and audit results. Treasury prepares a Government-wide annual statement.

- Every major Federal agency now completes its PAR within 45 days of the end of the fiscal year.
- Before the Bush Administration's emphasis on improved financial management, agencies took as long as five months to complete their financial reports.
- Agencies also produce interim financial statements throughout the year.

Material Weakness Internal Controls. These are flaws in internal management controls that could lead to financial risk.

- The number of auditor-reported material weaknesses has declined significantly.
- This result exceeds the Government-wide performance target of a 10-percent annual reduction in repeat auditor-identified material weaknesses.

Erroneous Payments. This refers to erroneous payments made by Government benefit programs.

- Guidance was issued by OMB for implementing the "Improper Payment Information Act" and for preparing annual reports on departmental progress.
- Federal agencies were required to assess the risk of, estimate the extent of, and put in place a strategy to reduce erroneous payments.
- Initially, the effort was focused on agencies with programs making payments in excess of $2 billion annually.
- Since the initial report in 2004, additional programs have been made subject to review.
- Examples of improvements include:

  - The Department of Health and Human Services (HHS) once had an error rate for Medicare exceeding 10 percent. This rate has been reduced to less than five percent.
  - The Department of Agriculture (USDA) continues to reduce the error rate for its Food Stamp program.
  - The Social Security Administration's (SSA) Old Age, Survivors and Disability Insurance program also reduced annual errors by hundreds of millions of dollars.

Federal Charge Cards. The Federal government sponsors more than 3.1 million credit cards for the purchase of goods and services, and for Federal employees to use when traveling on official Government business.

- In response to reports of credit card abuse, OMB issued guidance as Appendix B ("Improving the Management of Government Charge Card Programs") to OMB Circular A-123, "Management's Responsibility for Internal Control," on August 5, 2005.
- This has resulted in historically low delinquency and increased rebates.
- These programs continue to demonstrate the improved efficiencies of charge card use, through administrative savings, refunds earned, and streamlined processes.

Recovery Auditing. Recovery auditing is the process for auditing agency progress in recovering erroneous payments made to Government contractors.

- The Defense Authorization Act for FY 2002, Section 831 ("Recovery Auditing Act"), requires OMB to submit a report to Congress on recovery audit efforts at Executive agencies.
- OMB issued guidance in January 2003 to assist the agencies in implementing recovery auditing and recovery activity as part of their internal controls over

contract payments. This guidance required agencies that award $500 million or more in contracts annually to report for three consecutive years beginning not later than December 31, 2004.

Government Structure for Financial Management

Responsibilities Defined in the Chief Financial Officers Act of 1990. Public Law 101-576, the Chief Financial Officers Act of 1990 (CFO Act), laid the foundation for the wide-ranging reform of Federal financial management. The Act created a leadership matrix, established guidelines for long-term planning, established a requirement for audited financial statements, and strengthened accountability for Federal financial reporting. All Cabinet departments and the following agencies are subject to the Act:

- Agency for International Development (USAID)
- Environmental Protection Agency (EPA)
- General Services Administration (GSA)
- Federal Emergency Management Agency (FEMA)
- National Aeronautics and Space Administration (NASA)
- National Science Foundation (NSF)
- Nuclear Regulatory Commission (NRC)
- Office of Personnel Management (OPM)
- Small Business Administration (SBA)
- Social Security Administration (SSA)

In recognition of the key role of strong centralized leadership, the CFO Act established the following structure:

Deputy Director of OMB for Management. Although the Act emphasized financial management, it charged the Deputy Director for Management with overseeing the Government's general management functions, including information policy, procurement policy, property management, and productivity improvement. This individual, appointed by the President, is the Government's chief officer responsible for financial management and has specific responsibilities to:

- Provide Executive branch direction on financial management matters;
- Advise the Director of OMB on the resources required for financial systems;
- Review agency proposals for consistency with OMB financial management plans;
- Make recommendations to agency heads on their structure for financial management;
- Maintain qualification standards for agency CFOs and Deputy CFOs;
- Provide advice to agency heads on the selection of agency CFOs and Deputy CFOs;

- Provide advice to agencies on financial management personnel issues;
- Assess the adequacy of the professional qualifications of agency financial management staffs;
- Settle differences regarding the implementation of financial management policies; and,
- Communicate with state and local government financial officers concerning standards, techniques, and processes.

Office of Federal Financial Management (OFFM). This organization within OMB supports the Deputy Director and is headed by the Controller, who is appointed by the President and is responsible for managing day-to-day operations to guarantee that Federal financial operations are properly carried out. An annual report, the Federal Financial Report, is prepared to identify problems and includes a plan for fixing the problems. OFFM has specific responsibilities to:

- Implement the financial management improvement priorities of the President;[4]
- Establish Government-wide financial management policies of Executive agencies;[5] and,
- Carry out the financial management functions of the CFO Act.[6]

OFFM is comprised of two branches:

- The Financial Standards and Grants Branch; and,
- The Financial Analysis and Systems Branch.

The Financial Standards and Grants Branch is charged with:

- Developing financial management policies for Federal agencies and grant recipients;[7]
- Facilitating the development of timely, accurate, and useful financial information to support management decisions;[8] and,
- Ensuring accountability and effective customer service for Federal grants programs.[9]

The following key issues are within the purview of the Financial Standards and Grants Branch:

- **Financial Reporting.** All Executive agencies are required to prepare and submit audited financial statements to OMB and the Congress. As mentioned

---

[4] "Office of Federal Financial Management." Whitehouse.gov. 15 February 2010.
  http://www.whitehouse.gov/omb/financial_default/
[5] Ibid.
[6] Ibid.
[7] "Office of Federal Financial Management: Financial Standards and Grants Branch." Whitehouse.gov. 15
  February 2010. http://www.whitehouse.gov/omb/financial_fin_branch/
[8] Ibid.
[9] Ibid.

above, agencies are required to present a comprehensive, integrated account of financial and performance information in a single document (PAR) annually.[10] "Office of Federal Financial Management: Financial Reporting."

- **Financial Standards.** OMB actively participates in the financial standard setting process as one of the creators and sponsors of the Federal Accounting Standards Advisory Board (FASAB), which develops Federal accounting standards. OMB defines the form and content of agency financial statements.[11]

- **Financial Statement Audits.** OMB issues guidance on auditing agency financial statements and provides independent analysis of issues affecting the Inspector General (IG) community, working with agency IGs to maximize efficiency and effectiveness. OMB also issues guidance for auditing recipients of Federal funds.[12]

- **Grants Management.** OMB develops Government-wide policies to ensure the proper management of grants and the lawful distribution of Federal monies.[13]

- **Single Audit.** A single audit is intended to provide one cost-effective audit for non-Federal entities—including State, local and tribal governments; colleges and universities; and, other non-profit organizations—in lieu of multiple audits of individual programs. All non-Federal entities that expend $500,000 or more of Federal awards in a year are required to obtain an annual audit.[14]

The following key issues are within the purview of the Financial Analysis and Systems Branch:

- **Asset Management.** OMB is responsible for the management of assets owned, leased, or managed by Federal agencies—including real property, personal property, and financial assets—through comprehensive inventories, accurate assessments of asset value, and improved links between agency missions and acquisition and disposal plans.[15]

- **Debt Management.** OMB is responsible for the management of Federal agency debts—including loan repayments; duplicate or erroneous grant or entitlement payments; and, fines or penalties—and is especially focused on improving performance in the collection of outstanding debts.[16]

---

[10] "Office of Federal Financial Management: Financial Reporting." Whitehouse.gov. 15 February 2010. http://www.whitehouse.gov/omb/financial_fin_report/
[11] "Office of Federal Financial Management: Financial Standards Development." Whitehouse.gov. 15 February 2010. http://www.whitehouse.gov/omb/financial_fin_standards/
[12] "Office of Federal Financial Management: Financial Statement Audits." Whitehouse.gov. 15 February 2010. http://www.whitehouse.gov/omb/financial_fin_statement/
[13] "Office of Federal Financial Management: Grants Management." Whitehouse.gov. 15 February 2010. http://www.whitehouse.gov/omb/financial_fin_grants/
[14] "Office of Federal Financial Management: Single Audit." Whitehouse.gov. 15 February 2010. http://www.whitehouse.gov/omb/financial_fin_single_audit/
[15] "Office of Federal Financial Management: Asset Management." Whitehouse.gov. 15 February 2010. http://www.whitehouse.gov/omb/financial_fia_asset/
[16] "Office of Federal Financial Management: Debt Management." Whitehouse.gov. 15 February 2010. http://www.whitehouse.gov/omb/financial_fia_debt/

- **Improper Payments.** OMB is focused on strengthening financial management controls so that Federal agencies can better detect and prevent improper payments. An improper payment occurs when: the funds go to the wrong recipient; the recipient receives the incorrect amount of funds; or, the recipient uses the funds in an improper manner.[17]
- **Performance Measurement.** OMB tracks performance on key financial indicators to help guide financial management reforms and target resources to areas where better stewardship of funds is needed. OMB aims to provide the Congress, financial managers, and other stakeholders with the information they need to assess the overall financial health of the Federal government.[18]
- **President's Management Agenda (PMA).** OMB rates Federal agencies, according to a traffic light-style scoring system ("red," "yellow," and "green") on their efforts to improve in five Government-wide areas, including Improving Financial Performance. Critical success factors under this PMA initiative include: obtaining an unqualified audit opinion; eliminating material weaknesses; meeting financial reporting deadlines; and, using financial data to support daily and long-term management decisions.[19]
- **Travel and Purchase Cards.** OMB is focused on ensuring that all purchases made with Government-issued credit cards are appropriate, i.e. work-related, and that all credit card bills are paid timely, thereby increasing monthly rebates.[20]

Chief Financial Officer (CFO). In each Cabinet department and major agency designated in the Act, an officer appointed by the President with Senate confirmation, who reports to the department secretary or agency head, is designated as CFO. The CFO has specific responsibilities to:

- Oversee all financial management activities;
- Maintain accounting systems to all applicable standards;
- Monitor execution of the budget;
- Prepare an annual report on the financial condition of the department;
- Prepare an annual plan to implement the 5-year plan prepared by OMB; and,
- Review biennially the fees, royalties, rents, and charges set for services.

Chief Financial Officers Council (CFOC). The Council coordinates and advises on the activities of Federal agencies in matters such as the consolidation and modernization of financial systems, improved quality of financial information, financial data and information standards, internal controls, legislation affecting financial operations and

---

[17] "Office of Federal Financial Management: Improper Payments." Whitehouse.gov. 15 February 2010. http://www.whitehouse.gov/omb/financial_fia_improper/
[18] "Office of Federal Financial Management: Performance Management." Whitehouse.gov. 15 February 2010. http://www.whitehouse.gov/omb/financial_fia_performance/
[19] "Office of Federal Financial Management: President's Management Agenda." Whitehouse.gov. 15 February 2010. http://www.whitehouse.gov/omb/financial_fia_pma/
[20] "Office of Federal Financial Management: Travel and Purchase Cards." Whitehouse.gov. 15 February 2010. http://www.whitehouse.gov/omb/financial_fia_travel/

organizations, and other financial management matters. The composition of CFOC is as follows:

- The Deputy Director for Management at OMB chairs the Council;
- The CFOs and Deputy CFOs of Federal departments and agencies covered by the Act are members;
- Other members include the Controller, Office of Federal Financial Management, and the Fiscal Assistant Secretary of the Treasury; and,
- The CFOs of the Executive Office of the President (EOP) and the Corporation for National and Community Service (CNCS) also participate in the Council.

Financial Systems Integration Office (FSIO). This organization within the Government Services Administration (GSA) has three major areas of responsibility, including:

- Core financial systems requirements development, testing and product certification;[21] "About the Financial Systems Integration Office."
- Supporting the Federal financial community on priority projects;[22] and,
- Conducting outreach through an annual financial management conference and other related activities.[23]

FSIO focuses on:

- Developing performance measures (e.g., cost, quality, and timeliness) to assess the performance of financial services offered by Federal financial organizations;[24]
- Developing standard business processes, data specifications, and business rules for core financial management functions (e.g., funds management, payments, receipts, and reporting) to be adopted by all Federal agencies;[25] and,
- Working with Federal agencies to implement a uniform, Government-wide accounting code structure, including an applicable set of definitions and the layout, to which agencies' new financial systems must adhere.[26]

Additionally, FSIO delineates core competencies for the following Federal financial personnel:[27]

- Accountants
- Program Managers

---

[21] "About the Financial Systems Integration Office." FSIO.gov. 15 February 2010.
http://www.fsio.govfsiofsiodata/about.shtml
[22] Ibid.
[23] Ibid.
[24] Ibid.
[25] Ibid.
[26] Ibid.
[27] "Core Competencies." FSIO.gov. 15 February 2010.
http://www.fsio.gov/fsio/fsiodatadocs_corecompetencies.shtml

- Budget Analysts
- Financial System Analysts
- Information Technology Personnel Implementing Financial Systems
- Financial Management Analysts and Financial Specialists
- Project Managers Implementing Financial Systems

Federal Management Service (FMS). This organization within Treasury has specific responsibilities to:[28]

- Provide central payment services to Federal agencies;
- Operate the Federal government's collections and deposit systems;
- Provide Government-wide accounting and reporting services; and,
- Manage the collection of delinquent debt owed to the Government.

---

[28] "Welcome to FMS." FMS.Treas.gov. 15 February 2010. http://www.fms.treas.gov/

Chapter 12

Government Settlements with the Private Sector

Legal disputes between the Federal Government and private sector litigants (an individual or an organization) generally concern contract claims, easement or land use, environmental crimes, or discrimination. Settlements may arise from cases involving alleged violations of either civil or criminal laws. Often, the issues are settled through compromise and agreement. In most cases, the settlement involves monetary compensation.

Either party may initiate settlement negotiations in order to dispose of the pending litigation. Such a settlement must be approved by a court and is binding on both parties. Neither party may reopen the case unless the other party breaks the agreement. Settlements offer a good alternative to a court judgment when the outcome is not clear. If a ruling could go either way, a settlement may be beneficial to both parties in the dispute.

Budget Pressures and Government Settlements

Every year the Federal Government is confronted with budget pressures from an increased national deficit. Cost overruns, unexpected defense expenditures, War on Terror spending, and increases in Medicare and Medicaid costs have all contributed to the current record Federal deficit. Additionally, as the deficits rise, the Federal Government is called upon by the public to provide increased public accountability and transparency in Federal spending. Increased costs invariably lead to increased scrutiny on those non-governmental agencies and private sector contractors that provide goods and services to the Federal Government. Therefore, budget pressures which lead to increased scrutiny result in more Federal prosecutions (criminal) and Federal claims (civil) against private sector service providers.

Government as Plaintiff—Civil Settlements

The U.S. Department of Justice (DOJ) initiates civil suits on the behalf of the Federal Government in many areas, including anti-trust and price fixing-schemes, fraud, healthcare-related suits (such as large tobacco settlements), and increasingly false Medicare and Medicaid claims. Generally, it is more common that the Government will initiate causes of action against corporations rather than individual actors. As litigation with private sector corporations can prove to be costly and time consuming, the Government will often enter into settlements rather than resolve matters through the trial process.

The following cases offer examples of settlements concerning actions initiated by DOJ under the Obama Administration. These cases provide examples of how the recent budget pressures have increased scrutiny on health care issues, Medicaid and Medicare fraud, and Government accountability and therefore, have resulted in increased prosecution of fraudulent claims for health care costs. In the following matters, the Government sued to recover funds paid for fraudulent medical claims. These matters were all prosecuted by the civil division of the DOJ and provide examples of how the federal government acts as a private citizen—that is bringing civil actions rather than prosecuting criminally.

- Rush University Medical Center agreed to pay a settlement of $1.547 million (plus interest) to resolve allegations that the facility violated the False Claims Act. Rush is alleged to have submitted false claims to Medicare during the period 2000 through 2007 by entering into certain leasing arrangements for office space in violation of a which prohibits a hospital from profiting from patient referrals made by a physician with whom the hospital has an improper financial arrangement.

- Atlanta-based Mariner Health Care Inc. and SavaSeniorCare Administrative Services LLC, as well as their principals, Leonard Grunstein, Murray Forman and Rubin Schron, agreed to pay the United States and several states $14 million. This settlement arose from allegations of the United States that the several defendants solicited kickback payments from Omnicare, the nation's largest pharmacy that specializes in dispensing drugs to nursing home patients, in exchange for agreements by Mariner and Sava to continue using Omnicare's pharmacy services for 15 years. Approximately $7.84 million of the settlement proceeds will go to the United States, while $6.16 million has been allocated to certain state Medicaid programs.

- Brookhaven Memorial Hospital Medical Center, a Long Island, N.Y.-based hospital, agreed to pay $2.92 million, plus interest, to settle allegations that the hospital defrauded Medicare. The government alleged that the hospital fraudulently inflated its charges to Medicare patients to obtain enhanced reimbursement from the federal health care program.

- Mercy Hospital Inc. (d/b/a Mercy Medical Center) of Springfield, Mass., agreed to pay the United States $2,799,462 to settle claims that it violated the False Claims Act between 2005 and 2006 by failing to provide, or failing to document that it provided, the minimum number of hours of rehabilitation therapy required under Medicare guidelines.

Another type of civil case often initiated by the Government involves the recovery of funds spent cleaning up property on the Environmental Protection Agency (EPA) Superfund site list from the party that caused the contamination. Funds recovered from potentially responsible parties (PRPs) go into the Superfund Trust Fund and are available for further cleanup work after appropriation action. Civil penalties in these cases go to offset the expense of the DOJ and EPA investigations.

For example, in Granite City, Illinois in 1998, the Government reached a $60 million settlement with six PRPs (Allied-Signal, Inc., Exide Corporation, General Battery Corporation, GNB Technologies, Inc., Johnson Controls, and Lucent Technologies, Inc.). Some things the firms agreed to were:

- Take over and complete $22 million in cleanup work that the EPA had begun.
- Pay $9 million in costs incurred by the Government on the site.
- Pay $400,000 in civil penalties for the violation of EPA's 1990 cleanup order.
- Fund a $2 million lead paint abatement program in homes near the site.

Government as Plaintiff—Criminal Settlements

In the criminal context, settlements are a result of the defendant entering into a plea bargain with the Government. That is, the prosecuted party agrees to plead guilty to the alleged offense(s) in return for avoiding a trial and possible harsher penalties. In criminal cases prosecuted by the DOJ, settlements include fines for engaging in criminal activity, along with other monetary penalties. Additionally, settlements may involve a probation period during which the business or organization is prohibited from engaging in the activities at issue. The court may also order the defendant to perform remedial measures. This penalty is common in the settlement of criminal environmental prosecutions.

Criminal prosecutions which result in settlements often involve environmental crimes and violations of the Foreign Corrupt Practices Act. Similarly to civil matters, criminal prosecutions can be costly and time-consuming. Therefore, where the government is able, a plea bargain is often the preferable resolution to criminal prosecutions. The following cases are examples of instances where the Government opted to settle criminal prosecutions rather than continue the matter through the trial and penalty phase.

- In March 2010 BAE Systems plc (BAES) was sentenced to pay a $400 million criminal fine after pleading guilty in U.S. District Court in the District of Columbia to conspiring to defraud the United States by impairing and impeding its lawful functions, to make false statements about its Foreign Corrupt Practices Act (FCPA) compliance program, and to violate the Arms Export Control Act (AECA) and International Traffic in Arms Regulations (ITAR). This fine was one of the largest criminal fines in the history of DOJ's effort to combat overseas corruption in international business and enforce U.S. export control laws.

- Fleet Management Ltd. was ordered to pay $10 million for its role in causing the *Cosco Busan* oil discharge and a subsequent cover-up after the ship struck the San Francisco Bay Bridge in November 2007 after pleading guilty to a criminal violation of the Oil Pollution Act of 1990 as well as felony obstruction of justice and false statement charges for creating false and forged documents after the crash at the direction of shore-based supervisors with an intent to deceive the U.S. Coast Guard. Fleet was also ordered to implement a comprehensive compliance plan that would include heightened training and voyage planning for ships engaged in trade in the United States. The training will focus on better preparing masters for command of Fleet's vessels, providing classroom and shipboard navigation training to those who navigate Fleet's vessels, and ensuring that all Fleet vessels calling in U.S. ports create a thorough plan for how they will navigate in those ports.

Government as Defendant

Any citizen, corporation, trade association, environmental, or industry group can challenge the Government through the court system. Allegations most commonly seen involve unjust land takings, inaction of enforcing a law or regulation (see related section), or discrimination against a certain class or race of people. The Justice Department and counsel working for the Government's agencies and departments defend lawsuits brought by the public and decide whether to settle or litigate.

With respect to race and discrimination, many agencies have established programs such as EPA's Environmental Justice Program. This program aims to ensure equality in the applications of regulations. The program's oversight also applies when a private party seeks agency approval for a regulation that involves minority interests.

- An example is the settlement of a discrimination case that began in 1999 when a group of black farmers brought a class-action lawsuit against the U.S. Department of Agriculture (Pigford v. Glickman). The farmers alleged that the USDA was guilty of discrimination in the way it dealt with their applications for farm subsidies. Although the settlement did not set new policy for the USDA, it did make strides toward improving Government-minority relations.

It also brought this issue to the attention of Congress, which urged USDA to discipline or fire employees who may have discriminated against minority farmers.

- The litigation matter known as Pigford II, a continuation of Pigford v. Glickman was settled in February 2010. The settlement agreement reached, which is contingent on appropriation by Congress, provided a total of $1.25 billion to African American farmers who alleged that they suffered racial discrimination in USDA farm loan programs.

Cases brought against the Government often take a long time to resolve. The reasons vary from case to case, but the timing may be influenced by the Government's vast resources (money and Lawyers), which it can use to delay settlements by claiming problems in determining the value of a claim.

- An example is the case initiated by 19 San Joaquin, California, family farmers that took 16 years to resolve. In 1986, the families charged that the Interior Department's Bureau of Reclamation had not provided drainage systems required under previous contracts. As a result, their farm land was damaged due to the accumulation of large salt deposits. Finally, in late 2002, the case was resolved when the Government agreed to purchase the land for $107 million.

Regulation through Litigation

Regulation through litigation occurs when a court-ordered settlement or consent decree forces the Government to take an unplanned action or to unexpectedly stop a planned action. Numerous lawsuits are filed every year that attempt to dictate the policies of agencies. When the court encourages the parties to settle or to negotiate a settlement (such as a court-approved consent decree), policy and rulemaking are resolved through the judicial process rather than through normal legislative or regulatory processes.

When successful, these lawsuits and the resulting settlements serve to give the force of law to the social and regulatory policy preferences of the groups suing the Government. The key public policy issue thus becomes whether the courts and the legal system should be prescribing regulations or whether the advocacy groups should be required to accomplish their goals through legislative and agency channels.

- Opponents of litigation believe that the setting of public policy is the job of an agency directed by a democratically-elected legislature or the President.
- Proponents argue that the legislative and executive branches of Government often fail to deal with public policy issues in a timely or adequate manner and they therefore have no choice but to pursue resolution of the issues through the courts.

There is no indication that the trend toward more issues being resolved through the court system will change anytime soon.

Budgetary Treatment of Settlements

When a Government agency, department, or program receives money in a settlement the funds may go directly to the affected agency or program, if that is provided for under law. Even when the funds go into an account accessible by the agency, an appropriations act is often necessary to make the recovered funds available for spending.

- In some cases, such as EPA's Superfund, the Government's action is to recover money the agency has already spent. In such cases, the monies collected have a direct impact on the effectiveness of the program (in the Superfund case, the rate at which additional cleanups can be made).
- This benefit makes settlement a useful tool for collecting money more rapidly than would otherwise occur if the issue were litigated. Funds returned to the Superfund Trust Fund must be appropriated before they may be used for new cleanup projects.
- For Government claims against contractors, the money is returned to the appropriation account from which the contract funds were obligated if the funds in the appropriation are still available for obligation. These funds may then be used for a new contract to obtain the needed service without further Congressional action. If the period of availability has expired, the funds go into a miscellaneous receipts account in the Treasury and are not available to the agency or department that awarded the contract.

In other instances, monies are awarded to the states (in the case of tobacco legislation) or to damaged individual parties (such as citizens). In the highly publicized state tobacco lawsuits settled in November, 1998, via a "litigation tax," states are expected to receive a total of $246 billion over 25 years from the tobacco industry. This money is to be utilized by the states involved on a number of services, including healthcare and education.

Most settlements that require payment from the Federal Government are paid from the Judgment Fund in the Department of the Treasury. It is a mandatory account with an indefinite appropriation, which means that funds are always available to pay claims without further Congressional action. The Judgment Fund was established in 1956. Prior to 1956, judgments against the United States required specific appropriations from Congress in order to be paid.

- The Fund is used for most court judgments, settlement agreements, and administrative claims.

- Payments from the Fund include claims for back pay for Federal employees, judgments from district courts, judgments from the U.S. Court of Appeals for the Federal Circuit, and judgments of the U.S. Court of Federal Claims.
- Awards that cannot be paid from the Judgment Fund include tax judgments, judgments against the Postal Service, land condemnation judgments, and judgments against government corporations, such as Amtrak and the Tennessee Valley Authority.
- When a settlement or judgment involves a claim against a Government contract, the agency that awarded the contract is required to reimburse the Judgment Fund for the amount of the payment.
- Total claims paid in 2009 were $2.3 billion. In 2010 the claims are projected at $4.3 billion including $3.4 billion for settlement of a long-standing suit from Indian tribes about the management of Indian lands. After 2010, the claims are estimated to be less than $1 billion annually.

Chapter 12: Government Settlements with the Private Sector

Chapter 13

Applied Ethics for Budget Officials

The overriding ethics rules and policies for Federal budget officials as well as all other Federal employees whether from the Executive, Legislative, or Judicial branches are fully discussed in our companion publication, <u>Understanding the Ethics Policy of the United States Government</u> (The EOP Foundation, 2006). Specific concepts and standards for ethical conduct within the Federal budget process are highlighted in this chapter. These concepts have taken on increased importance due to the significant segment of the lobbying industry focused on the budget. Stakeholders have daily business with Government officials as they seek to add, change, or eliminate funding throughout the President's budget formulation and Congress' appropriation processes.

Decision-Making: Psychological Pitfalls

Federal budget officials' roles require them to find a balance between programmatic, technical, regulatory, and political requirements associated with formulation and execution of the Federal budget. The difficulty of a Budget official's task is increased when these requirements come in conflict.

The conflicts and an explanation of the underlying heuristics and biases that influence budget officials' decision-making framework are discussed below.

- **Heuristics.** All budget officers and Government decision-makers generally rely upon heuristics. These rules of thumb, whether consciously or subconsciously, are used to conduct "gut analysis." In our everyday lives, we all use heuristics because they are important for navigating routine decisions efficiently. Because we utilize this process so frequently, we develop an intuitive reliance. Unfortunately, the heuristics that are reliable for routine decisions often lead a budget officer to act on his or her personal biases when conducting relatively complex budget-related analysis and decision-making.

Heuristic biases come from the budget officer's past experiences and aggregated knowledge, or "institutional memory." Influences such as a prior place of employment or programmatic experience could have a significant subconscious impact in the framework within which a career official operates. A budget officer must avoid one-sided gut analysis. A budget officer must be capable of evaluating data and analysis provided by program officials before finalizing budget decision-making documents for political decision-makers.

An ethical challenge may arise as a budget officer is faced with the challenge of meeting a significant workload-demand without the assistance of heuristics to quicken the analytical process. From a manager's perspective, this can be especially challenging. Managers also face the pressure of deadlines and likely recognize that balanced decision-making is necessary to maintain the trust of the key players in the budget process. Managers may face the added dilemma of having to deal with heuristics bias of subordinates who are not consciously aware (and may reject the idea) their biases are playing a role in the process.

- **Buck Passing.** The complex hierarchies within Federal agencies can create environments in which "bucks," or responsibility, are passed throughout an organization. For instance, the trust authority heuristic means a budget officer might trust their program managers' perspectives too much based on their expertise versus the data. The danger is that a budget official may not want to take the heat associated with going against the grain.

Senior managers may be positioned or programmed to make an otherwise unpopular decision. Conversely, political officials will sometimes leave a decision they know will have political repercussions to the career bureaucracy. Thus, they do not have to take the political heat. The budget officer is often the only defense between this dynamic being actualized.

This phenomenon occurs in Government and industry from the top down as well as the bottom up. Passing the buck creates ethical challenges for budget officers. Psychologists, organization theorists, and economists alike note how the dynamics associated with agreeing versus disagreeing with one's colleagues given an objective read of the data creates issues for an individual working in an institutional setting. Loyalties become entangled and personal responsibility gives way to fear of banishment to another job or delay of promotion. The chains of command not only tie people's hands, they cloud their minds and consciences as well.[1] The budget officer must demonstrate loyalty to the integrity of the process and honesty notwithstanding these pressures.

A *slippery slope* heuristic explains how a decision-makers' incremental changes over time can result in outcomes which would otherwise be rejected.

---

[1] David J. Luban, *supra n.* 2 at 4

- **Groupthink.** Scholars have shown that decision-makers working in groups can face significant peer pressure and submit to groupthink. Groupthink takes place when powerful social pressures are brought to bear by members of a working group of career officials. In other words, the viewpoint of a popular member or momentum toward consensus can result in agreement by group members who, in the absence of 'going along' would have contributed additional analysis that resulted in a different or more robust viewpoint. The ethical dilemma arises when group members believe or understand that conformity is valued more than differing opinions and that they risk alienating themselves from the group if they express opposition. Resolving this dilemma ethically will likely require a budget officer to overcome the temptation to succumb to groupthink, present alternatives in a constructive manner so as to avoid being labeled a dissenter, and address systemic issues through official channels external to the group.

- **Agency Capture**. Some experts argue that unhealthy relationships between agency decision-makers and their relevant constituencies can result in "agency capture," when agencies can be "captured" (i.e. biased) either for or against other agencies or groups they are expected to govern or regulate. One outcome under this scenario occurs when regulators of a very specific industry could become so intertwined in that industry's intricacies that the "big picture" regulatory mission becomes compromised. To cite a common colloquialism, regulators may become so concerned with a certain tree they overlook the forest.

As decision-makers become cognizant of these pitfalls and how to avoid them, they can become more ethical and effective decision-makers. Understanding the underlying psychological drivers of bias is critical to operating appropriately efficiently in the decision-making process, especially given the ethical conflicts that surface in the formulation and execution of the Federal budget. An overview of these ethical conflicts is provided below.

Ethical Conflicts

- **Objective Analysis vs. Biased Institutional Analysis**

When preparing issue papers, writing budget proposals, and other support documents, Federal budget officers must perform objective/technical analysis. This requires them to prevent institutional biases from affecting their work product. Their objective/technical analytical capabilities are improved by their institutional memory and professional training. A budget officer must rely on evaluation, comparative, stakeholder, and performance data. The most effective analysis is straightforward and cognizant of all externalities that may affect decision-makers. Increasingly, this efficiency-related data are being relied upon as the baseline materials for budget/policy option papers prepared by budget officers. The infusion of institutionally biased information in the process is the ethical issue for budget officers.

- **Professional vs. Political Performance**

A career budget officer must always strive for professional excellence. Excellence is achieved by performing on the basis of criteria associated with neutral competence. This boils down to objective, unbiased analysis of alternatives. It is their duty to ensure that budget-related materials and analysis are presented in a straightforward and simple manner. Budget officers must guard against unwarranted spin proposed by political officials whose advocacy in budget-related materials would diminish the quality and credibility of budget-related materials. These political pressures require career professionals to insist that any political spin does not stray from reasonable interpretation of analytical or performance-related facts. They must also be vigilant to ensure that their personal political views, or those of their colleagues and superiors, do not impact the integrity of the budget materials.

Senior administration officials are appointed due to their political compatibility with the views of the President. They provide guidance to career officials throughout the budget process. However, budget-related documents are expected to contain technical substance that is accurate. The written or spoken spin to increase, decrease, and neutralize political sensitivities are expected in testimony, Q&A, and other justification materials. However, there is a credibility line between politically sensitive and politically directed documents. The latter is a blatant dismissal of the facts in favor of politically driven agenda. Maintaining the professional quality of budget-related materials is the ethical issue for a budget officer. Responsible advocacy that spins the political realities is acceptable as part of the justification of the Administration's initiatives. The intent is to increase the chances that the desired level of funding is enacted. Budget officers are relied on to ensure that the line between advocacy and partisanship is not crossed.

- **Administrative Priorities vs. Congressional Priorities**

In the State of the Union and State of the Economy speeches, the President provides an overview of the key economic issues and policies that the upcoming fiscal year's Budget will address. The goals, objectives, and issues are stated in macro terms and most importantly, reflect the President's priorities. Conversely, Members of Congress seek to build a record for fiscal and budget driven priorities consistent with loyalty to their political party and micro, or area specific goals and objectives of their state and district constituencies. The President's Budget is formulated with two constituencies in mind. The first is the President's political base and core constituency. The second is the Executive Branch's career, professional bureaucracy. This perspective is amplified when different political parties control the White House and Congress. Budget officers' understanding of the Administration's position and the Congress' position is critical to their success. A budget officer's ethical challenge is to accurately and articulately explain and implement budget decisions with due respect to an opposing view.

- **Government Perspectives vs. Stakeholder Perspectives**

Budget officials must maintain accountability to varying constituencies. As civil servants, budget officers must prevent informational asymmetries by keeping the public informed. This duty, however, is limited in practice by Executive Branch rules, which are intended to maintain a certain level of secrecy in the formulation process. A budget officer's ethical dilemma is *what* and *how much* can be publicly disclosed without compromising the secrecy of the formulation and execution processes. On the other hand, stakeholders provide extremely valuable data and information that program officials often do not have. Further, there is valuable data and information available from other Federal agencies. However, stakeholders will typically aim to influence the budget process to result in a conclusion which benefits their own objectives. They may seek influence over what programs are to be established, continued, expanded, or terminated.

Regardless of the decisions reached, once the policy direction is established budget officers are duty bound to explain the associated rationale to external stakeholders and, ultimately, Congress.

Budget officers must be prepared to present stakeholder perspectives as alternatives during the formulation process, respond to critics during the Congressional process, and implement Congressional/Executive Branch direction in the execution process. To the extent that Congressional and Executive Branch direction conflict, the budget officer's job is to ensure political officials resolve the issues. The budget officer must be a purist in presenting the President's proposal without tipping the scale in discussing alternatives. Achieving these goals often presents several ethical issues for the budget officer.

- **Agency Position vs. OMB Position**

Federal budget officials must find and maintain the neutral ground on conflicts that arise between their respective agencies and OMB. This conflict is encompassed in their duties with respect to three distinct groups: departmental program officials, departmental political officials, and OMB/White House officials. It is incumbent on budget officials to employ the appropriate advocacy throughout the budget formulation process, including during the late-phase of the appeals process to ensure that the associated decision-making does not result in OMB using its institutional powers to thwart the protections built into the formulation and execution processes.

There is a set of rules that result in staying within the White House's guidelines while permitting the department to implement the programs under its authority. This includes internal and other reprogrammings requiring OMB and Appropriation Committee approval.

OMB issues guidance (OMB Circular A-11) on budget proposals that departments must follow at all phases of the budget process. The Circular articulates how OMB exercises its institutional authority. Failure to follow the guidance can lead to inconsistencies throughout the process. The most significant areas which highlight potential conflicts are reprogramming, response to Congressional direction in Committee reports, and interpretation of Administration/Congressional intent.

OMB enforces the President's policy direction to departments regarding specific programs and their overall funding levels. Once departments submit budget proposals, OMB informs departments of the President's decision via a written passback. Agencies may appeal the passback via a confidential document. The appeal process addresses the areas in which the department believes the President should take a second look at budget decisions. It is important to address differences between Presidential and departmental priorities in this manner because divergence from the President's decisions after the appeals phase has concluded are not normally tolerated and usually result in the resignation of an offender.

OMB also enforces unauthorized spending from approved budget allocations. Budget execution occurs after an appropriations bill becomes law. Funds are expended as provided for in the appropriations and authorization acts. Desired changes to the budget authority create conflicts and must be provided for in the legislation. Conflicts arise for a variety of reasons: the President may not want to spend the money, the full amount of available funding may not be needed, it may not be feasible to use the funds immediately, or a new requirement may develop which requires funding not provided for in the act, to name a few.

Maintaining the Highest Ethical Standard

In general, budget officers maintain the highest ethical standards. Regardless of position—budget officer for a program, base, agency, or department—the rules are the same. Whether interfacing with a career senior executive, a political senior executive, the Secretary, a Congressman, or a Senator, the rules are the same. The statutes governing the budget process (see Chapter 2) and certain other publications provide most of the guidance required. However, the axioms presented here should help a budget officer maintain an ethical standard in performing their duties. In addition to the statutes referenced earlier, several other reference documents are directed at increasing transparency and objectivity in Federal budgetary decision-making:

- the Administrative Procedures Act of 1974,
- Executive Order 12866,
- the OMB's Good Guidance Practices, and
- the Office of Government Ethics' *Standards of Ethical Conduct*.

One of the most important documents for improved Government decision-making and regulation is the **Administrative Procedures Act** (APA). Sanctioned by the Attorney General in 1974, the two most important principles of the APA are:

- The requirement to keep the public currently informed of the Government's organization, procedures, and rules; and
- The requirement to provide for public participation in the rulemaking process.

These purposes go a long way in addressing some of the key problems of the decision-makers by creating a public forum that is open to public regulation. Now, decision-makers cannot operate in an environment that fosters groupthink, institutional bias, or where assumptions go unchallenged. The APA also created policy and legal structures designed to ensure objective decision-making for issues that are common amongst political and professional players. The APA unified the standards for the conduct of formal rulemaking and adjudicatory proceedings. This requirement prevents agencies from implementing varying operational guidelines for constructing rules and adjudicatory procedures that favor their biases or special interest groups.

Since the adoption of the APA, an executive order (EO) has been issued that further illustrates Government action to remove discretion and subjective elements from agency decision-making. **EO 12866** reaffirms the regulatory review function of OMB and establishes economic efficiency as the primary yardstick by which regulations are to be judged. This executive order also structures a process for agency supervision centered on OMB review and approval. OMB's director meets with agency representatives annually to learn each agency's regulatory priorities and to coordinate regulatory efforts on a Government-wide basis for the upcoming year. EO 12866 also expanded the responsibilities of the Office of Information and Regulatory Affairs (OIRA).

OIRA was established in 1980 under the Paperwork Reduction Act. It is charged with reviewing the collection of information. EO 12866 expanded OIRA's responsibilities to reviewing draft regulations and developing and overseeing the implementation of Government-wide policies. OIRA also established a system of peer review of agency practices. In the future OIRA will oversee and enforce the proposed rules of increasing transparency and objectivity amongst Federal decision-makers through OMB's Good Guidance Practices.

The office within the Executive Branch that monitors the ethical behavior of its employees and former employees is called the Office of Government Ethics (OGE). OGE was established by the Ethics in Government Act of 1978 and was originally placed in the Office of Personnel Management. OGE became a separate agency on October 1, 1989 after Congress passed the OGE Reauthorization Act in 1988. OGE deals solely with the ethical behavior of Executive Branch employees. OGE's mission is to prevent conflicts of interest that may occur and can interfere with budget-related processes. OGE works with the ethics offices at the agency level to proffer advice to prevent conflicts of interest and to uphold the public's confidence that Government business is conducted with impartiality and integrity.

According to OGE, the ethical standards to which a non-career political appointee or career employee must adhere are generally the same for all levels of employment. The standard is that all Executive Branch employees, regardless of rank, are subject to the same standards. High-level officials must disclose potential conflicts of interest as part of the Senate confirmation process and are expected to restrict their contact with agencies and recuse themselves from working on matters they have associated with after leaving Government service. Many high-ranking officials are required to submit various forms annually which display their sources of income and any stock or interest in outside corporations.

The two "core concepts" that OGE regulations, governing laws, and executive orders uphold are:

- Employees should not use public office for private gain; and
- Employees should act impartially and avoid preferential treatment whether for a private organization or individual.

Regarding specific regulations, Table 13-1 summarizes the ethical standards by which an Executive Branch employee must abide. There are additional ethical requirements dictated by different agencies as well as special conditions that regulate particular classes of Executive Branch employees who sit on appointed commissions, advisory boards, and other panels who maintain outside employment. As with any rule, there are exceptions to some of the broad statements outlined in the table. However, the ethical requirements listed here summarize the basic guidelines that an employee should follow.

Ensuring Responsible Spending of Recovery Act Funds

Under the Obama Administration, the ethics of lobbying activities have received heightened attention. This manifested itself in a series of memoranda from the White House addressing responsibilities and restrictions associated with Executive branch officials and lobbyist activities regarding Recovery Act—otherwise known as the American Recovery and Reinvestment Act—funds. Although these rules apply to deployment and thus are not strictly speaking an aspect of the budget formulation process, they reflect the Administration's policy priorities and may be incorporated in future rules and/or legislation directly impacting the ethics of budget formulation.

The documents—herein referred to collectively as the "Recovery Act Ethics Memos"—containing these rules are:

- OMB Director Peter R. Orszag, Memorandum for the Heads of Executive Departments and Agencies regarding Initial Implementing Guidance for Re-

Table 13-1
Ethical Requirements by Employee Type

Ethical Requirement or Standard	General Schedule GS 1-15	Accepted Positions Schedule A,B, or C	Senior Executive Service Levels I-IV	Senior Executive Service Levels V-VI	Presidential Appointee Not Subject to Senate Confirmation	Presidential Appointee Subject to Senate Confirmation
Gift restrictions from outside interests seeking official action from employee's agency.	x	x	x	x	x	x
Gift restrictions from immediate family or personal friends.						
May accept invitations to gatherings when attendance is of interest to agency (widely attended gatherings rule).	x	x	x	x	x	x
May participate in political events or fundraising activities (indirectly) provided they do not solicit co-workers or subordinates.	x	x	x	x	x	x
Prohibited from participating in a matter that will directly affect any personal financial interest.	x	x	x	x	x	x
Prohibited from using non-public information in an inappropriate manner.	x	x	x	x	x	x
May provide public information to outside interests.	x	x	x	x	x	x
Prohibited from using Government property for unauthorized purposes.	x	x	x	x	x	x
May not misuse official time.	x	x	x	x	x	x
May not have conflicting outside employment (varies with agency specific guidelines and exceptions)	x	x	x	x	x	x
May maintain enrollment in former employer's pension, retirement, or profit-sharing plan (exceptions exist for stock plans, disclosure rules apply).	x	x	x	x	x	x
May not receive direct payroll payment from previous employers while a Government employee for compensation of previous services.	x	x	x	x	x	x
Two year restriction on working with agency on matters directly under the employee's control after service.	x	x	x	x	x	x
One year strict "cooling off" period from lobbying agency after service.				x	x	x
One year strict restriction from aiding or advising foreign governments.				x	x	x
Permitted to furnish scientific or technical knowledge under established agency procedures.	x	x	x	x	x	x
Must file confidential financial disclosure forms if working directly (in a decision-making capacity) on contracting or procurement issues.	x	x	x	x		
Must file public financial report detailing holdings of self, family (with the exception of grown children).			x	x	x	x
Must file public financial reports with Senate.						x
Must comply with agreements made during confirmation process within 90 days of placement or appointment (settlement of conflicts, recusal issues and blind trusts).	x	x	x	x	x	x

covery Act,[2] 02/18/2009, The Executive Office of the President, Office of Management and Budget (OMB).[3]

- President Barack Obama, Memorandum for the Heads of Executive Departments and Agencies regarding Ensuring Responsible Spending of Recovery Act Funds, 03/20/2009, The White House, Office of the Press Secretary.
- OMB Director Peter R. Orszag, Memorandum for the Heads of Executive Departments and Agencies regarding Updated Guidance Regarding Communications with Registered Lobbyists About Recovery Act Funds, 07/24/2009, The Executive Office of the President, OMB.

Additionally, several posts to the White House blog by Norm Eisen, Special Counsel to the President for Ethics and Government Reform, contained updates, guidance, and explanations associated with the Recover Act Ethics Memos.

The following policy priorities for the Recovery act were evident in the President's Recovery Act Memos:

- Create jobs;
- Restore economic growth; and
- For environment/energy sector companies, modernize the nation's infrastructure and jumpstart American energy independence.

The Recovery Act Ethics Memos set forth accountability objectives and include detailed requirements to ensure Federal executives use their *discretion* and *judgment* (institutional expertise) to determine merit-based decision-making criteria as the basis for decision-making. Further, there are requirements for a written record of communications, and the transparency of that record. The Recovery Act Ethics Memos were intended to ensure fast and efficient Recovery Act funds distribution while achieving reductions in fraud, waste, error, and abuse. The memoranda discuss departmental and agency actions and responsibilities for transparency and reporting inclusive of performance criteria from complimentary perspectives.

The memos specifically address restrictions on registered lobbyists, accountability for federal officials, and transparency requirements. They include no restriction on registered lobbyists providing policy issue assistance to departments and agencies as long as (a) it is not provided during the period of review or decision-making for deployment of Recovery Act funds; and, (b) scheduling requests and associated document requirements are met.

---

[2] P.L. 111-5. American Recovery and Reinvestment Act of 2009.
[3] The guidance is issued under the authority of 31 U.S.C. 1111; Reorganization Plan No. 2 of 1970; Executive Order 11541; the Chief Financial Officers Act of 1990 (P.L. 101-576); the Office of Federal Procurement Policy Act (41 U.S.C. Chap. 7); and the Federal Funding Accountability and Transparency Act of 2006 (P.L. 109-282).

The restrictions against influencing or attempting to influence Administration officials during merit-based review of Recovery Act funding opportunities were clarified in the memorandum *regarding Updated Guidance Regarding Communications with Registered Lobbyists About Recovery Act Funds*. Specifically, oral communications during the period between the dates of submission and award of grant or other competitive Federal finance are prohibited with two exceptions—for logistical questions and at *widely attended gatherings*.[4]

Stakeholder Interactions

The ethics behind the budget process are not limited to regulations associated with the decision-making framework of budget officials and agency supervisors, but are also integrated with the scale and scope of interactions between non-governmental organizations (NGOs), lobbyists, special interest groups, and Federal decision-makers.

Dealing with the Federal Government on important issues such as the budget is a critical venture for many NGOs. A significant segment of the lobbying industry and much of the daily business that goes on in Washington, DC involves advocating positions and discussing different aspects of the Federal budget with Executive branch employees.

Organizations outside of the Government seek a certain degree of stability and reassurance when dealing with the Government, especially if a program or budget function deals specifically with their markets or core businesses. Companies that take in significant portions of their yearly revenues from goods and services supplied to the Federal Government will naturally pay close attention to funding increases/decreases and agency and departmental budget requests. Communicating with budget and other Government officials is integral to their business operations such as forecasting revenues and achieving certainty needed to sustain business operations.

In order to facilitate an open communications process with Federal officials, certain rules must be adopted to ensure the process is clear and scrupulous. The Executive Branch must monitor itself appropriately and the lobbying community must make sure that is stays within ethical boundaries to maintain the integrity of the budget process and the administration of public funds.

---

[4] 5 C.F.R. § 2635.204(g)(2). *Widely attended gatherings. A gathering is widely attended if it is expected that a large number of persons will attend and that persons with a diversity of views or interests will be present, for example, if it is open to members from throughout the interested industry or profession or if those in attendance represent a range of persons interested in a given matter.* [excerpt]

Chapter 14

Regulatory Policy and the Budget

In addition to the taxes and other costs paid directly by the public to the Government, the public indirectly pays for the costs of carrying out regulations issued by the Government. These regulations affect the domestic economy, international trade, the workplace, the environment, and tax policy compliance. The private sector, state and local governments, and Federal agencies bear the cost of implementing the regulations.

A regulation is a means for the Government to divert public and private resources to meet public objectives. Federal regulations run the gamut from governing internal operations of Federal agencies and departments, to governing the way citizens file and pay taxes, to governing the type of pollution control equipment that must be installed at a manufacturing facility.

Regulation and Government spending can be close substitutes in providing public services. For example, if the Government wants to encourage universal healthcare, it can pay for the entire cost of such a system, or it can shift some of the program costs onto workers and employers by mandating that all employers provide health insurance.

Congress has granted over 70 different Federal agencies or parts of agencies the authority to issue regulations. Agencies publish over 10,000 regulatory actions each year. While many of these actions are minor, the cumulative effect is considerable. For some agencies, issuing, monitoring, and enforcing regulations to achieve certain goals is the primary objective. For most agencies, regulations are one of the many tools they use to carry out their primary missions. Creating, enforcing, and implementing regulations comes with considerable cost to the Federal Government and to the private sector.

- Cost to the Government to operate the regulatory system: Veronique de Rugy and Melinda Warren[1] performed a detailed examination of the President's budget to estimate how much the Government spends each year to develop, issue, and enforce regulations. Their estimate of these costs leads to the conclusion that about nine percent of all Federal discretionary nondefense spending goes for operating the regulatory system.
- Cost to comply with Federal regulations: When the Government sets regulations, the private sector, state and local governments, and Federal departments and agencies must comply. It is estimated that the annual cost of compliance is as high as 11 percent of the Gross Domestic Product (GDP).

Regulatory agencies receive a fair amount of scrutiny due to the inherent uncertainties surrounding regulatory analysis. The sources of this scrutiny are often:

- The costs cannot be measured easily.
- The most significant costs, domestic economic regulations, are determined indirectly. Although it appears to be the best estimate for these types of regulations, it contains considerable uncertainly.
- The other costs are based on detailed analyses of regulatory costs.
- Very little is known about actual costs; almost all Government reports use estimates prepared before the regulations took effect. Those estimates were made for benefit-cost analyses to demonstrate that the expected benefits would exceed the expected costs. Many analysts believe that Government agencies tend to understate costs.

In addition to the costs that have been estimated, there may be indirect costs in terms of international competition, economic growth, and jobs.

- Studies by the World Bank and the Organization for Economic Cooperation and Development (OECD) have concluded that countries with less regulated economies show higher rates of economic development.
- Reforms in regulation tend to increase investment, innovation, productivity, and employment rates according to the OECD analysis.

Purpose of Regulation

Regulations are issued for internal management purposes and for implementing statutory requirements.

---

[1] Veronique de Rugy and Susan Dudley & Melinda Warren, **Regulatory Agency Spending Reaches New Height:** *An Analysis of the U.S. Budget for Fiscal Years 2008 and 2009 August 2008,* Mercatus Center George Mason University, Arlington, VA and Weidenbaum Center, Washington University St. Louis, MO.

- Internal Management. Departments and agencies use regulation as a means of managing their own actions as well as those of members of the public who deal with those agencies. Uses of such regulations include:

  - Personnel management;
  - How the public is to apply for certain benefits or permits; and
  - How the Government acquisition process works.

- Implementing statutory requirements. Most regulations are in response to requirements in authorizing legislation that require a department or agency to issue regulations that implement the provisions of the statute. The Clean Air Act is an example in which the Environmental Protection Agency was required to issue regulations in accordance with the provision of the Act.

Why Statutes Include Regulatory Requirements

Regulations issued in response to statutory requirements fall into the following categories.

- **Market Failure.** A market failure is when the free market results in socially inefficient outcomes. Market failures commonly addressed through regulation include:

  - Natural monopolies. These exist where the good being sold is such that multiple participants in a market cannot survive. As a result, the single remaining firm can restrict supply and charge monopoly prices. One example of a natural monopoly is the electricity distribution system. It would not make sense for two companies to build competing infrastructure to deliver electricity to your home or business. In instances such as this, governments step in to regulate prices.
  - Common property. Issues occur where no clear property rights – or no clear way of enforcing them – exist. Since nobody "owns" the resource, there is no way to ensure that it is being used most efficiently. For example, since nobody "owns" the fish in a particular fishery, the fishery could easily become over fished if a licensing system were not put in place to restrict use.
  - Externalities. These occur when market prices do not reflect some aspect of a transaction. If the price of a good fails to include all costs to society associated with the production and consumption of that good, the market will produce too much of that good. Conversely, if the price fails to include all benefits to society from a particular good, the market will produce too little. Pollution is an example of a negative externality. Those bearing the cost of the pollution are likely to be different from the producer of the pollution. As a result the price of the good will not reflect the cost to

society of the pollution and too much of the good will be produced. Regulation can restrict production of the good or reduce the pollution associated with the production to reach a more efficient outcome.

- Information inequalities. These are situations where participants in a transaction do not have the same, or sufficient, information to make an efficient decision. For example, purchasers of a refrigerator may not have sufficient information on the energy consumption of that refrigerator to weigh its true costs of ownership against that of other refrigerators. In this instance, the government may be able to improve the efficiency of such transactions by requiring that information be provided to consumers on energy consumption. However, not all cases of imperfect information represent a failure of the market. Sometimes information is too expensive to obtain, or simply insignificant to the decision at hand.

- Fairness or Equity. Regulations may be used to address issues of fairness or inequality that do not result from inherent market inefficiency. For example, Federal Procurement Regulations exist to try to make it "fair" for all competitors trying to do business with the Government. Similarly, regulations promulgated under the Americans with Disabilities Act and other civil rights legislation seek to address inequalities created by history, accident, or birth.
- Standardization. The Government may use regulations to reduce transactions costs through standardization. For example, all taxpayers file the same tax forms to reduce the cost of collecting taxes and enforcing tax law.

Regulations are developed through formal rulemaking or informal rulemaking processes.

- Formal rulemaking. This is usually associated with independent regulatory agencies such as the Federal Communications Commission. Regulations are developed in this process through formal hearings that are judicial in nature, with independent commissioners hearing testimony and releasing rulings in response to the evidence received.
- Informal rulemaking. This is associated with agencies such as the Environmental Protection Agency and the Department of Agriculture that are under control of the President. This process takes place through "notice and comment," whereby agencies publish their intentions in the *Federal Register* and allow the interested public to comment on the agency's ideas. Agencies are required to respond to public comment before issuing a final rule.

The remainder of this chapter focuses on "informal rulemaking" that is under the control of the President.

The Movement to Centralized Regulatory Review

Before 1970, most Federal regulations were "economic" regulations, or actions that set the price and/or quantity of goods sold in major industries. The Federal Government regulated energy, telecommunications, airline, railroad, trucking, and other major markets. While these regulations had substantial impact on the economy, the political impact to the President was minimal. Most of the regulatory agencies were independent commissions not under the direct control of the President (e.g., Interstate Commerce Commission and the Federal Communications Commission). Since 1970, Congress has eliminated many Federal economic regulations.

Now, the most sweeping regulations are "social" regulations to improve the health, safety, and environmental conditions for workers and the public. Because the agencies that issue these regulations, mainly EPA and OSHA, are part of the Executive Branch, the President has responsibility for their actions. Recent Administrations, therefore, have sought to ensure that agency actions are consistent with Presidential priorities.

The trend toward centralized regulatory review is not limited to the United States. When the United States adopted a more formal regulatory review process in 1981, it was one of only three or four countries to have such a system. By 2001, a majority of all nations with highly-developed economies had a government entity to review draft regulations, requirements to analyze the impacts of draft regulations, and stated principles to guide national regulatory efforts.

Managing the Regulatory Review Process

The first regulatory reform statute was the Administrative Procedure Act (APA) signed in 1946. The APA gives the public the opportunity to oversee regulatory activity through the notice and comment process. Agencies must base their regulatory decisions on the record and avoid decisions that are arbitrary and capricious. The APA also provides recourse to the public to take agencies to court for decisions that violate this standard – thus providing the Judiciary Branch of Government with a regulatory oversight role.

A number of measures have been taken that require agencies to look at the economic and policy consequences of their regulatory activities. Executive Order No. 12291, signed by President Reagan on April 1, 1981, established economic efficiency as the primary yardstick by which regulations were to be judged. In 1993, President Clinton replaced that Executive Order with Executive Order No. 12866, "Regulatory Planning and Review," which expanded the issues to be considered in judging regulations but retained economic efficiency remained the key factor.

In 1996, Congress passed the Congressional Review Act in 1996. This Act provides Congress direct oversight of the regulatory process by giving Congress 60 days to overturn any Federal Regulation. This authority has been used only once since the Act was passed: in 2001, the Congress passed a joint resolution overturning the Department of Labor's ergonomics standards.

On January 18, 2007, President George W. Bush further amended Executive Order No. 12866 to add three new requirements:

- The substantive requirements of the Executive Order now apply to significant guidance documents – this addresses the fine line between guidance and regulations mentioned earlier in this chapter;
- Agency heads must designate a political appointee to be the agency's Regulatory Policy Officer. This requirement ensures that all regulations have, at least, one political review before a rule is submitted to the Office of Management and Budget; and
- Agencies must state in writing what market failure the regulation is intended to address.

Since 1981, OMB has managed the White House's centralized regulatory review. OMB provides oversight of the regulatory activities of Executive Branch agencies, provides guidance to the agencies, and assists the President, Vice President, and other policy advisors in regulatory planning and in reviewing individual regulations.

Within OMB, the Office of Information and Regulatory Affairs (OIRA) is responsible for oversight of regulatory matters. Executive Order 13258 of February 28, 2002 shifted responsibility for regulatory planning and interagency appeal to the Director of OMB and the White House Chief of Staff, respectively.

Executive Order 12866 directs the Executive Branch agencies to submit for a 90-day inter-agency review all proposed and final "significant" regulatory actions that meet one of the following criteria:

- Have an annual effect on the economy of $100 million or more or adversely affect, in a material way the economy, a sector of the economy, productivity, competition, jobs, the environment, public health or safety, or state, local, or tribal governments or communities;
- Create a serious inconsistency or otherwise interfere with an action taken or planned by another agency;
- Materially alter the budgetary impact of entitlements, grants, user fees, or loan programs or the rights and obligations of recipients thereof; or
- Raise novel legal or policy issues arising out of legal mandates, the President's priorities, or the principles set forth in this Executive order.

OIRA limits its review to regulations classified as "economically significant" (an annual effect on the economy of $100 million or greater), or "significant" because they meet one or more of the other three Executive Order 12866 criteria.

Executive Order 12866 does not apply to the following regulations or rules:

- Issued in accordance with the formal rulemaking provisions;
- Pertaining to a military or foreign affairs function of the United States, other than procurement regulations and those involving the import or export on non-defense articles and services; and
- Limited to agency organization, management, or personnel matters.

Policies Governing the Regulatory Review Process

OMB Circular A-4, *Regulatory Analysis,* provides guidance to Federal agencies on the development of regulations as required under Executive Order 12866. The Circular also provides guidance to agencies on the regulatory accounting statements that are required under the Regulatory Right-to-Know Act.

As defined by OMB, a regulatory analysis should include the following three basic elements:

(1) A statement of the need for the proposed action;
(2) An examination of alternative approaches; and
(3) An evaluation of the benefits and costs—quantitative and qualitative—of the proposed action and the main alternatives identified by the analysis.

To evaluate properly the benefits and costs of regulations and their alternatives, departments and agencies must do the following:

- Explain how the actions required by the rule are linked to the expected benefits. For example, indicate how additional safety equipment will reduce safety risks. A similar analysis should be done for each of the alternatives.

  - Since the late 1960s, benefit-cost analysis has been the primary tool for judging the effectiveness of regulatory decisions. A benefit-cost analysis (BCA) is used to estimate the positive results associated with the Government's action in relation to the resources the Government is requiring to be spent to achieve those results. To the extent possible, Federal agencies are to choose those alternatives that "maximize net benefits to society."
  - Cost-effectiveness analysis (CEA) is another tool used to measure the economic utility of Government action. OMB suggests that regulatory agencies use both BCA and CEA to support analysis of regulatory alternatives. Specifically, CEA is used for major rules for which the primary benefits are improved public health and safety or when benefits cannot be expressed in monetary terms.

- Identify a baseline. Benefits and costs are defined in comparison with a clearly stated alternative. This normally will be a no action baseline: what the world will be like if the proposed rule is not adopted. Comparisons to a next best alternative are also especially useful.

- Identify the expected undesirable side-effects and ancillary benefits of the proposed regulatory action and the alternatives. These should be added to the direct benefits and costs as appropriate.

Each Administration has issues that it considers to be more important than others. Recent Administrations have used the regulatory review process as a means of ensuring that such issues receive attention. For example, the President may issue an Executive Order requiring agencies to consider the issue as part of their regulatory development. Examples include the following:

- **Impact on Children.** In 1997, President Clinton signed Executive Order 13045, "Protection of Children from Environmental Health Risks and Safety Risks." This Executive Order requires agencies to estimate the potential risks and benefits to children from significant regulatory actions and why the selected alternative is preferable to other alternatives.
- **Impact on Energy Supplies, Production, and Consumption.** The Bush Administration issued a new requirement for agencies and OIRA in May, 2001. Under Executive Order 13211, agencies must analyze how their draft regulations affect U.S. energy supplies, distribution, and consumption. Agencies must prepare "Statements of Energy Effects" for each significant regulation. Regulations with "significant" energy impacts will undergo additional scrutiny.

In December of 2000, Congress expanded the interagency review process through passage of the Data Quality Act ("DQA"), which required OMB to issue standards for information quality. In January 2002, OIRA published the final version of its *Guidelines for Ensuring and Maximizing the Quality, Objectivity, Utility, and Integrity of Information Disseminated by Federal Agencies* (the "Guidelines"). The Guidelines require each Federal agency to:

- Issue information quality guidelines that maximize the quality, objectivity, utility, and integrity of information that it disseminates;
- Establish administrative mechanisms to allow the public to seek and obtain correction of agency information maintained or disseminated that does not comply with the OMB or agency guidelines; and
- Report periodically to OMB the number and content of complaints received regarding the accuracy of its information and the disposition of such complaints.

The public can file a petition with an agency challenging the utility, objectivity, or integrity of information that agency has disseminated.

Peer review of scientific analyses supporting a regulation is a requirement. OMB Memorandum (M-05-03) issued on December 16, 2004 provided OMB's "Final Information Quality Bulletin for Peer Review." This Bulletin applies stricter requirements for the peer review of highly influential scientific assessments.

Cost Benefit Analysis

Cost benefit analysis is a method for regulatory review employed with more regularity in the last few Administrations. During the past two decades, cost-benefit analysis has become the dominant method used by policymakers to evaluate government intervention in the areas of health, safety and environment. As conceived in theory, cost-benefit analysis:

- Enumerates *all* possible consequences, both positive and negative, that might arise in response to the implementation of a candidate government policy;
- Estimates the probability of each consequence occurring;
- Estimates the benefit or loss to society should each occur, *expressed in monetary terms,* where possible;
- Computes the *expected* social benefit or loss from each possible consequence by multiplying the amount of the associated benefit or loss by its probability of occurrence; and
- Computes the net *expected* social benefit or loss associated with the government policy by summing over the various possible consequences. The reference point for these calculations is the state of the economy in the absence of government policy, termed the "baseline".

Steps in the Development and Approval of Regulations

- **Developing a Regulatory Plan and Agenda**. OIRA coordinates the centralized, Government-wide regulatory planning process. This planning process consists of two major components, the Regulatory Plan and the Unified Regulatory Agenda.

  - **Regulatory Plan.** Under Executive Order 12866, the Director of OMB meets with agency representatives annually to learn their regulatory priorities and to coordinate the regulatory efforts on a Government-wide basis for the upcoming year.

    * By June 1st, agencies provide to OIRA a draft regulatory plan that describes the significant regulations they plan to issue during the upcoming fiscal year. OMB may suggest through use of a Prompt Letter the need for additional regulation that could yield improvements in

environmental, safety, or health protections and to suggest that agencies remove or modify current regulations that are no longer needed.

* OIRA and other advisors review the plan to determine whether the proposed actions will interfere with another agency's rules or established regulations, or if there is a potential conflict with the Administration's priorities and objectives.

* The final regulatory plan published in October describes the most significant regulatory actions that each agency expects to issue in proposed or final form during the current fiscal year or shortly thereafter.

- **Unified Regulatory Agenda.** The *Unified Agenda*, published twice each year in April and October in the *Federal Register*, identifies all rules and proposed rules that each agency expects to issue during the next six months.[2] The *Regulatory Plan* is published as part of the October *Unified Agenda*.

• **Agency Rulemaking Development**. When agency staffs are drafting a proposed regulation, they consult with OIRA staff to determine if a draft regulation is "significant" under Executive Order 12866 and subject to OMB review. While an agency may contest OIRA's classification, the Executive Order gives OIRA the final decision authority. Regulations that are economically significant are automatically reviewed. Many regulations that might otherwise qualify for examination under the other criteria undergo an "informal" analysis to determine whether or not they warrant a formal interagency review.

• **OIRA Review**. OIRA reviews a draft regulation using the following criteria:

- <u>**Social Benefits Must Justify the Social Costs.**</u> The most significant regulatory principle is that the social benefits of a rule should justify its social costs.

- <u>**Impact on Small Businesses.**</u> Regulations must minimize the burden on all sizes of businesses. In addition, and the Regulatory Flexibility Act requires the agencies to fashion regulatory requirements appropriate to the size of the enterprises affected. In 2002, President Bush announced an agreement between SBA and OIRA to strengthen SBA's participation during OIRA's review.

- <u>**Impact on State and Local Governments and Indian Tribal Governments.**</u> Agencies must certify, and OIRA must concur, that they have adequately consulted with state and local governments (E.O. 13132 "Federalism") and with Indian Tribal Governments (E.O. 13175 "Consultation and Coordination with Indian Tribal Governments"). The 1995 Unfunded Mandates Reform Act also requires agencies to consult and to prepare specific benefit-cost analyses for large regulatory mandates (greater than $100 million in any one year).

---

[2] 5 USC Sec. 602, Regulatory agenda

OIRA seeks the views of other affected Federal agencies on the draft regulation. If other agencies have problems with the proposed regulation, OIRA oversees an interagency review of the draft action.

- **OIRA Action on Proposed Regulation**. At the end of OIRA's review, the draft regulation is either approved or returned to the agency for additional consideration or modification. If a draft regulation is returned, the agency may modify it and re-submit it to OIRA for further review. If no change is recorded on the conditions or facts of the regulatory action, OIRA has 45 days to complete its review. If OIRA determines that more consideration of the action by the issuing agency is needed, OIRA can return the proposal to the agency again.

- **Congressional Review**. Prior to becoming a final rule, the Congress is given an opportunity to review all economically significant regulations under the provisions of the 1996 Small Business Regulatory Enforcement Fairness Act (SBREFA).[3] The issuing agency must provide Congress a copy and summary of the rule, the determination as whether it is a significant action, the effective date of the rule, and any relevant analyses. The Congress has 60 days to disapprove the regulation. If the Congress takes no action within the 60-day period, the rule goes into effect. Congress can stop the regulation by passing a joint resolution of disapproval. The President can veto the resolution. If either house of Congress fails to override the veto or takes no action within 30 session days of receiving the veto, the rule then takes effect.

  Since passage of this law, Congress has overturned only one of the thousands of agency rulemakings. In March 2001, Congress passed a joint resolution overturning the Department of Labor's final ergonomics standards.

- **Publishing the Final Regulation**. The final rule is published in the Federal Register. That can occur before Congressional action takes place, but the rule cannot go into force until completion of the congressional review.

Public Access to Rulemaking Actions

To increase public participation and the transparency of OIRA's communications with the public, OIRA maintains the following:

- A publicly-available list, accessible through the Internet, that describes all regulations currently under formal review by agency, title, date received, and the completion date.

---

[3] 5 USC Sec. 801, Congressional review

- A list of all meetings, attendees, and conversations between OIRA officials and the public (including Congress) pertaining to a regulatory action that is on file in OIRA's public docket room in Washington and on the Internet.

Once a regulation is published in the *Federal Register*, all draft regulations, economic analyses, and documents exchanged between OIRA and the agency are made available.

Annual Report on Regulatory Activities

Each year, OMB must produce a report detailing the actions taken on significant regulations and the estimated benefits and costs of the rules. The report does not include the details of rules promulgated by independent agencies.

Chapter 15

Politics of the Budget

On the occasion of Obama's second budget submission to Congress, it is appropriate to note that the politics surrounding deliberations on the budget are not only visible to the American public, but also unusually divisive!

The Congressional Democratic majority has been amazingly successful delivering the President's budget priorities. However, the President's agenda has spurred an uncharacteristically vitriolic debate with the Republican minority. The Congressional Republicans have attempted to gain enough votes to defeat various budget proposals through dialogue with Democrats who would normally oppose the President's priorities. The Republicans' attempts have largely failed; their spirited effort has highlighted the divisions within the Democratic Party but has not resulted in the President's call for adoption of Republican proposals. Nonetheless, bipartisan action has been the President's rhetoric.

The President has relied on the Democratic Congressional leadership to work through intra-party issues, but made strong unprecedented attempts to gain Republican support for his priorities. However, most recently the President has become more hands-on due to the potential for Republican success at picking off votes required to enact his agenda on the most contentious issues. Politically, not only has this approach been necessary but has included the demonstration of the skillful application of both the President's constitutional and political levers. The Congressional leadership has similarly been emboldened to use its most controversial processes and procedures to match the President's maneuvers. As a result, an increasing number of American voters are becoming more aware and educated on the politics of the budget. Phrases such budget reconciliation, CBO scoring rules, budget gimmicks, and logrolling are becoming more commonplace.

Republicans have been equally effective by achieving political solidarity in opposition to the President's budget priorities as well as mounting a campaign to expose the procedural mechanisms Democrats are using to highlight the shortcuts the majority and the President have utilized to enact their priorities.

Which party is connecting most with the voters will be known following the upcoming off-year elections. However, current indicators can determine general mood by examining the results of the most recent gubernatorial and special Congressional elections. Those races have favored Republicans. In fact, the nation's most respected pollsters are predicting that the Republican message will resonate with the voting public. Thus, notwithstanding the debate, controversy and acrimony associated with the state of the economy, unemployment, energy and environmental initiatives, healthcare reform and Federal bailout of banks, insurance companies and car manufacturers, the President is still winning.

The key issues in this year's budget debate are the same issues that were most prominent during the 2008 Presidential election campaign. During President Obama's campaign, his main focus was to promise voters a sweeping reform in healthcare. Following his election, President Obama again reiterated the fact that healthcare reform would be his and the Democratic Party's top budget and legislative priority. Current statistics make clear that there are approximately 35 million Americans without healthcare. Further, this number is expected to rise should the current budget and program remain in place.

On March 21st, 2010, the House passed its version of the healthcare bill by a vote of 219-212, with President Obama signing it on the following day. Although the Senate passed their version of the bill in December of 2009, a separate package of changes was also passed by the House in order to satisfy a handful of members that had reservations with the Senate bill. Senate Republicans had forced further action in the House based on procedural defects in the House bill. While the House re-enacted their bill bowing to the procedural defects, in the end, the Democratic majority achieved their goal. The back and forth is the largest showing of partisanship related to budgetary matters in U. S. history.

The only way the healthcare bill could be enacted was by using the reconciliation process. The reason Democrats used reconciliation to pass the bill was because the process only requires 51 votes. Many Republicans also felt that it was the best way to stop it. Any change made to the bill in the Senate meant it would require the House to call for another vote. Under reconciliation, an unlimited number of amendments can be offered.

Historically, in the 23 times reconciliation has been used, only once has the Senate bill not been changed and sent back to the House.

Since 1980, reconciliation has been used on the following occasions[1]:

- Nine times when Republicans controlled both the House and the Senate,
- Six times when Democrats controlled both the House and the Senate,
- Once when the Democrats controlled the Senate and the Republicans the House, and
- Seven times when the Republicans controlled the Senate and the Democrats the House.

To ensure that all provisions of the bill have a budgetary impact, the rules of reconciliation allow Republicans to raise 19 different types of objections. The most commonly used objection is known as the "Byrd Rule." The Byrd Rule can declare a provision to be ineligible for reconciliation in six different events:

- It does not produce a change in outlays or revenues;
- It produces an outlay increase or revenue decrease when the instructed committee is not in compliance with its instructions;
- It is outside the jurisdiction of the committee that submitted the title or provision for inclusion in the reconciliation measure;
- It produces a change in outlays or revenues which is merely incidental to the non-budgetary components of the provision;
- It would increase the deficit for a fiscal year beyond those covered by the reconciliation measure, though the provisions in question may receive an exception if they in total in a Title of the measure net to a reduction in the deficit; and
- It recommends changes in Social Security.

Thus, the debate on the Hill continues regarding the passing of healthcare reform. At the time of writing, the bill had been passed back to the Senate for the reconciliation process.

President Obama's FY 2011 Budget Message

While America is still recovering from its worst recession for over 70 years, President Obama has continually conveyed the message of hope and change to the American public. His FY 2011 Budget and his State of the Union address strengthened his unrelenting and determined efforts to ease the burdens faced by the nation.

In his budget message to the Congress of the United States, President Obama acknowledged that the heart of the Administration's efforts is to move the United States from recession to recovery, and ultimately to prosperity. The President's Budget sub-

---

[1] http://en.wikipedia.org/wiki/Reconciliation_(United_States_Congress)

mission and address provides the following blueprint for the Administration and focuses on the following six major topic areas:

Investing in Job Creation

- Provide small business access to credit: The Budget provides funds to support $17.5 billion in loan guarantees to help small business expand and operate.
- Refocus Troubled Asset Relief Program (TARP) Funds to assist small busi-ness: The Treasury is redirecting TARP to focus on preserving homeownership and supporting small business lending.
- Eliminate capital gains tax on investments in small businesses: The Budget eliminates capital gains taxes on long-term investments in many small busi-nesses.
- Promote American exports to fuel economic growth: The Budget provides $534 million to promote exports for small businesses, help enforce free trade agreements with other nations, eliminate barriers to sales of U.S. products, and improve the competitiveness of U.S. firms.
- Invest in science research and development: The Budget includes $61.6 billion for civilian research and development.
- Foster job creation and economic growth in Rural America: This initiative in-cludes several investments to promote economic growth and job creation in rural communities.

Build Infrastructure for Job Creation

- Create a national infrastructure innovation and finance fund: The Budget pro-vides $4 billion to invest in projects of regional or national significance.
- Invest in a smart, energy-efficient, and reliable energy grid: The Budget con-tinues to support modernization of the Nation's electric grid.
- Support clean water infrastructure investments: The Budget provides $3.3 bil-lion for the Clean Water and Drinking Water State Revolving Funds.
- Establish a new federal transit safety program: The Budget invests $30 million for this program.
- Modernize the Air Traffic Control system: The Budget provides $1.14 billion for the system.
- Invest in America's water resources infrastructure: This initiative seeks to ensure the safe and reliable operation and maintenance of key facilities of the Army Corps of Engineers and Bureau of Reclamation.

Educate the Workforce for the jobs of the 21st Century

- Reform schools: The Budget aims to reform elementary and secondary school funding by setting high standards, encouraging innovation, and rewarding suc-cess.

- Grow high-performing charter schools and other innovative public schools: The Budget provides $490 million to increase the number of these schools.
- This initiative will increase the number of effective teachers and principles: President Obama envisions this as being the key to high-quality education.

Create a Clean Energy Economy

- Transform energy supply and slow global warming: The Administration will work to enact and implement a comprehensive market-based policy that will reduce greenhouse gas emissions by 17 percent in 2020 and by more than 80 percent by 2050.
- Advance the development of carbon capture and storage technologies: The Budget provides $545 million in funding will help reduce greenhouse gas emission by focusing resources to develop carbon capture technologies.
- Eliminate funding for inefficient fossil fuel subsidies: The proposed Budget will reduce taxpayer dollars on incentives that run counter to this national priority.

Keep America Safe and Maintain Global Leadership

- Support mission in Afghanistan, Pakistan, and Iraq: The Budget provides funding for 30,000 additional troops to deploy to Afghanistan while U.S. combat forces continue drawing down in Iraq.
- Strengthen Homeland Security: The Budget continues investments in homeland defenses that are targeted to meet priority needs.
- Increase funding for the Department of Defense: The Budget requests $548.9 billion.
- Prevent the Proliferation of Nuclear weapons: The Budget provides $2.7 billion for this program

Health Care Reform

- Increase investment in patient-centered health research: The Budget provides $286 million for research.
- Expand affordable primary and preventative care: The Budget includes $2.5 billion for health centers.
- Medicare, Medicaid, and the Children's Health Insurance Program: The Budget seeks to reduce fraud, waste, and abuse.
- Increase the number of primary health care providers: The Budget includes $169 million for the National Health Service Corps.

Presidential Action on Stimulating the Economy

Since the onset of the financial crisis, there has been a great deal of debate over what types of actions should be taken by the Federal Government and at what expense to the taxpayer. In general, most agreed that the Government should take action and some taxpayer money would be placed at risk. Because appropriation of taxpayer money required action by Congress, it was decided to pass a number of stimulus bills to jumpstart the waning economy.

Following negotiations between both parties, the Senate agreed to the Economic Stimulus Act of 2008 (H.R. 5140) on February 7, 2008, by a vote of 81 to 16. The House quickly approved the bill that evening by an overwhelming vote of 380 to 34. President George W. Bush, a strong advocate for the legislation, signed it on February 13 immediately after it reached his desk. The package included rebates, which were up to $600 for individuals and up to $2,400 for couples. The rebates were the centerpiece of the $152 billion package designed to jumpstart the U.S. economy. In addition to rebates, the new law included $44.8 billion in business incentives and help for homeowners facing fore-closure because of the mortgage meltdown.

Later that year, it became apparent that the earlier stimulus package did not provide enough help for homeowners struggling to make mortgage payments. More action was needed. On July 30, President Bush signed the Housing and Economic Recovery Act of 2008. This authorized the Treasury to guarantee up to $300 billion in mortgages held by Government Sponsored Entities (GSEs) like Fannie Mae and Freddie Mac and reformed regulatory supervision of the GSEs.

The crisis hit a boiling point in September of 2008. Amid panic in the markets and stern calls to action across the Government, President Bush signed the Emergency Eco-nomic Stabilization Act on October 3, 2008. This gave the Treasury broad authority to spend up to $700 billion to stabilize the markets under the new Troubled Asset Relief Program (TARP). About half was spent right away and half was deferred to early 2009. This legislation was enacted in the weeks leading up to a heated presidential election in which the economy dominated debate.

Following President Obama's election, The President and the Democrat-controlled Congress rushed to enact the American Recovery and Reinvestment Act (ARRA). This Act had three immediate goals[2]:

- Create new jobs and save existing ones;
- Spur economic activity and invest in long-term growth; and
- Foster unprecedented levels of accountability and transparency in Govern-ment spending.

ARRA intended to achieve these goals by providing $288 billion in tax cuts and ben-efits for families and business, $224 billion of funding for education and health care, and $275 billion for Federal loans, grants and contracts. The Administration wanted the law passed as quickly as possible because of the severity of the economic crisis and

---

[2] www.recovery.gov

argued that the package would only be effective if enacted immediately. This belief, however, was not shared by the Republicans who argued that the package contained too many pet projects and did too little to create jobs in the short run. Democrats felt that the public works, green energy, and education components of the packages would spur immediate job growth while simultaneously addressing other problems. Following heated debate, no Republicans in the House and only three Republicans in the Senate voted for the bill. President Obama signed the $787 billion bill on February 17, 2009.

The Jobs Bill, passed by the Senate on February 24, 2010, was one of the few examples of bipartisanship shown between the Democratic and Republican parties recently. Thirteen Republicans joined Democrats in passing the bill by a vote of 70 – 28, with only one Democrat voting against the measure. The bill will create a $13 billion program to give relief to companies by allowing them to not pay Social Security taxes for new employees for the remainder of the year. Further, should the new employees remain on the company's payroll for at least a year; the company would receive a $1,000 tax credit per employee. The bill also reauthorizes the Highway Trust Fund and an expansion of the Build America Bonds Program. Many House Republicans believe that the Democratic Party is using budget gimmicks to pass the bill and argue that the bill violates PAYGO rules by not offsetting the complete spending package with cost saving measures. Senator Tom Coburn (R – OK) summed up his frustration by saying "These kinds of budget gimmicks would send any businessman to prison, but in Washington it is common practice to hide the true costs from taxpayers.[3]"

The Politics of Partisan Political Parties

Partisan differences receive the most media coverage. The Administration always articulates its sharp policy differences with the other party's officials and vice versa. However, the current debate is full of gimmickry and spin from both sides.

Regardless of which party occupies the White House, the President's Budget message delivers the President's allocations and economic expectations, delineates his themes, and sets out his spending priorities. The FY 2011 Budget will be closely analyzed and critiqued by both Republicans and Democrats, media, special interests, NGO's, and various institutions seeking to voice their viewpoints.

Typically, and regardless of which party proposes the Budget, opposing party leaders label presidential priorities and program policy objectives as unacceptable for America's future and pronounce the Budget *"dead on arrival."* However, this year the President's party holds the majority in both houses of Congress. Thus, even though the opposing party continues to vigorously object to the proposed budget, the President's fellow party leaders will extol praise on the President's Budget and work to develop support for its proposals.

The parties' different perspectives on budget programs, allocations, and policy objectives are numerous and can be analyzed within various frameworks including, scope, political

---

[3] http://www.nytimes.com/2010/02/25/us/politics/25jobs.html

ideology, political rhetoric, and program magnitude. The new Administration will employ every technique of political leverage to win for the President.

The Politics of State & Local/NGOs (Non-Governmental Organizations) and Special Interests

Societies and their institutions are typically designated as one of three categories: public (or, government), for-profit (or, corporate), or nonprofit (or, independent). This number is sometimes reduced to two—as in, public versus private. In this setup, the public sector includes governmental institutions, while the private includes both for-profit and nonprofit organizations. Institutions within the nonprofit sector are often referred to as nongovernmental organizations (NGOs). The issues NGOs address transcend partisan politics because they are committed to addressing social needs and improving the human condition. As such, supporters transcend party ideology and unite to advance a policy agenda despite that their position runs contrary to the Administration or their own party leaders.

With the rise of the modern nation state, social development has increasingly been viewed as a government responsibility. The growth of social democracies and the welfare state during the twentieth century clearly reflects this belief. Despite massive investment in social programs, however, governments have not fully addressed many needs of the citizenry; nor are these needs often met by the corporate sector. NGOs have emerged in large part to bridge the gap between what governments and corporations can do and what societies need or expect.

The Politics of Institutional Government

Savvy elected and appointed officials control the partisan process, but the Federal career bureaucracy controls institutional politics. Their influence over discharge of Federal projects and programs that benefit the American public exceeds any other. The simple reason is formulation and implementation process is the domain of institutional politics. Thus, career employees in the Executive Branch who develop program plans, provide information to the political officials, and implement the approved programs are preeminent. These employees constitute the organization's institutional memory, provide analytic capability, and are organizationally secure and network driven.

In the context of this macro view of politics, this section attempts to address the following questions:

- Who are the most powerful, controlling, and influential players in the budget process?

    - The President, the Office of Management and Budget (OMB), and the Executive Branch; or

- The Congressional leadership, the appropriations committees, the Congressional Budget Office (CBO), and the rest of the legislative branch.

- What roles do the following institutions play in the Executive Branch process associated with the formulation and execution of the budget?

    - OMB;
    - The departmental budget office; and
    - The agency budget office.

Addressing these questions requires an understanding of the overall process and rules described in previous chapters, what the rules do and do not permit, knowing how to apply budgetary techniques, and the motivations of the players in the process.

- **Rules of the game**. In many ways, the budget process is like a game of chess in which strategy and technical knowledge both play important roles. Knowledge of technical rules allows a strategist to be aware of all options and use rules to their advantage.

    - An agency needing additional funds for a new requirement might propose a new or increased user fee to cover the cost of the service that could be included in the appropriation bill and be counted as an offset to the cost. Recently proposed examples of these user fees include DHS's border and transportation security conveyance, passenger, and merchandise processing fees. Other examples of user fees include pesticide registration fees and nuclear security and regulatory fees.

- **Realism versus theory in the process.** The rules and regulations describe the budget and implementation processes in great detail for each stage in the process. However, experienced practitioners often find considerable room to apply the flexibility inherent in the rules and regulations.

    - For instance, there is no definition in law as to what constitutes an emergency for purposes of providing funds above levels set in law or Congressional Budget Resolution. The Congress and the President have been able to use emergency authority to get around annual discretionary appropriations limits.

- **Budgetary techniques and their implication.** Preparing budgetary documents is especially important. OMB issues guidance on the types of information that must be submitted with a department's request. Each department and agency develops, generally in concert with the staff of the congressional committees, the formats and information to include in congressional budget justification books. This guidance to the program/project offices describes the minimum information required. Each major element can submit, in addition to the required materials, information that explains and justifies a program's benefits and costs in the best possible manner. The manner in which a program and its benefits are described has a significant effect on the political decision-makers and the outcome of the budget process.

– For example, an agency, with OMB approval, might provide committees with a detailed benefit-cost analysis supporting the budget request for a specific project.

• **The players and their motivations and pressures.** The pressures on the decision-makers from various sources play a major role in the process. These pressures can come from inside the organization and from the White House and Congress, as well as from stakeholders outside the Government. If the players are motivated to achieve certain ends they will work harder to see those ends accomplished. Without that motivation, good programs can be eliminated from the budget due to a lack of commitment.

– For instance, a motivated manager with an idea or proposal for solving an issue of concern to the White House and/or Congress will take the initiative to push that proposal forward and be rewarded with program funding if the proposal is accepted.

Budget Process Overview

Each program goes through a circular process, or program life cycle, with respect to organizational involvement in the budget process. Each step in this process is an important part of the institutional processes of the Executive and Legislative Branches. Partisan politics are injected into these processes through discussions, memos, and meetings among political appointees in the Administration and Members of Congress or as spelled out in congressional committee reports and bills. Each step is described below and summarized in Figure 15-1.

• **Program/project office**

– The program or project office develops an initial proposal including costs and benefits consistent with the agency's overall mission and goals.
– Budget justification relating the project to the agency's goals, describing costs, benefits, and schedules is prepared.

• **Agency/bureau**

– For most departments, the budget generally goes to an agency or bureau to which the program office is attached.
– The agency/bureau will integrate the project into its budget submission as appropriate given the programs costs, benefits, and contribution to agency objectives.

Figure 15-1
Organizational Involvement in the Budget Process

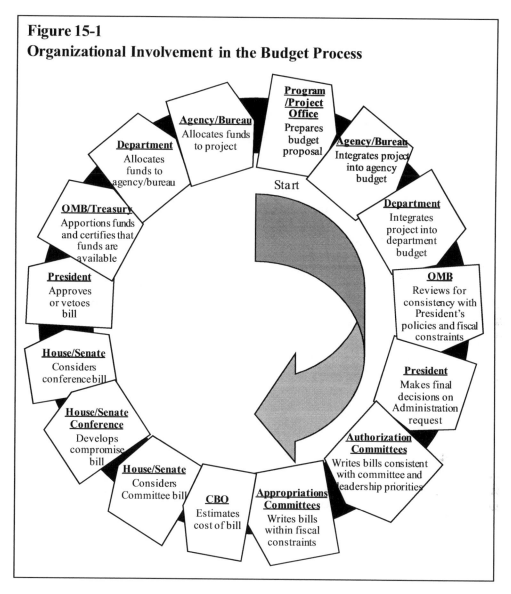

- **Department**

  - The departmental headquarters considers the program proposals in the context of the department's mission, trade-offs with other agencies and programs within the department, and overall resource constraints issued to the department by the White House.
  - Legislative and judicial branches also develop budget requests.

- **OMB**

  - OMB reviews the requests from each Executive Branch department and agency in the context of overall governmental missions, resource constraints, and presidential priorities.
  - OMB reviews proposals from legislative and judicial branches only for technical accuracy and not for substance.
  - As a specific new initiative by the President and the Director, OMB will now be a more significant force in the formulation of the Administration's policy.

- **President**

  - The President reviews the OMB recommendations, obtains views from White House staff, hears departmental appeals of OMB recommendations, and makes final decisions on what is to be included in the Budget for each Executive Branch department and agency.
  - Because there are always more ways to spend money than there is money, these reviews take account of assessments of programs costs, benefits, and urgency.
  - The President's review and decisions take into account likely congressional reaction, consistency with the President's political promises, and the strategy for dealing with the Congress.
  - Legislative and judicial branches budget proposals are included in the Budget as provided without adjustment.

Congress pursues its agenda by going to the bully pulpit in response to the President's Budget message, the hearings process, and by questions and answers to partisan and emotional issues which are aired on C-SPAN and other media outlets. All of these avenues are intended to build a sufficient record of issues and concerns with the President's proposals. The American public will either side with them or be neutral. This then paves the way for Congress to act on their agenda where it differs from the President's.

- **Congressional authorizers**

  - Authorizing committees in each house of Congress review budget proposals from the context of that committee's priorities, urgency, long-term benefits, political acceptability, and consistency with congressional leadership priorities.
  - Most of the staff work would be described as institutional politics because it involves program evaluation, and the systematic evaluation of information provided by the Executive Branch departments and agencies.
  - This step can become partisan from the standpoint of differences between presidential and congressional leadership priorities, especially when the President and the majority of one or both houses of Congress are from different political parties.

- **Congressional appropriators**

  - Appropriations subcommittees consider departmental budget proposals for the upcoming fiscal year by taking into account overall fiscal constraints, feasibility of spending plans, prior year experience and spending, leadership priorities, and Member's requests.
  - This step often includes a strong dose of partisan politics since this is where issues of discretionary spending priorities between the Administration and congressional committees surface.
  - Agencies prepare capability statements which outline the full time equivalent employee requirements to implement a congressional increase or decrease to the budget to provide an indication of the institutions' view of the proposed congressional action.
  - OMB provides a Statement of Administration Policy stating whether or not the President's senior advisors would recommend the committee bill be vetoed.

- **CBO**

  - The CBO estimates the costs of each bill proposed by a committee before it goes to the floor of either house for consideration.
  - This scoring will be the basis for a potential point of order during floor debate if the bill would exceed the limits established in the most recent Budget Resolution Congress.

- **House/Senate**

  - Each bill drafted by a committee goes to the floor of that house for consideration.
  - Partisan issues are debated on the floor and generally some Member of the President's party will offer an amendment that would make the bill acceptable to the Administration if strong objections or a veto threat has been registered.

- **House/Senate Conferences**

  - After both houses of Congress pass bills addressing a specific issue or one of the appropriations bills, a conference of Members selected by each house is formed to develop a compromise bill.
  - This step often involves partisan politics in that many of the issues involve either policy differences between the legislative and Executive Branches or member interest items.

- **House/Senate**

  - The conference bill goes to each house for final consideration.

- **President**

  - Once both houses pass the conference bill, it is presented to the President.
  - OMB prepares an enrolled bill memorandum, which includes the recommendation of each relevant department head and the President's senior advisors in the White House.

- **Treasury/OMB**

  - Before any obligation of funds can take place, OMB must apportion the funds provided in appropriations acts to the relevant departments and agencies, and the Treasury Department must issue a warrant that certifies the amount of funds available for expenditure.

- **Department**

  - The department allocates the funds as apportioned by OMB to each agency and operating unit within its purview.

- **Agency/Bureau**

  - The agency receives the funds allocated by the department and makes further allocations to the programs and projects.

- **Program/Project**

  - Individual programs and projects receive allocations and obligate the funds as provided in the appropriations

- **Honesty.** Political appointees need honest advice. Honesty throughout the process is essential to build the credibility required for helpful relations within the budget fraternity. Career employees will be around for years and the bureaucracy will remember who is and who is not credible. Honesty is also important for effective relations with key careerists in other departments and in the legislative branch. Views and information are passed through networks of key people who can trust each other. The careerist must make sure to provide:

  - Honest evaluations of existing programs,
  - Honest pricing,
  - Honest project evaluations,
  - Honest people requirements, and
  - Honest experience-based advice.

- **Creativity and responsiveness.** Players throughout the process need creative solutions to the issues and problems they face. They also need solutions that respond to the specific situation faced and in a timely manner. The careerist will have seen many prior attempts to improve the organization, improve processes, and obtain funding for controversial new programs and have a sense for which ones worked and which did not work and why. A careerist should never say never. The organization must attempt to do what the Administration is asking.

The careerist should stay abreast of politically significant words and phrases which are appropriate for their programs and projects and never miss an opportunity to rewrite the base program in a more politically sensible way.

The people who will want and can benefit from the careerist's information and knowledge, include the following:

- **Agency stakeholders.** The stakeholders should be continually informed about the status of the process and the programs in which they are interested. This will help them do their jobs successfully and at the same time build the careerist's reputation as a team player and helpful individual.
- **Departmental policymakers and the career chain of command**. They need to be kept informed in order to react and manage situations as they develop rather than having to fight fires. Political officials should find useful any ideas based on the careerist's in-depth knowledge of the process. Facts associated with project/program budget activities within the careerist's purview should be routinely provided.
- **External stakeholders.** Information should be provided only on request. For most programs, they are the Government's real customers. When they request information they should be given whatever is available and releasable.

- **Budget justification materials should be thorough**. For most people, this information is all that they will know about a project. If it does not tell a coherent story, the reader cannot be expected to translate it into meaningful information. A poorly prepared or inaccurate presentation will result in the program not receiving the consideration it would otherwise get. If errors in the material are discovered after it is submitted, a revision sheet should be provided. As budget levels become more constrained, the writing of good justification will take on increasing importance.

- **The chain of command must be aware of and approve any budgetary gimmicks before they are used.** These gimmicks could include delayed obligations to reduce estimated outlays or lease rather than buy options to reduce budget authority requirements. The use of budgetary gimmicks generally is not well received by professionals in the budget process whether they are in the Executive Branch or the Congress. The CBO will discover most budget gimmicks and inform the Congress. Unless the department's decision-making authorities have approved the proposed gimmick, departmental officials are likely to be embarrassed when the gimmick is made public and the career employee will be held accountable.

- **Political or career managers must not reallocate budget authority without appropriate clearances.** There are rules for moving resources from one program to another during budget execution. The rules for these reprogrammings and transfers among appropriations have been developed over the years and are closely monitored by the Congress. Political appointees need to be aware of the rules and the flexibility they have within the rules for reprogrammings. If reprogrammings are made without the appropriate clearances, the careerist and the agency will lose credibility and likely pay a heavy price in terms of additional congressional controls and oversight.

  In order to properly transfer funds, most situations dictate that proper authorities have to be consulted to not only transfer the funds but to gauge the political clearance for the transfer itself. Without addressing the political significance of transferring funds from one program to another program, a career manager could simply stamp out one problem while creating a more significant political and financial problem for another program within the agency.

Motivations of the Players

There are a large number of players in the budget process. Where the players are organizationally structured will have a lot to do with how they view a project. People in the program office can be expected to be program advocates while those in higher headquarters faced with allocating limited resources may take a more analytical approach to evaluating that program. Understanding the characteristics of the players will make it easier to both support them and to understand their positions.

- **Political executives (appointees)**

  - **Personal agenda**. Each sought the position, usually because he or she wants to see a particular issue or an agenda of issues resolved in a certain way.
  - **No loyalty to the process.** The political executive's interest is in getting certain issues resolved. For the most part, they do not understand the process though they may have a desire to use the process to achieve their objectives.
  - **Short-tenure.** Most appointees are in their positions for about two years. Few last the full term of an administration.
  - **Limited knowledge**. Many appointees do not have wide knowledge of the programs for which they are responsible. They may, however, have a great deal of knowledge about certain programs they want to see changed or protected.
  - **Highly biased.** Appointees are often highly biased because of their backgrounds. These biases may be the reason they sought the position.

- **Initial distrust of career bureaucrats.** Bureaucrats may be considered as roadblocks to progress and incapable of performing useful work. Sometimes they are viewed as holdovers from the previous administration and not to be trusted. In some situations, the careerists may not be trusted because of their relations with congressional staff. The careerists have to demonstrate their utility and loyalty before they will be trusted.
- **Not interested in details of most programs – just hot items.** Many details will be left to the careerists even though the new appointee may have questions about the careerist's loyalty.

- **Departmental career executives**

  - **Loyal to process not programs, sensitive and responsive to political executives.** The careerist lives by processes, which transcend the tenure of political executives and administrations. They will be sensitive to the needs of the political executives and show them how to use the process.
  - **Bonded with congressional officials.** The processes require that career officials work with congressional staff. This network relies on credibility of the participants and adherence to process.
  - **Want to trust agency/program budget official but often disappointed.** Although the budget official will attempt to be helpful, a department's resource demands almost always exceed available funds and some programs will receive less funding than requested. Departmental program executives may at times view the decision process as arbitrary.

- **Departmental budget analysts**

  - **Loyal to the process and projects/programs.** Their work life revolves around meeting requirements and deadlines. This takes precedence over the merits of a particular program.
  - **Bonded to OMB and congressional officials.** Their contacts tell them about hot, upcoming issues in OMB and in Congress. These contacts make them valuable to political appointees, but also a potential threat.
  - **Gate keepers for data; job is both qualitative and quantitative.** Budget staff often is the most well informed staff in the department. They can provide information to departmental officials, both career and political, in a timely and comprehensive manner. This often frustrates other agency officials who tend to be advocates of certain programs and do not have the depth of information available in the budget office.
  - **Often frustrated given pressures of the process without understanding big picture.** Some analysts can get so wrapped up in details of their assigned areas that they are not aware of the big picture. This can lead to unpleasant situations if budget recommendations are not consistent with that macro view.
  - **Unique analytical requirements such as pricing projects, estimating person year requirements, quality and credibility of performance/ projections.** The analysts must collect a variety of information for budget

purposes. This information makes the analyst helpful to the political officials in evaluating agency projects.

- **Program/policy analysts**

    - **Believe they are superior to budget analysts.** They believe they are doing serious policy analysis that will provide the vision for the agency in the coming years. The mission of the budget analyst, in their view, is to obtain the funds needed to support the policy analyst's findings and not to question the findings.
    - **Not generally loyal to the budget process.** It is not their process. In addition, they believe changes should be made whenever their analysis indicates a change is appropriate rather than waiting for the decision points in the budget process. Participation in the budget process also requires a lot of detailed information that policy analysts often do not have.
    - **Analysis steeped in quantitative methods, including economic and engineering models**. Many analytical techniques used are not readily understandable to other people in the agency. Reliance on theoretical models sometimes leads to distrust of analysts by departmental officials overseeing the program areas. Policy analysts need to work with budget staff in order to use the budget lever as a way to implement their findings.

- **OMB analysts**

    - **Loyal to process.** The President's Budget is one of the principal products of OMB. Much staff work is focused on meeting deadlines required by the process and making sure the departments also meet deadlines.
    - **Taught to be analytical and policy/budget neutral.** The OMB Director wants to be able to tell the President what works and what does not work because the funding demands from agencies greatly exceed the funds available. This strong emphasis on analytical work makes OMB staff a devil's advocate for all sides of all issues.
    - **Work for the President but do not face stakeholder pressures the departments and agencies must address**. This permits the staff to be politically neutral in their budget analysis. Downside of this is that the OMB staff often has little comprehension of or appreciation for the intensity of the politics surrounding an issue.

- **Congressional staffers**

    - **Loyal to process.** They control the process for their committee's area of responsibility. Staffers know the rules of their respective houses and can help the committee chair steer bills through the process.
    - **Job is to build chairman's record.** Their tenure and power is based on support from the chairman. It is important that the hearing record and staff evaluations support the committee's recommendations.

- **Clout is in the base/details**. Agency budgets contain more details than an elected official can master and also serve his or her constituency. The congressional staff knows the programs almost as well as agency staff. Because of the little time members spend on these issues, staffers accumulate more clout in the process than people at similar levels within the Executive Branch.

Process Considerations

Political and career officials must be aware of certain conditions in the budget process that have a bearing on how the players can react, especially when dealing with the Congress and the public.

Most important in dealing with the Congress is whether a meeting is on-the-record or off-the-record. An administration official has more flexibility when the meeting is off-the-record, but the official still must be careful. Points to consider include the following.

- **Formal hearing (on-the record)**

    - Whatever is said will be recorded.
    - Support for the Administration's position is mandatory. An official must not volunteer a personal opinion. Only if directly asked is an administration official to provide a personal opinion.
    - Written testimony and questions and answers must be cleared by the department and OMB before they are provided to the Congress.
    - Accuracy, timeliness and quality are extremely important. This includes all papers provided to Congress — budget requests, justifications, questions and answers, testimony, white papers, memoranda, execution documents.

- **Informal (off-the-record)**

    - Discussions with other stakeholders inside the Government (department, OMB, Congress)

        * Questions are answered, but information is not volunteered.
        * An official will provide a personal opinion on request only.
        * An official should be credible. If a question cannot be answered on the spot, the official should say so and quickly seek the answer.

    - Discussions with external stakeholders

        * As in internal meetings, the official should not volunteer information, but should answer the questions asked.
        * The official should be clear on the Government's position.
        * Credibility of stakeholders and personal comfort with them should be analytically determined before a meeting.

* External stakeholders should not be provided advice on how to proceed with an issue.
* Stakeholders should be clear about what you can do with the information they provide - both who may and may not receive the information.

Process Implications of Lobbying

Although an official might be tempted to lobby for a particular position, that is forbidden. The career executive also must avoid the appearance of lobbying because his or her credibility may be at stake.

The official must be careful to draw a line that defines the boundary between providing information and lobbying. That line is not always clear. A statement on-the-record supporting the Administration's position, cleared as appropriate and quoted as written is not lobbying. The official is safe so long as he or she offers no personal agenda and only supports the Administration's proposal and provides direct answers to questions.

It is often easier to discuss lobbying violations. This would include statements along the following lines:

* Personal animus to current or past administrations;
* Personal animus toward a political executive or colleague; and
* Personal animus toward project/program initiatives.

Politics of Increases to the Budget Base

The annual debate on the budget focuses on programs slated for increase and decrease. As a general rule, the budget changes substantially from one year to the next only on the margin. Therefore, the majority of each stakeholder's effort is targeted to increase.

Information is the key to superior performance. Whether the sponsoring agency or an interested external stakeholder, the following guidance appears appropriate:

* Pack as much substance, analysis, and facts as possible into budget papers;
* Summarize key points in one page and provide additional information as attachments;
* Talk about successes in the base program (where there are few successes elaborate on the milestones, challenges and plans/program and only if pressed); and
* Quality check the facts included throughout the written materials.

GPRA and the recent emphasis on performance budgets should play a substantial role in describing increases in terms of the expected results in quantitative terms.

Chapter 16

Internet Resources for the Federal Budget

Use cutting-edge technologies to create a new level of transparency, accountability, and participation for America's citizens.

— Excerpt from the White House Policy on Technology

General Internet Resources for the Budget

This section provides contact information for sites providing information on the Federal Budget:

- **Viewing and obtaining copies of the Budget**

    - To view the President's current Budget and supporting documents in full, visit: http://www.whitehouse.gov/omb/budget
    - To purchase a hard copy of the Budget, or a copy on cd-rom, go to: http://bookstore.gpo.gov/collections/budget.jsp
    - To view current and previous FYs of the U.S. Government Budget, go to: http://www.gpoaccess.gov/usbudget/browse.html

- **Executive Branch offices heavily involved in the Budget Process**

    - White House Office of Management and Budget (OMB): http://www.whitehouse.gov/omb/
    - The Department of the Treasury: http://www.treasury.gov/

- **Congressional Offices heavily involved in the Budget process**

    - Congressional Budget Office (CBO): http://www.cbo.gov/
    - Government Accountability Office (GAO): http://www.gao.gov/
    - House Committees on Rules: http://www.rules.house.gov/budget_pro.htm

    - Appropriations Committees
      House: http://appropriations.house.gov/
      Senate: http://appropriations.senate.gov/

    - Budget Committees
      House: http://www.house.gov/budget/
      Senate: http://www.senate.gov/~budget/

    - Tax Committees
      House: http://waysandmeans.house.gov/
      Senate: http://finance.senate.gov/

    - Government process laws and reform
      House: http://oversight.house.gov/
      Senate: http://hsgac.senate.gov/public/

- **Independent research and policy organizations**

    - Center on Budget and Policy Priorities:
      http://www.cbpp.org/pubs/fedbud.htm
    - National Center for Policy Analysis: http://www.ncpa.org/
    - OMB Watch: http://www.ombwatch.org/
    - TruthandPolitic.org: http://www.truthandpolitics.org/budget-basics.php
    - The Heritage Foundation: http://www.heritage.org/
    - Urban Institute: http://www.urban.org/
    - American Economic Association: http://www.aeaweb.org/

Specific Budget References

What follows are Internet sites with additional information on the topics in the chapters of this book. There are many sites on each topic. The reader might use these references as a place to begin when delving deeper into topic areas.

- **Chapter 5: Overview of the Budget Process and Rules**

    - For a more complete discussion of issues and options surrounding the expiration of budget enforcement procedures, visit:
      http://www.cbo.gov/showdoc.cfm?index=4032&sequence=7

- Introduction to the Federal Budget process:
  http://www.cbpp.org/3-7-03bud.htm

- **Chapter 7: Formulation of the President's Budget**

  - Office of Management & Budget: http://www.omb.gov
  - Congressional Budget Office: http://www.cbo.gov
  - The Heritage Foundation:
    http://www.heritage.org/Research/Taxes/wm994.cfm
  - To find out more about the Macroeconomic Advisors' study on dynamic scoring, go to http://www.macroadvisers.com/
  - A Short Guide to Dynamic Scoring: http://www.cbpp.org/7-12-06bud2.htm
  - To view the GPRA in full, see:
    http://govinfo.library.unt.edu/npr/library/misc/s20.html
  - GPRA and Performance Management:
    http://www.john-mercer.com/index.htm

- **Chapter 10: Budget Execution**

- EPA Budget Execution Strategies: http://www.epa.gov/cfo/modernization/
- IMF Guidelines for Public Expenditure Management:
  http://www.imf.org/external/pubs/ft/expend/guide4.htm

- **Chapter 11: Federal Financial Management Systems**

- Chief Financial Officer Act of 1990: http://govinfo.library.unt.edu/npr/library/misc/cfo.html

- **Chapter 12: Government Settlements with the Private Sector**

  - The Department of Treasury's Judgment Fund:
    http://www.fms.treas.gov/judgefund/
  - The Superfund Program and related settlements:
    http://www.epa.gov/superfund/

- **Chapter 13: Applied Ethics for Budget Officials**

  - The Lobbying Disclosure Act of 1995:
    http://lobbyingdisclosure.house.gov/lda.html
  - United States Office of Government Ethics: http://www.usoge.gov/

- **Chapter 14: Regulatory Policies and Procedures: Impact on the Budget Process**

  - To find, review, or make comments regulations still in their comment period, go to: http://www.regulations.gov/
  - A selective guide to resources at Columbia University Libraries and on the Internet, for conducting research on the U.S. Federal regulatory process: http://www.columbia.edu/cu/lweb/indiv/usgd/regulation.html
  - Center for Progressive Reform work on issues concerning the regulatory process: http://www.progressivereform.org/regPolicy.cfm
  - Reginfo.gov, a website produced by OMB and GSA: http://www.reginfo.gov/public/
  - The Federal Register catalogues regulations: http://www.archives.gov/federal_register/

Chapter 17

Glossary of Budget Terms

This glossary provides an extensive list of terms used in daily practice by budget professionals in Federal agencies, the Office of Management and Budget, the General Accounting Office, the Congressional Budget Office, and Congressional appropriations offices when communicating about Federal budgeting and the budget process. The emphasis in developing this list is on providing understandable, common-sense definitions.

ACCRUAL ACCOUNTING - System of accounting in which revenues are recorded when earned and outlays are recorded when goods are received or services performed, even though the actual receipt of revenues and payment for goods or services may occur at a different time.

ACCRUED EXPENDITURES - Charges during a given period that reflect liabilities incurred for: (a) service performed by employees, contractors, and others; (b) goods and other property received; and (c) amounts becoming owed under programs for which no current service or performance is required, such as annuities and other benefit payments. Expenditures accrue regardless of when cash payments are made.

ACTIVITY/PROGRAM BUDGET - The budget for a specific and/or discrete program or program activity performed by a governmental unit to accomplish its objectives. For example, the budget for food inspection is managed as an activity performed in the discharge of the health function.

ACTUAL EXPENDITURE(S) - Actual spending for a prior fiscal year, as opposed to a budget estimate.

ADJUSTED GROSS INCOME (AGI) - Income subject to taxation under the individual income tax after reducing total income for certain items, such as alimony payments and contributions for individual retirement accounts. Personal exemptions and the standard or itemized deductions are subtracted from AGI to determine taxable income.

ADVANCE APPROPRIATION - Budget authority provided in an appropriation act that will become available in a fiscal year after the fiscal year for which the appropriation is passed. The amount is not included in the budget totals for the year in which the appropriation is enacted but it is included in the budget totals for the fiscal year in which the amount will become available for obligation.

ADVANCE FUNDING - Appropriations of budget authority in an appropriations act that can be used, if necessary, to cover obligations incurred late in the fiscal year for benefit payments in excess of the amount specifically appropriated in the act for that year. The budget authority is charged to the appropriation for the program for the fiscal year following the fiscal year for which the appropriations act is passed.

AGENCY - The governmental entity for which there is a total allocation of budgetary resources; often used interchangeably with department. There is no single definition of the term agency. Any given definition usually relates to specific legislation. Generally, an "executive agency" means any Executive Branch department, independent commission, board, bureau, office, or other establishment of the Federal Government, including independent regulatory commissions and boards. (The term sometimes includes the municipal government of the District of Columbia).

AGGREGATE DEMAND - Total purchases of a country's output of goods and services by consumers, businesses, government, and foreigners during a given period.

ALLOTMENT - An authorization by the head (or other authorized employee) of an agency to his/her subordinates to incur obligations within a specified amount. The amount allotted by an agency cannot exceed the amount apportioned by the Office of Management and Budget (OMB). Exceeding an allotment results in an anti-deficiency violation.

ALLOWANCES - Amounts included in the President's Budget request or projections to cover possible additional proposals, such as statutory pay increases and contingencies for relatively uncontrollable programs and other requirements. Allowances are also used to indicate savings required to meet budget totals. As used by Congress in the Concurrent Resolution on the Budget, allowances represent a special functional classification designed to include amounts to cover possible requirements, such as civilian pay raises and contingencies. Allowances remain undistributed until they become firm, then they are distributed to the appropriate functional classification(s).

ALTERNATIVE MINIMUM TAX (AMT) - A tax intended to limit the extent to which higher-income taxpayers can reduce their tax liability through the use of preferences in the tax code. Taxpayers subject to the AMT are required to recalculate their tax liability on the basis of a more limited set of exemptions, deductions, and tax credits than would normally apply. The amount by which a taxpayer's AMT calculation exceeds his or her regular tax calculation is that taxpayer's AMT liability.

ANNUAL AUTHORIZATION - Legislation that authorizes appropriations for a single fiscal year. Programs with annual authorizations must be authorized each year and for a definite sum of money.

ANNUAL PERFORMANCE PLAN - A plan required by the Government Performance and Results Act that shows the outcomes and outputs expected during a specific year at the proposed budget level.

ANNUAL PERFORMANCE REPORT - A report required by the Government Performance and Results Act that compares the actual performance to (1) the performance proposed in the budget and (2) the performance expected at enacted appropriations levels, and that explains the variance and possible corrective measures.

ANTI-DEFICIENCY ACT - The law that prohibits the incurring of obligations or expenditures (outlays) in excess of the amounts available in appropriations or funds, or in excess of the amounts authorized for obligation in apportionments.

APPEALS PROCESS - The process for seeking a change to a budget decision within an agency/department or the OMB. In recent years the incentive to department and agency heads is to resolve appeals at the OMB Program Associate Director level rather than to plead a case to the Director or the President. Under the reinventing government initiative, agencies have greater flexibility to set their own priorities, so long as they are generally consistent with the President's priorities and do not violate budget scorekeeping requirements.

APPORTIONMENT - A distribution made by OMB of amounts available for obligation, including budgetary reserves established pursuant to law, in an appropriation or fund account. Apportionments divide amounts available for obligation by specific time periods (usually quarters), activities, projects, objects, or a combination thereof. The amounts apportioned are a limit on the amount of obligations that may be incurred. In apportioning any account, some funds may be reserved to provide for contingencies or to affect savings, pursuant to the Antideficiency Act; or may be proposed for deferral or rescission pursuant to the Impoundment Control Act of 1974. The apportionment process is intended to prevent accruing obligations in a manner that would require deficiency or supplemental appropriations and to achieve the most effective and economical use of the funds available for obligation.

APPROPRIATED ENTITLEMENT - An entitlement whose source of funding is in an annual appropriation act. Because the entitlement is created by law, eligible recipients may have legal recourse if Congress does not appropriate adequate funds to cover the payments.

APPROPRIATION - A provision in law authorizing expenditures for a specific purpose. The appropriation represents a limitation of the amounts that agencies may obligate for certain activities during the period of time specified in the appropriation act. Although an appropriation generally provides funds for one year only, an appropriation act may make the funds for some capital investment programs available for more than one year. Several types of appropriations are not counted as budget authority, since they do not provide authority to incur additional obligations. Examples of these are: appropriations to liquidate contract authority; appropriations to reduce outstanding debt; and appropriations for refunds of receipts.

APPROPRIATION ACCOUNT/FUND ACCOUNT - An account established in the Treasury for each appropriation and/or fund.

APPROPRIATIONS ACT - A statute, initially drafted under the jurisdiction of the House and Senate Committees on Appropriations that provides authorization for Federal agencies to incur obligations and to make payments out of the Treasury for specified purposes. An appropriation act generally follows enactment of authorizing legislation which permits, but does not require, subsequent appropriations. Currently, there are 13 regular annual appropriation acts. From time to time, Congress passes supplemental appropriations. Generally, funding in appropriation acts is considered "discretionary."

APPROPRIATION (EXPENDITURE), RECEIPT, AND FUND ACCOUNTS - An account from which expenditures can be made or receipts deposited. Some accounts are used only for accounting purposes, e.g., transfer appropriation accounts, foreign currency accounts, receipt clearing accounts, and deposit fund accounts.

APPROPRIATIONS LIMITATION - A statutory restriction in an appropriations act that establishes the maximum or minimum amount that may be obligated or expended for specified purposes.

AUTHORIZATION ACT - Legislation under the jurisdiction of a committee other than the House and Senate Committees on Appropriations that establishes or continues the operation of a Federal program or agency, either indefinitely or for a specified period of time. An authorization act may suggest a level of budget authority needed to fund the program or agency, which is then provided in a future appropriation act. For some programs, the authorization may provide the budget authority.

AUTHORIZING COMMITTEE - A standing committee of the House or Senate with legislative jurisdiction over the laws that set up or continue the operations of Federal programs or agencies. It can propose direct spending authority to fund programs or make funding subject to subsequent appropriations action. An authorizing committee also has jurisdiction in those instances where backdoor authority is provided in the substantive legislation.

AUTHORIZING LEGISLATION - Substantive legislation that establishes or continues the operation of a Federal program or agency either indefinitely or for a specific period of time, or sanctions a specific type of obligation or expenditure within a program. Authorizing legislation is normally a prerequisite for appropriations. It may place a limit on the amount of budget authority to be included in appropriations acts or it may authorize the appropriation of "such sums as may be necessary." Authorizing legislation may provide authority to incur debts, or to mandate payment to particular persons or political subdivisions of the country.

BACKDOOR AUTHORITY - Budget authority provided in legislation outside the normal (Appropriations Committee) appropriations process. The most common forms of backdoor authority are authority to borrow (also called borrowing authority or authority to spend debt receipts) and contract authority. Section 401 of the Congressional Budget and Impoundment Control Act of 1974 (2 U.S.C. 651) specifies certain limits on the use of backdoor authority.

BALANCED BUDGET - A fiscal year budget in which receipts are equal to or greater than outlays.

BALANCED BUDGET AND EMERGENCY DEFICIT CONTROL ACT - Originally known as Gramm-Rudman-Hollings, the law established specific deficit targets and a sequestration procedure to reduce spending if the targets were estimated to be exceeded. The Deficit Control Act was amended and extended several times — most significantly by the Budget Enforcement Act of 1990 (BEA). The BEA established the pay-as-you-go procedure for legislation affecting direct spending and revenues and annual spending limits for discretionary spending. The sequestration procedure — originally applicable to overall deficit targets — was restructured to enforce the discretionary spending limits and pay-as-you-go process separately. On September 30, 2002, the discretionary spending caps and the sequestration procedure to enforce those caps expired, and the OMB and CBO were no longer required to record the five-year budgetary effects of legislation affecting direct spending or revenues.

BALANCES OF BUDGET AUTHORITY - Amounts of budget authority that have not been outlayed. Unobligated balances are amounts that have not been obligated and remain available for the following year.

BASELINE - A benchmark projection that generally reflects the receipts, outlays, and deficit or surplus that will result if all current laws are continued through the period covered by the budget. Congress uses the CBO baseline to conduct its analysis of budget issues and for budget debate with the Executive Branch. The baseline reflects budget trends using expected inflation rates, provisions of law and other factors. The baseline has been used for measuring expenditure reductions in the reconciliation process and for projecting future budget conditions.

BASIS POINT - One-hundredth of a percentage point. (For example, the difference between interest rates of 5.5 percent and 5.0 percent is 50 basis points.)

BIENNIAL BUDGET – A budget covering a two-year period. This could apply to the President's budget request, the budget resolution adopted by Congress, or the period covered by appropriations acts. There have been proposals to shift the Federal Government's budget process to a two-year cycle and in 1988 and 1989 the Department of Defense began submitting 2-year budget requests. However, appropriations for all agencies remain an annual event.

BEA - The Budget Enforcement Act of 1990, as amended. See Balanced Budget and Emergency Deficit Control Act of 1985.

BLUE CHIP CONSENSUS FORECAST - The average of about 50 private-sector economic forecasts compiled and published monthly by Aspen Publishers, Inc.

BOOK PROFITS - Profits calculated using book (or tax) depreciation and standard accounting conventions for inventories. Different from economic profits, book profits are referred to as "profits before tax" in the national income and product accounts.

BORROWING AUTHORITY - Statutory authority that permits a Federal agency to incur obligations and to make payments for specified purposes out of borrowed monies.

BREACH - The amount by which new discretionary budget authority or outlays within a category of discretionary appropriations for a fiscal year exceeds the legal cap for that year.

BUDGET - The Budget of the United States Government that sets forth the President's comprehensive financial plan and indicates the President's priorities for the Federal Government. (See President's Budget).

BUDGET AMENDMENT - Revision to a pending appropriations request.

BUDGET AND ACCOUNTING ACT OF 1921 – Legislation that required the President to submit an annual budget request to Congress for the entire Federal Government rather than allowing all agencies to submit their own budgets. This centralization of authority to the White House resulted in the creation of what is now the Office of Management and Budget (OMB). Following this legislation, Congress also acted to strengthen its budgetary oversight by establishing what is now the Government Accountability Office (GAO).

BUDGET AUTHORITY - Authority becoming available during the year to enter into obligations that will result in immediate or future outlays of Federal Government funds.

The basic forms of budget authority are appropriations, authority to borrow, contract authority, and authority to spend certain receipts. Budget authority may be classified by the period of availability (1-year, multiple-year, no-year), by the type of congressional action (current or permanent), or by the manner of determining the amount available (definite or indefinite).

BUDGET BASELINE - An estimate that assumes Federal spending and revenue levels based on current policies will continue unchanged in the upcoming fiscal year. For revenue levels and entitlement program spending, the budget baseline assumes continuation of current laws. For discretionary spending, the baseline assumes an adjustment for inflation (GDP deflator) added to the previous year's discretionary spending levels. The baseline includes funds to cover a Federal pay comparability raise.

BUDGET DEFICIT - The amount by which the Government's Budget outlays exceed budget receipts for a given fiscal year.

BUDGET ENFORCEMENT ACT OF 1990 (BEA) - See Balanced Budget and Emergency Deficit Control Act of 1985.

BUDGET ESTIMATES - Estimates of budget authority, outlays, receipts, or other budget measures that cover the current and future budget years, as reflected in the President's Budget and budget updates.

BUDGET EXAMINER - Standard position title for employee of OMB responsible for the oversight of program implementation, policy formulation, legislative formulation, clearance of testimony and other congressional submissions and development of the President's Budget for a specific set of programs or appropriation accounts.

BUDGET FUNCTION - One of 20 categories into which budgetary resources are grouped so that all budget authority and outlays can be presented according to the national interests being addressed.

BUDGET HEARINGS - Congressional opportunity to question Executive Branch and other witnesses about program needs, costs, and results; to challenge or support decisions reached within the Executive Branch; and to build a record for proposed changes to the requested program and budget.

BUDGET HIGHLIGHTS - A summary of significant proposals included in a department/agency budget submission which is prepared in advance of the congressional justification. The document is released when the President's Budget is submitted to Congress.

BUDGET RESOLUTION - See Concurrent Resolution on the Budget.

BUDGET SURPLUS - The amount by which Government receipts exceed outlays for a given fiscal year.

BUDGET TARGETS (GUIDANCE) - Letter from the Director of OMB which sets forth agency budget ceilings for the upcoming budget formulation cycle. OMB transmits budget policy letters to the Executive Branch departments and agencies or provides guidance and directives to heads of departments at Cabinet meetings.

BUDGET TESTIMONY - Elaboration and defense of the President's Budget generally by members of the Cabinet and other political officers of the Administration.

BUDGET TOTALS - The totals for budget authority, outlays, and receipts included in the budget. Some presentations in the budget distinguish between on-budget totals and off-budget totals. On-budget totals reflect the transactions of all Federal Government entities except those excluded from the budget totals by law. Off-budget totals reflect the transactions of Government entities that are excluded from the on-budget totals by law. Currently excluded are the social security trust funds (Federal Old -Age and Survivors Insurance and Federal Disability Insurance Trust Funds) and the Postal Service Fund. The on-and off-budget totals are combined to derive a unified total for Federal activity.

BUDGET UPDATES - Amendments to, or revisions in, budget authority requests, estimated outlays, deficit estimates and estimated receipts for the ensuing fiscal year. The President is required to transmit a mid-session review update to Congress by July 15th of each year. However, the President may also submit budget updates at other times during the fiscal year.

BUDGET YEAR - The fiscal year for which a budget is proposed.

BUDGETARY RESERVES - Portions of budgetary resources set aside (withheld from apportionment) by the OMB by authority of the Antideficiency Act (31 U.S.C. 1512) and the Budget Impoundment and Control Act of 1974 to (a) provide for contingencies, (b) achieve savings made possible by or through changes in requirements or greater efficiency of operations, or (c) as specified by law.

BUDGETARY RESOURCES - All forms of funds available for obligation including new budget authority, unobligated balances of budget authority, direct spending authority, and obligation limitations.

BUREAUS - The principal subordinate organizational units of an agency.

BUSINESS CYCLE - Fluctuations in overall business activity accompanied by swings in the unemployment rate, interest rates, and corporate profits. Over a business cycle, real activity rises to a peak (its highest level during the cycle), then falls until it reaches a trough (its lowest level following the peak), whereupon it starts to rise again, defining a new cycle. Business cycles are irregular, varying in frequency, magnitude, and duration.

BUSINESS FIXED INVESTMENT - Spending by businesses on structures, equipment, and software. Such investment is labeled "fixed" to distinguish it from investment in inventories.

BYRD RULE – A rule of the Senate allowing senators to strike extraneous provisions in reconciliation language or related conference reports. A provision can be considered "extraneous" if it does not produce a change in outlays or revenues.

CAP - Term commonly used to refer to legal limits on the budget authority and outlays for each fiscal year for each of the discretionary appropriation categories. A sequester of budget authority is required if an appropriation for a category causes a breach in either the budget authority or outlay cap.

CAPABILITY STATEMENT - Response to direct congressional inquiries concerning a program's capability to spend resources above the President's request.

CAPACITY UTILIZATION RATE - The seasonally adjusted output of the nation's factories, mines, and electric and gas utilities expressed as a percentage of their capacity to produce output. The capacity of a facility is the greatest output it can maintain with a normal work pattern.

CAPITAL - Physical capital is land and the stock of products set aside to support future production and consumption. In the national income and product accounts, private capital consists of business inventories, producers' durable equipment, and residential and nonresidential structures. Financial capital consists of funds raised by governments, individuals, or businesses by incurring liabilities such as bonds, mortgages, or stock certificates. Human capital is the education, training, work experience, and other attributes that enhance the ability of the labor force to produce goods and services. Bank capital is the sum advanced and put at risk by the owners of a bank; it represents the first "cushion" in the event of loss, thereby decreasing the willingness of the owners to take risks in lending.

CAPITAL BUDGET - Budget providing for separate financing of (a) capital or investment expenditures and (b) current or operating expenditures. Investments in capital assets generally would be excluded from calculations of the budget surplus or deficit. The Federal Government has never had a capital budget in the sense of financing capital or investment-type programs separately from current expenditures.

CAPITAL GAINS AND LOSSES - The increase or decrease in the value of an asset that comes from the increase or decrease in the asset's market price since it was purchased. A capital gain or loss is "realized" when the asset is sold.

CAPITAL INCOME - Income derived from wealth, such as stock dividends, realized capital gains, or the owner's profits from a business.

CAPITAL SERVICES - A measure of how much the stock of physical capital contributes to the flow of production.

CASH ACCOUNTING - A system of accounting in which revenues are recorded when actually received and outlays are recorded when payment is made.

CASH EQUIVALENT TRANSACTION - A transaction in which the Government makes outlays or receives collections in a form other than cash, or in which the outlays or receipts recorded in the budget differ from the cash because the cash does not accurately measure the value of the transaction.

CATEGORIES OF DISCRETIONARY APPROPRIATIONS - See Spending Caps.

CBO BASELINE - CBO version of a current services baseline that is generally used as the baseline by Congress for the Concurrent Resolution on the Budget.

CENTRAL BANK - A government-established agency responsible for conducting monetary policy and overseeing credit conditions. The Federal Reserve System fulfills those functions in the United States.

CHIEF FINANCIAL OFFICER (CFO) – Under the CFO Act of 1990, every agency is required to establish a CFO to provide individual financial accountability. The CFO's responsibilities include establishment of a financial leadership structure, long-range planning, and issuance of audited financial statements. In addition, the CFO Act established the Chief Financial Officer Council, an interagency group focused on Federal financial management reform.

CIVILIAN UNEMPLOYMENT RATE - Unemployment as a percentage of the civilian labor force — that is, the labor force excluding armed forces personnel.

CLOSED ACCOUNT - A budget account for which the expired budget authority has been canceled.

COLLECTIONS - Money collected by the Federal Government that the budget records as a receipt, an offsetting collection, or an offsetting receipt. Collections are classified into two major categories:

- *Budget receipts* - Collections from the public based on the Government's exercise of its sovereign powers, from payments by participants in certain voluntary Federal social insurance premiums, and court fines, certain licenses, and deposits of earnings by the Federal Reserve System. Gifts and contributions (as distinguished from payments for services or cost-sharing deposits by state and local governments) are also counted as budget receipts. Budget receipts are compared with the total outlays in calculating the budget surplus or deficit.

- ***Offsetting collections*** - Collections from Government accounts or from transactions with the public that are of a business-type or market-oriented nature. They are classified into two major categories: (a) collections credited to appropriation or fund accounts, and (b) offsetting receipts (i.e., amounts deposited in receipt accounts). In general, the "collections credited to appropriation or fund accounts" can be used to pay for program costs, whereas funds in "receipt accounts" cannot be used without being appropriated. Offsetting collections are deducted from disbursements in calculating total outlays.

COMMITMENT – An administrative reservation of allotted funds in anticipation of their obligation.

COMMITTEE ALLOCATION - Recommended appropriation level following congressional subcommittee and full committee action.

COMMITTEE HEARINGS - Forum in which Executive Branch witnesses (generally political officers within the Administration) defend the President's Budget proposals and the members of the committee (often prompted by the staff) build the record that justifies their position on the President's proposals.

COMMITTEE MARK-UP - The meeting of a congressional committee to markup draft legislation for presentation to the whole House or Senate.

COMMITTEE PRINT - A draft bill prepared for markup by the full committee.

COMMITTEE REPORT - A report including directives, instructions, congressional reasoning and intent that supports and clarifies a bill. While not legally binding on the Executive Branch, most political and program manager's view report language as binding.

COMMUNITY DISASTER LOAN (CDL) – Federal loans administered through FEMA that provide operational funding to help local governments that have incurred a significant loss in revenue, due to a presidentially declared disaster that has or will adversely affect their ability to provide essential municipal services. In response to Hurricanes Katrina and Rita, The CDL Act of 2005 authorized up to $1 billion in direct loans to local governments.

COMMUNITY DEVELOPMENT BLOCK GRANT (CDBG) - A Federal entitlement program administered by HUD's Community Planning and Development Office. The purpose of CDBG funds is to improve communities by providing decent housing, a suitable living environment, and expanding economic opportunities—principally for persons with low and moderate incomes. Since the program began in 1974, more than $55 billion has been appropriated. CDBG funds have been a critical vehicle for providing Federal relief to states struck by Hurricanes Katrina and Rita.

COMPARATIVE STATEMENT OF NEW BUDGET AUTHORITY – A table accompanying a regular or supplemental appropriations act in a report of the House or Senate Appropriations Committee. This table compares the amount recommended for each account in the act to both the President's request and the amount enacted in the previous fiscal year.

COMPENSATION - All income due to employees for their work during a given period. In addition to wages, salaries, bonuses, and stock options, compensation includes fringe benefits and the employer's share of contributions to social insurance programs, such as Social Security.

CONCURRENT RESOLUTION ON THE BUDGET (Budget Resolution) - A resolution passed by both Houses of Congress, but not requiring the signature of the President, setting forth or revising the Congressional Budget for the United States Government for one or more fiscal years. The resolution, due April 15th, sets spending targets for the entire Government, and subdivides them into congressional committee allocations. It is to be passed by Congress before appropriations bills move forward.

CONFEREES - Congressional members from both Houses appointed to resolve differences between House and Senate versions of legislation.

CONFERENCE COMMITTEE - Committee of House and Senate members appointed to resolve differences in House and Senate versions of legislation.

CONGRESSIONAL BUDGET - The budget as set forth by Congress in a concurrent resolution on the budget. By law the resolution includes:

- The level of total budget outlays and new authority for the coming fiscal year;
- An estimate of the appropriate levels of budget outlays and new budget authority for each major functional category, for undistributed intergovernmental transactions, and for such other matters relating to the budget as may be appropriate to carry out the purpose of the 1974 Congressional Budget and Impoundment Control Act;
- The amount of the surplus or deficit in the budget;
- The recommended level of Federal receipts; and
- The appropriate level of the public debt.

CONGRESSIONAL JUSTIFICATION - The formal materials prepared by the Executive Branch that present, explain and defend the President's Budget. The format and technical information are presented as dictated by the Clerk of the Appropriation's Subcommittee.

CONSTANT DOLLARS - A dollar value adjusted for changes in prices. Constant dollars are derived by dividing current dollar amounts by an appropriate price index, a process generally known as deflating. The result is a constant dollar series as it would presumably exist if prices were the same in all years as in the base year. Any changes in such a series reflect only changes in the real volume of goods and services. Also known as "real dollars."

CONSUMER CONFIDENCE - An index of consumer optimism based on surveys of consumers' attitudes about current and future economic conditions. One such index, the index of consumer sentiment, is constructed by the University of Michigan Survey Research Center. The Conference Board constructs a similar index, the Consumer Confidence Index.

CONSUMER PRICE INDEX (CPI) - An index of the cost of living commonly used to measure inflation. The Bureau of Labor Statistics publishes the CPI-U, an index of consumer prices based on the typical market basket of goods and services consumed by all urban consumers during a base period, and the CPI-W, an index of consumer prices based on the typical market basket of goods and services consumed by urban wage earners and clerical workers during a base period.

CONSUMPTION - In principle, the value of goods and services purchased and used up during a given period by households and governments. In practice, the Bureau of Economic Analysis counts purchases of many long-lasting goods (such as cars and clothes) as consumption even though the goods are not used up. Consumption by house-holds alone is also called consumer spending.

CONTINGENT LIABILITY - For the purpose of Federal credit programs, a contingent liability is a conditional commitment that may become an actual liability because of a future event beyond the control of the Government. Contingent liabilities include such items as loan guarantees and bank deposit insurance.

CONTINUING RESOLUTION - An appropriations act that provides budget authority for Federal agencies and/or specific activities to continue in operation until the regular appropriations are enacted. Continuing resolutions are enacted when action on an appropriations act is not completed by the beginning of a fiscal year. The continuing resolution usually specifies a maximum rate at which the obligations may be incurred, based on the rate of the prior year, the President's Budget request, or an appropriation bill passed by either or both Houses of Congress. The Congress sometimes uses a Continuing Resolution as an omnibus measure to pass a number of appropriations bills.

CONTRACT AUTHORITY - Statutory authority that permits obligations to be incurred in advance of appropriations, often in anticipation of receipts to be credited to a revolving fund or other account. Contract authority must subsequently be funded by an appropriation to liquidate the obligations incurred under the contract authority or by the collection of receipts.

CONTROLLABLE SPENDING - The ability of Congress and the President to increase and decrease budget outlays or budget authority in the year in question, generally the current or budget year. Relatively uncontrollable refers to spending that the Federal Government cannot increase or decrease without changing existing substantive law. For example, outlays in any one year are considered to be relatively uncontrollable when the program level is determined by existing law or by contract or other obligations.

CORE INFLATION - A measure of the rate of inflation that excludes changes in the prices of food and energy.

COST - This term is used in many contexts. Generally, it is the price or cash value of the resources used to produce a program, project, or activity. For Federal credit programs, cost means the estimated long-term cost to the Government of a direct loan or loan guarantee, calculated on a net present value basis, excluding administrative costs and any incidental effects on governmental receipts or outlays.

COST-BENEFIT ANALYSIS - Cost-benefit analysis is the process of weighing the total expected costs of investments, programs, or policy actions against the total expected benefits in order to maximize economic efficiency.

COST ESTIMATES - An estimate of the 5-year cost of legislation reported by congressional committees. The estimate is prepared by the Congressional Budget Office as required by Section 403 of the Congressional Budget Act (2 U.S.C. 639) and is included in the report accompanying the measure.

CPI – See Consumer Price Index.

CREDIT AUTHORITY - Authority to incur direct loan obligations and loan guarantee commitments. New credit authority must be approved in advance in an appropriations act.

CREDIT BUDGET - The levels of total new direct loan obligations, total new primary loan guarantee commitments, and total new secondary loan guarantee commitments set forth in a budget resolution. These levels form the basis for limitations on direct and guaranteed loans in appropriation bills.

CREDIT CRUNCH - A sudden reduction in the availability of loans and other types of credit from banks and capital markets at given interest rates. The reduced availability of credit can result from many factors, including an increased perception of risk on the part of lenders, an imposition of credit controls, or a sharp restriction of the money supply.

CREDIT LIMIT - The limitation in an appropriations act on the total amount of direct or guaranteed loans that can be made in a year.

CREDIT PROGRAM ACCOUNT - An account that receives an appropriation for the cost of a direct loan or loan guarantee program, and from which such cost is disbursed to a financing account for the program when the loan or guarantee is disbursed.

CREDIT REFORM - Budget process change included in the Budget Enforcement Act of 1990 that required the up-front funding of the full contingent liability of the government for subsidized credit programs.

CREDIT SUBSIDY - The estimated long-term cost to the Federal Government of a direct loan or loan guarantee. That cost is calculated on the basis of net present value, excluding Federal administrative costs and any incidental effects on revenues or outlays. For direct loans, the subsidy cost is the net present value of loan disbursements minus repayments of interest and principal, adjusted for estimated defaults, prepayments, fees, penalties, and other recoveries. For loan guarantees, the subsidy cost is the net present value of estimated payments by the government to cover defaults and delinquencies, interest subsidies, or other payments, offset by any payments to the government, including origination and other fees, penalties, and recoveries.

CROSS WALK - Any procedure for expressing the relationship between budget data from one set of classifications to another, such as between appropriation accounts and authorizing legislation or between the budget functional structure and congressional jurisdictions. This term is commonly used to refer to allocations made pursuant to Section 302 of the Congressional Budget Act.

CURRENT-ACCOUNT BALANCE - The net revenues that arise from a country's international sales and purchases of goods and services plus net international transfers (public or private gifts or donations) and net factor income (primarily capital income from foreign property owned by residents of that country minus capital income from domestic property owned by nonresidents). The current-account balance differs from net exports in that it includes international transfers and net factor income.

CURRENT DOLLARS - The value of goods and services in dollar costs experienced in that year.

CURRENT POLICY - An estimate of the budget authority and outlays required to continue existing programs in the next or future fiscal years based on its priority within the President's Budget. Programs whose spending is fixed in law would not be adjusted for inflation. Other programs may be increased, reduced, or remain constant reflecting the President's priorities.

CURRENT SERVICES ESTIMATES - Presidential estimates of budget authority and outlays for future fiscal years based on continuation of existing levels of service. These estimates reflect the anticipated effects of inflation on the cost of continuing

Federal programs and activities at present spending levels without policy changes. The estimates assume no new initiatives, presidential or congressional, that are not yet law. (See Budget Baseline.) These estimates, accompanied by the underlying economic and programmatic assumptions upon which they are based (such as the rate of inflation, the rate of economic growth, the unemployment rate, program caseloads, and pay increases) are required to be transmitted by the President to the Congress with the President's Budget. CBO produces a similarly prepared baseline that is used by the Congress.

CURRENT YEAR - Fiscal year for which funds are being obligated and expended.

CYCLICAL DEFICIT OR SURPLUS - The part of the federal budget deficit or surplus that results from the business cycle. The cyclical component reflects the way in which the deficit or surplus automatically increases or decreases during economic expansions or recessions.

CYCLICALLY ADJUSTED BUDGET DEFICIT OR SURPLUS - The level of the federal budget deficit or surplus that would occur under current law if the influence of the business cycle was removed—that is, if the economy operated at potential gross domestic product.

DEBT - The total value of outstanding securities issued by the Federal Government is referred to as Federal debt or gross debt. It has two components: debt held by the public (Federal debt held by non-Federal investors, including the Federal Reserve System) and debt held by Government accounts (Federal debt held by Federal Government trust funds, deposit insurance funds, and other Federal accounts). There is a statutory limit on Federal debt that applies to all gross debt, except a small portion of the debt issued by the Department of the Treasury and debt issued by other Federal agencies (primarily the Tennessee Valley Authority and the Postal Service). Unavailable debt is debt that is not available for redemption, or the amount of debt that would remain outstanding even if surpluses were large enough to redeem it. Such debt includes securities that have not yet matured (and will be unavailable for repurchase) and non-marketable securities, such as savings bonds.

DEBT HELD BY THE GOVERNMENT - Holdings of Federal trust funds and other special government funds. Surplus funds in Federal trust funds, such as the Old Age and Disability Retirement Trust Fund, are invested in government securities.

DEBT HELD BY THE PUBLIC - Value of Federal debt held by individuals, institutions, and others outside the Federal Government.

DEBT MANAGEMENT - Operation of the U.S. Treasury Department that determines the composition of the Federal debt. Debt management involves determining the amounts, maturities, other terms and conditions, and schedule of offerings of Federal debt securities. This is accomplished in a manner that raises the cash needed at least cost to the taxpayer and minimizes the effect of government operations on financial markets and on the economy.

DEBT SERVICE - Payment of scheduled interest obligations on outstanding debt.

DEFERRAL OF BUDGET AUTHORITY - Any action or inaction by an officer or employee of the United States Government that temporarily withholds, delays, or effectively precludes the obligation or expenditure of budget authority, including authority to obligate by contract in advance of appropriations as specifically authorized by law. Pursuant to the Congressional Budget and Impoundment Control Act 1974, the President must provide advance notice to the Congress on proposed deferrals.

DEFICIENCY APPORTIONMENT - A distribution by the Office of Management and Budget of available budgetary resources for the fiscal year that anticipates the need for supplemental budget authority. Such apportionments may only be made under certain specified conditions provided for in law (Antideficiency Act, 31 U.S.C. 665 (e)). In such instances, the need for additional budget authority is usually reflected by making the amount apportioned for the fourth quarter less than the amount that will actually be required. Approval of requests for deficiency apportionment does not authorize agencies to exceed available resources within an account.

DEFICIENCY APPROPRIATION - An appropriation made to an expired account to cover obligations that have been incurred in excess of available funds. Deficiency appropriations are rare since obligating in excess of available funds generally is prohibited by law. Deficiency appropriation is sometimes erroneously used as a synonym for supplemental appropriation.

DEFICIT - The amount by which outlays exceed governmental receipts in a given fiscal year.

DEFICIT FINANCING - A situation in which the Federal Government's excess of outlays over receipts for a given period is financed primarily by borrowing from the public.

DEFINITE AUTHORITY - Authority which is stated as a specific sum at the time the authority is granted. This includes authority stated as "not to exceed" a specified amount.

DEFLATION - A drop in general price levels that results in price indexes, such as the consumer price index, to register continuing declines. Deflation is usually caused by a collapse of aggregate demand.

DEPARTMENT - See agency.

DEOBLIGATION – Cancellation or downward adjustment of previously incurred obligations.

DEPOSIT FUND - An account established to record amounts held temporarily by the Government until ownership is determined (for example, earnest money paid by bidders for mineral leases) or as an agent for others (for example, state and local income taxes withheld from Federal employees' salaries and not yet paid to the state or local government). Deposit fund transactions are excluded from the budget totals because the funds are not owned by the Government. Since increases in deposit fund balances reduce Treasury's need to borrow, they are a means of financing a deficit or a surplus.

DEPOSIT INSURANCE - The guarantee by a Federal agency that an individual depositor at a participating depository institution will receive the full amount of the deposit (up to $100,000) if the institution becomes insolvent.

DEPRECIATION - Decline in the value of a currency, financial asset, or capital good. When applied to a capital good, depreciation usually refers to loss of value because of obsolescence, wear, or destruction (as by fire or flood). Book depreciation (also known as tax depreciation) is the depreciation that the tax code allows businesses to deduct when they calculate their taxable profits. It is typically faster than economic depreciation, which represents the actual decline in the value of the asset. Both measures of depreciation appear as part of the national income and product accounts.

DEVALUATION - The act of a government to lower the fixed exchange rate of its currency. The government devalues a currency by announcing that it will no longer maintain the existing rate by buying and selling its currency at that rate.

DIRECT LOAN - A disbursement of funds under a contract that requires repayment with or without interest. It includes direct Federal participation in loans privately made or held and purchase of private loans through secondary markets. Transactions similar to direct loans are sometimes displayed in the budget, e.g., the sale of Federal assets on credit terms for more than 90 days duration; investments in obligations or preferred stock of any privately owned enterprises; and deferred or delinquent interest that is capitalized.

DIRECT SPENDING - Spending, also known as mandatory spending, that consists of entitlement authority, the budget authority for the food stamp program, and budget authority provided in law other than annual appropriations acts.

DISBURSEMENT - Cash expenditure.

DISCOUNT RATE - The interest rate that the Federal Reserve System charges on a loan it makes to a bank. Such loans, when allowed, enable a bank to meet its reserve requirements without reducing its loans.

DISCOURAGED WORKERS - Jobless people who are available for work but not actively seeking it because they think they have poor prospects of finding a job. Discouraged workers are not included in measures of the labor force or the unemployment rate.

DISCRETIONARY APPROPRIATIONS - A category of budget authority that comprises budget authority and budgetary resources (except those provided to fund direct-spending programs) provided in annual appropriations acts.

DISCRETIONARY SPENDING - A category of spending (budget authority and outlays) subject to annual appropriations.

DISCRETIONARY SPENDING LIMITS (OR CAPS) - Ceilings imposed on the amount of budget authority that can be provided in appropriation acts in a fiscal year and on the estimated outlays in that fiscal year. The limits were first established in the Budget Enforcement Act of 1990 and enforced through sequestration. On September 30, 2002, all discretionary spending limits, and the sequestration process to enforce them, expired.

DISINVESTMENT - A term that is sometimes used to refer to the status of national physical infrastructure. Disinvestment occurs when the rate of deterioration of physical infrastructure exceeds the rate of new investment in rehabilitation and improvements in infrastructure.

DISPOSABLE PERSONAL INCOME - Personal income—the income that individuals receive, including transfer payments— minus the taxes and fees that individuals pay to governments.

DOMESTIC DEMAND - Total purchases of goods and services, regardless of their origin, by U.S. consumers, businesses, and governments during a given period. Domestic demand equals gross domestic product minus net exports.

DYNAMIC ANALYSIS - A comprehensive assessment of the potential economic effects of a legislative proposal that includes estimates of the response of macroeconomic aggregates, such as gross domestic product, and of the impact those economic effects may have on the Federal budget. Such an assessment typically involves multiple outcomes that reflect the uncertainty associated with such responses and the use of alternative assumptions about fiscal and monetary policy.

DYNAMIC SCORING - A method of scoring the budgetary impact of legislation that would reflect all the economic effects of the proposal or law that can be estimated, including its effects on overall economic activity, such as employment, inflation, and output.

E-GOVERNMENT – Refers to the Federal government's use of information technologies (such as mobile computing and the Internet) to exchange information and services with citizens, businesses, and with government.

EARMARKING – Designation of funds for a specific purpose or program. This can refer to either designation by law, meaning it is actually included in the legislation, or non-binding commitment of funds specified by language included in congressional committee reports. The latter amounts to a political commitment among members of Congress.

ECONOMIC GROWTH AND TAX RELIEF RECONCILIATION ACT
OF 2001 (PUBLIC LAW 107-16) - This law, also known as EGTRRA, significantly reduced tax liabilities (the amount of tax owed) over the 2001–2010 period by cutting individual income tax rates, increasing the child tax credit, repealing estate taxes, raising deductions for married couples who file joint returns, increasing tax benefits for pensions and individual retirement accounts, and creating additional tax benefits for education. The law phased in many of those changes over time, including some that are not fully effective until 2010. Although some of the law's provisions have been made permanent, most are scheduled to expire on or before December 31, 2010.

ECONOMIC INDICATORS - A set of statistical series that have had a systematic relationship to the business cycle. Each indicator is classified as leading, coincident, or lagging, depending on whether the indicator generally changes direction in advance or, coincident with, or subsequent to changes in the overall economy.

ECONOMIC PROFITS - Corporations' profits, adjusted to remove distortions in depreciation allowances caused by tax rules and to exclude the effect of inflation on the value of inventories. Economic profits are a better measure of profits from current production than are the book profits reported by corporations. Economic profits are referred to as "corporate profits with inventory valuation and capital consumption adjustments" in the national income and product accounts.

EFFECTIVE TAX RATE - The ratio of taxes paid to a given tax base. For individual income taxes, the effective tax rate is typically expressed as the ratio of taxes to adjusted gross income. For corporate income taxes, it is the ratio of taxes to book profits. For some purposes — such as calculating an overall tax rate on all income sources — an effective tax rate is computed on a base that includes the untaxed portion of Social Security benefits, interest on tax-exempt bonds, and similar items. It can also be computed on a base of personal income as measured by the national income and product accounts. The effective tax rate is a useful measure because the tax code's various exemptions, credits, deductions, and tax rates make actual ratios of taxes to income very different from statutory tax rates.

EMERGENCY APPROPRIATION - An appropriation in a discretionary category that the President and the Congress have designated as an emergency requirement. There is no definition in law as to what constitutes an emergency. Such appropriations result in an adjustment to the Budget Enforcement Act cap for the category.

EMERGENCY SPENDING - Spending that the President and the Congress have designated as an emergency requirement. Such spending is not subject to the limits on discretionary spending, if it is discretionary spending, or the pay-as-you-go rules, if it is direct spending.

EMPLOYMENT COST INDEX (ECI) - An index of the weighted-average cost of an hour of labor — comprising the cost to the employer of wage and salary payments, employee benefits, and contributions for social insurance programs. The ECI is structured so that it is not affected by changes in the mix of occupations or by changes in employment by industry.

ENROLLED BILL - Final bill transmitted by the Congress to the President for approval or disapproval.

ENROLLED BILL MEMO - Memorandum to the President recommending approval or disapproval of spending authority by the agency's staff through OMB. Requires sign off by the Cabinet officer prior to presentation to the President.

ENTITLEMENT - A legal obligation of the Federal Government to make payments to a person, group of persons, business, unit of government, or similar entity that is not controlled by the level of budget authority provided in an appropriation act. The Congress generally controls spending for entitlement programs by setting eligibility criteria and benefit or payment rules. The source of funding to liquidate the obligation may be provided in either the authorization act that created the entitlement or a subsequent appropriation act. The best-known entitlements are Social Security and Medicare.

ENTITLEMENT AUTHORITY - Legislation that requires the payment of benefits (or entitlement) to any person or unit of government that meets the eligibility requirements established by such law. Budget authority for such payments is usually provided by authorization legislation and constitutes direct (or mandatory) spending. Entitlement legislation requires the subsequent enactment of appropriations unless the existing appropriation is permanent. Examples of entitlement programs are Social Security and veterans' compensation or pensions.

EXCHANGE RATE - The number of units of a foreign currency that can be bought with one unit of the domestic currency, or vice versa.

EXCISE TAX - A tax levied on the purchase of a specific type of good or service, such as tobacco products or telephone services.

EXPANSION - A phase of the business cycle that begins when gross domestic product exceeds its previous peak and extends until GDP reaches its next peak.

EXPENDITURE - Generally the same as an outlay, or a cash payment to settle an obligation.

EXPENDITURE ACCOUNT - An account established to record appropriations, obligations, and outlays that is usually financed from the associated receipt account.

EXPIRED ACCOUNT - A budgetary account in which the unobligated balances are no longer available for new obligations because the time available for incurring such obligations has expired. After 5 years, these accounts are canceled and are then considered to be closed accounts.

FACTS II - The Treasury Federal Agencies' Centralized Trial-balance System II. Departments and agencies use this system to electronically submit the accounting data that supports the SF 133 Report on Budget Execution and Budgetary Resources.

FAN CHART - A graphic representation of CBO's baseline projection of the budget deficit or surplus that includes not only a single line representing the outcome expected under the baseline's economic assumptions but also the various possible outcomes surrounding that line, based on the reasonable expectations of error in the underlying economic and technical assumptions.

FEDERAL CREDIT – Federal direct loans and loan guarantees.

FEDERAL FUNDS - The moneys collected and spent by the Government other than those designated as trust funds. Federal funds include general, special, public enterprise, and intra-governmental funds.

FEDERAL FUNDS RATE - The interest rate that financial institutions charge each other for overnight loans of their monetary reserves. A rise in the Federal funds rate (compared with other short-term interest rates) suggests a tightening of monetary policy, whereas a fall suggests an easing.

FEDERAL OPEN MARKET COMMITTEE - The group within the Federal Reserve System that determines the direction of monetary policy. The open market desk at the Federal Reserve Bank of New York implements that policy with open market operations (the purchase or sale of Government securities), which influence short-term interest rates — especially the Federal funds rate — and the growth of the money supply. The committee is composed of 12 members, including the seven members of the Board of Governors of the Federal Reserve System, the president of the Federal Reserve Bank of New York, and a rotating group of four of the other 11 presidents of the regional Federal Reserve Banks.

FEDERAL RESERVE SYSTEM - The central bank of the United States. The Federal Reserve is responsible for conducting the nation's monetary policy and overseeing credit conditions.

FINANCING ACCOUNT - An account that receives the payments from a credit program account and includes all cash flows to and from the Government resulting from direct loan obligations or loan guarantee commitments beginning in FY 1992. At least one financing account is associated with each credit program account. For programs with direct and guaranteed loans, there are separate financing accounts for direct loans and guaranteed loans. The transactions of the financing accounts are not included in the budget totals.

FISCAL POLICY - Federal Government policies with respect to taxes, spending, and debt management, intended to promote the nation's macroeconomic goals, particularly with respect to employment, gross domestic product, price stability, and equilibrium in the balance of payments. The budget process is a major vehicle for determining and implementing Federal fiscal policy. The other major component of Federal macroeconomic policy is monetary policy.

FISCAL YEAR - The Government's accounting period. It begins on October 1st and ends on September 30th, and is designated by the calendar year in which it ends.

FIXED APPROPRIATION ACCOUNT – An account in which appropriations are available for a definite period. This period can be one year or multiple years.

FOREIGN DIRECT INVESTMENT - Financial investment by which a person or an entity acquires a lasting interest in, and a degree of influence over the management of, a business enterprise in a foreign country.

FORWARD FUNDING - Appropriations of budget authority that become available for obligation in the last quarter of the fiscal year for the financing of grant programs that continue into the next fiscal year.

FULL FUNDING - Provision of budgetary resources to cover the total cost of a program or project at the time it is undertaken. Full funding differs from incremental funding in which budget authority is provided or recorded for only the portion of estimated obligations expected to be incurred during a single fiscal year. Full funding is generally discussed in terms of multi-year programs, whether or not obligations for the entire program are made in the first year.

FULL-TIME EQUIVALENT (FTE) EMPLOYMENT - The basic measure of the levels of employment used in the budget. It is the total number of hours worked (or to be worked) divided by the number of compensable hours applicable to each fiscal year.

FUNCTIONAL CLASSIFICATION - A classification of budget resources that permits all budget authority, outlays, loan guarantees, and tax expenditures to be related in terms of the national need being addressed (e.g., national defense, health). Appropriation accounts generally are placed in the single budget function that best reflects its major end purpose. A function may be divided into two or more subfunctions, depending on the complexity of the national need addressed by that function. There are 19 functional categories of national need (e.g., national defense, health) and one category for undistributed offsetting receipts.

FUND ACCOUNTING - The legal requirement for Federal agencies to establish accounts for segregating revenues and other resources with all related liabilities, obligations, and reserves. Fund accounting, in a broad sense, is required to demonstrate agency compliance with legislation for which Federal funds have been appropriated or otherwise authorized.

GDI - Gross Domestic Income.

GDP - Gross Domestic Product.

GDP GAP - The difference between potential and actual gross domestic product, expressed as a percentage of potential GDP.

GDP PRICE INDEX - A summary measure of the prices of all of the goods and services that make up gross domestic product. The change in the GDP price index is used as a measure of inflation in the overall economy.

GENERAL FUND - The account for receipts not earmarked by law for a specific purpose, the proceeds of general borrowing, and the expenditure of these moneys.

GENERAL PROVISIONS - Directives and instructions that Congress includes in an appropriations act.

GNP - Gross National Product.

GO ZONE BONDS – To assist in the rebuilding effort following Hurricanes Katrina, Rita, and Wilma, the states of Louisiana, Mississippi, and Alabama were authorized to issue up to $14.8 billion of a special class of private activity bonds called GO Zone Bonds outside the state volume caps. The States or municipalities may issue these bonds, with the proceeds used to pay for acquisition, construction, and renovation of non-residential real property. Low-income housing rules are relaxed, so more bond proceeds may be used to rebuild housing in the Zone. Mortgage revenue bonds may be used to repair homes (up to $150,000), with the first-time homebuyer rule waived. Interest payments are not subject to Alternative Minimum Taxes. This authority is good through December 31, 2010.

GOVERNMENT PERFORMANCE RESULTS ACT OF 1993 (Public Law 103-62) - The law that requires Federal agencies to create a framework and develop the information that will lead to more effective planning, budgeting, program evaluation, and fiscal accountability for Federal programs. Agencies must submit strategic and annual performance plans that clearly state performance goals and indicators for each program, and annual reports on actual performance against the goals and targets.

GOVERNMENT-SPONSORED ENTERPRISES (GSEs) - Financial institutions established and chartered by the Federal Government — as privately owned and operated entities — to facilitate the flow of funds to selected lending markets, such as those for residential mortgages and agricultural credit. Although they are classified as private entities for purposes of the Federal budget (their transactions are not included in the budget totals), GSEs retain a relationship with the Federal Government that confers certain advantages on them that would not be available to similar private entities that were not federally sponsored. Examples of GSEs are Fannie Mae and the Federal Home Loan Bank System.

GOVERNMENTAL RECEIPTS - Collections from the public that result primarily from the Government's exercise of its sovereign power to tax or otherwise compel payment. They include individual and corporation income taxes, social insurance taxes, excise taxes, compulsory user charges, customs duties, court fines, certain license fees, and deposits of earnings of the Federal Reserve System. Government receipts are compared to outlays in calculating a surplus or deficit.

GRAMM-RUDMAN-HOLLINGS (GRH) – The common name for the Balanced Budget and Emergency Deficit Control Act of 1985. The Act was named for Senators Phil Gramm, Warren Rudman, and Ernest Hollings.

GRANTS - Assistance awards in which substantial involvement is not anticipated between the Federal Government and the state or local government or other recipient during the performance of the contemplated activity. The two major forms of Federal grants are block and categorical.

- **Block grants -** grants given primarily to general purpose governmental units in accordance with a statutory formula and can be used for a variety of activities within a broad functional area. Formula grants allocate Federal funds to states or their subdivisions in accordance with a distribution formula prescribed by law or administrative regulation. Community Development Block Grants are an example.
- **Categorical grants -** formula, project, and formula-project grants that can be used only for a specific program and are usually limited to narrowly defined activities.

GRANTS-IN-AID - Grants from the Federal Government to state and local governments to help provide for programs of assistance or service to the public.

GROSS DOMESTIC INCOME (GDI) - The sum of all income earned in the domestic production of goods and services. In theory, GDI should equal GDP, but measurement difficulties leave a statistical discrepancy between the two.

GROSS DOMESTIC PRODUCT (GDP) - The total market value of goods and services produced domestically during a given period. The components of GDP are consumption (both household and government), gross investment (both private and government), and net exports.

GROSS INVESTMENT - A measure of additions to the capital stock that does not subtract depreciation of existing capital.

GROSS NATIONAL PRODUCT (GNP) - The total market value of goods and services produced during a given period by labor and capital supplied by residents of a country, regardless of where the labor and capital are located. GNP differs from GDP primarily by including the capital income that residents earn from investments abroad and excluding the capital income that nonresidents earn from domestic investment.

HOME EQUITY - The value that an owner has in a home, calculated by subtracting the value of any outstanding mortgage (or other loan) secured by the home from the home's current market value.

IDENTIFICATION CODES - 11 digit code assigned to each appropriation or fund account in The Budget of the United States Government that identifies: (a) the agency, (b) the account, (c) the timing of the transmittal to Congress, (d) the type of fund, and (e) the account's functional classification.

IMPOUNDMENT - Any action or inaction by an officer or employee of the Government that precludes the obligation of budget authority provided by Congress.

INCREMENTAL FUNDING - The provision of budget resources for an investment program or project that covers only the obligations that will be incurred during one fiscal year of a program spanning several years. This differs from full funding in which budget resources are provided for the total estimated obligations for a program or project in the initial year of funding.

INDEFINITE AUTHORITY - Authority for which a specific sum is not stated but is determined by other factors such as the receipts collected or the obligations incurred. Indefinite authority also includes authority to borrow that is limited to a specified amount that may be outstanding at any time, e.g., revolving debt authority is considered to be indefinite budget authority.

INFLATION - Growth in a general measure of prices, usually expressed as an annual rate of change.

INFORMAL HEARING - Discussions between congressional members and political appointees.

INFRASTRUCTURE - Government-owned capital goods that provide services to the public, usually with benefits to the community at large as well as to the direct user. Examples are schools, roads, bridges, dams, harbors, and public buildings.

INTRA-GOVERNMENTAL FUNDS - Accounts for business-type or market-oriented activities conducted primarily within and between government agencies and financed by offsetting collections that are credited directly to the fund.

INVENTORIES - Stocks of goods held by businesses for further processing or for sale.

INVESTMENT - *Physical investment* is the current product set aside during a given period to be used for future production—in other words, an addition to the capital stock. As measured by the national income and product accounts, *private domestic investment* consists of investment in residential and nonresidential structures, producers' durable equipment, and the change in business inventories. *Financial investment* is the purchase of a financial security, such as a stock, bond, or mortgage. *Investment in human capital* is spending on education, training, health services, and other activities that increase the productivity of the workforce. Investment in human capital is not treated as investment by the national income and product accounts.

INVESTMENT INITIATIVES - These include proposed budget increases for Federal programs that support infrastructure, technology, skills, and security—all of which yield public benefits in the future.

JOINT RESOLUTION – One of two forms of legislation:

- A congressional action either for a single appropriation for a specific purpose, increasing the statutory limit on the public debt, or continuing appropriations. For example, following the September 11, 2001 attacks on the U.S., Congress authorized the use of military force via joint resolution. This type of joint resolution becomes law in the same manner as any other law; it requires a simple majority in both houses of congress and must be approved by the President.

- A congressional action used to propose amendments to the Constitution. This does not require presidential approval, but requires a two-thirds majority in both houses of congress and must be ratified by three-fourths of the states.

JOINT FINANCIAL MANAGEMENT IMPROVEMENT PROGRAM (JFMIP) - The joint undertaking of the Department of the Treasury, the General Accounting Office, the OMB, and the Office of Personnel Management to improve financial management in the Federal Government.

JUDGMENT FUND - A permanent and indefinite appropriation in the Department of the Treasury that is available to pay final judgments, settlement agreements, and certain types of administrative awards against the United States when payment is not otherwise provided for.

LABOR FORCE - The number of people who have jobs or who are available for work and are actively seeking jobs. The labor force participation rate is the labor force as a percentage of the noninstitutional population age 16 or older.

LIMITATION - A restriction on the amount, purpose, or period of availability of budget authority. It typically is established through appropriations acts, but it can be included in authorization legislation.

LINE ITEM - In executive budgeting, this term usually refers to a particular item or expenditure such as travel costs or equipment. In congressional budgeting, it refers to particular accounts or programs assumed in the budget aggregates, functional allocations, or reconciliation instructions. Although line items are not specified in congressional budget resolutions, the aggregate functional classifications and reconciliation instructions reflect assumptions about such items. A line item may be a specific directive by Congress to set-aside spending for a specific purpose within an appropriation account.

LIQUIDATING ACCOUNT - An account that includes all cash flows to and from the Government resulting from direct loan obligations and loan guarantee commitments made prior to FY 1992.

LIQUIDATING APPROPRIATION - An appropriation to pay obligations incurred pursuant to substantive legislation, usually contract authority. A liquidating appropriation is not counted as budget authority.

LIQUIDITY - The ease with which an asset can be sold for cash. An asset is highly liquid if it comes in standard units that are traded daily in large amounts by many buyers and sellers. Among the most liquid of assets are U.S. Treasury securities.

LOAN GUARANTEE - An agreement by which the Government agrees to pay part or all of the loan principal and interest of a non-federal borrower to a non-federal lender or holder of a security, in the event of default by a third party borrower.

LOCKBOX - Any of several legislative mechanisms that attempt to isolate, or "lock away," funds of the Federal government for purposes such as reducing Federal spending, preserving surpluses, or protecting the solvency of trust funds.

LONG-TERM INTEREST RATE - The interest rate earned by a note or bond that matures in 10 or more years.

MANAGEMENT AGENDA - Initiatives proposed within the Executive Branch to improve overall program/project efficiency.

MANDATORY SPENDING - Spending for mandatory programs. Used synonymously with direct spending.

MARGINAL TAX RATE - The tax rate that applies to an additional dollar of income.

MARKET BASED SPECIAL – The rate a department or agency receives for fund balances based on the "best" mix of treasury securities available at the time to maximize returns for the uses of the fund (maturities expected usage cycles).

MARK-UP - Meeting of a congressional committee to work on the language of a specific bill or piece of legislation.

MAXIMUM DEFICIT AMOUNTS - Amounts specified in and subject to certain adjustments under law. If the deficit for the year in question is estimated to exceed the adjusted maximum deficit amount for that year by more than a specified margin, a sequester of budget authority to eliminate the excess deficit is required.

MEANS OF FINANCING - Means by which a budget deficit is financed or a surplus is used. Means of financing are not included in the budget totals. The primary means of financing is borrowing from the public. In general, the cumulative amount borrowed from the public (debt held by the public) will increase if there is a deficit and decrease if there is a surplus, although other factors can affect the amount that the government must borrow. Those factors, known as other means of financing, include reductions (or increases) in the government's cash balances, seigniorage, changes in outstanding checks, changes in accrued interest costs included in the budget but not yet paid, and cash flows reflected in credit financing accounts.

MEANS-TESTED PROGRAMS - Programs that provide cash or services to people who meet a test of need based on income and assets. Most means-tested programs are entitlements (such as Medicaid, the Food Stamp program, Supplemental Security Income, family support programs, and veterans' pensions). There a few means-tested programs (for instance, subsidized housing and various social services) for which the budget authority for the program is provided in annual appropriation acts.

MID-SESSION REVIEW OF THE BUDGET – An update of the President's Budget that contains revised estimates of budget receipts, outlays, and budget authority. Federal law requires the mid-session review to be submitted to Congress annually no later than July 15th.

MONEY SUPPLY - Private assets that can readily be used to make transactions or are easily convertible into assets that can. The money supply includes currency and demand deposits and may also include broader categories of assets, such as other types of deposits and securities.

MONETARY POLICY - Policies which affect the money supply, interest rates, and credit availability that are intended to promote national macroeconomic goals, such as price stability and full employment. Particular significance is assigned to employment, gross domestic product, price stability, and equilibrium in the balance of payments in policy development. Monetary policy is directed primarily by the Board of Governors of the Federal Reserve System and the Federal Open Market Committee. Monetary policy works by influencing the cost and availability of bank reserves.

MONTHLY TREASURY STATEMENT - A summary statement prepared from agency accounting reports and issued by the Department of Treasury. The MTS presents the receipts, outlays, and resulting budget surplus or deficit for the month and the fiscal year to date.

MULTI-YEAR APPROPRIATION - Budget authority that is available for a specified period of time in excess of one fiscal year. This authority may cover periods that do not coincide with the start or end of a fiscal year.

MULTI-YEAR BUDGET PLANNING - A budget planning process designed to make sure that the long-range consequences of budget decisions are identified and reflected in the budget totals. This process provides a structure for the review and analysis of long-term program and tax policy choices.

NATIONAL INCOME - Total income earned by U.S. residents from all sources, including employee compensation (wages, salaries, benefits, and employers' contributions to social insurance programs), corporate profits, net interest, rental income, and proprietors' income.

NATIONAL INCOME ACCOUNTS - Accounts prepared and published quarterly and annually by the Department of Commerce, which provide a detailed statistical description of aggregate economic activity within the U.S. economy. These accounts depict in dollar terms the composition and use of the Nation's output and the distribution of national income to different recipients. The accounts make it possible to trace fluctuations in economic activity.

NATIONAL SAVING - Total saving by all sectors of the economy: personal saving, business saving (corporate after-tax profits not paid as dividends), and government saving (the budget surplus). National saving represents all income not consumed, publicly or privately, during a given period.

NATURAL RATE OF UNEMPLOYMENT – The rate of unemployment arising from all sources except fluctuations in aggregate demand. Those sources include *frictional unemployment,* which is associated with normal turnover of jobs, and *structural unemployment,* which includes unemployment caused by mismatches between the skills of available workers and the skills necessary to fill vacant positions and unemployment caused when wages exceed their market-clearing levels because of institutional factors, such as legal minimum wages, the presence of unions, social conventions, or employer wage-setting practices intended to increase workers' morale and effort.

NET EXPORTS - Exports of goods and services produced in a country minus the country's imports of goods and services produced elsewhere (sometimes referred to as a trade surplus when net exports are positive or a trade deficit when net exports are negative).

NET FEDERAL GOVERNMENT SAVING - A term used in the national income and product accounts to identify the difference between federal current receipts and federal current expenditures (including consumption of fixed capital).

NET INTEREST - In the Federal budget, net interest comprises the government's interest payments on debt held by the public (as recorded in budget function 900) offset by interest income that the government receives on loans and cash balances and by earnings of the National Railroad Retirement Investment Trust.

NET NATIONAL SAVING - National saving minus depreciation of physical capital.

NEW MARKETS TAX CREDITS (NMTCs) – The New Markets Tax Credit program was established by Congress in December of 2000 and is administered by the CDFI Fund, a division of Treasury. The program allows individual and corporate taxpayers to receive a Federal income tax credit for making qualified equity investments in investment vehicles known as Community Development Entities (CDEs). The credit provided to the investor totals 39 percent of the cost of the investment and is claimed over a seven-year period. Substantially all of the taxpayer's investment must in turn be used by the CDE to make qualified investments in low-income communities. The GO Zone Act of 2005 authorized a special allocation of $1 billion in NMTCs for GO Zone counties and parishes.

NOMINAL - A measure based on current-dollar value. The nominal level of income or spending is measured in current dollars. The nominal interest rate on debt selling at par is the ratio of the current-dollar interest paid in any year to the current-dollar value of the debt when it was issued. The nominal interest rate on debt initially issued or now selling at a discount includes as a payment the estimated yearly equivalent of the difference between the redemption price and the discounted price. The nominal exchange rate is the rate at which a unit of one currency trades for a unit of another currency.

NONEXPENDITURE TRANSACTIONS - Intra-governmental transactions between appropriation and fund accounts that do not represent payments for goods and services received but serve only to adjust the amounts available in the accounts for making payments. Nonexpenditure transactions are not recorded as obligations or outlays of the transferring accounts or as reimbursements or as collections of the receiving accounts. The statutory restrictions on the purpose, availability, and use of appropriated funds by administrative agencies require that no change be made in the availability of funds by agencies through the use of nonexpenditure transactions unless specifically authorized by law.

OBJECT CLASSIFICATION - A uniform classification identifying the transactions of the Federal Government by the nature of the goods or services purchased (such as personnel compensation, supplies and materials, and equipment). Data on obligations by object classification are provided in the Object Classification Schedule along with the corresponding Program and Financing Schedule in the Budget of the United States Government.

OBLIGATED BALANCES - Amounts of budget authority that have been obligated but not yet outlayed. Unobligated balances are amounts that have not been obligated and that remain available for obligation under law.

OBLIGATION DELAY - Legislation that precludes the obligation of an amount of budget authority provided in law until some time after the first day on which that budget authority would normally be available. For example, language in an appropriation act for fiscal year 2004 that precludes obligation of an amount until March 1 is an obligation delay; without that language, the amount would have been available for obligation on October 1, 2003 (the first day of fiscal year 2004).

OBLIGATIONS - Binding agreements that will result in outlays, immediately or in the future. Budgetary resources must be available before obligations can be incurred legally.

OBLIGATIONAL AUTHORITY - Sum of (a) budget authority provided for a given fiscal year, (b) balances of amounts brought forward from prior years that remain available for obligation, and (c) amounts authorized to be credited to a specific fund or account during that year, including transfers between funds or accounts.

OBLIGATION-BASED BUDGETING - Financial transactions that record obligations when they are incurred, regardless of when the resources acquired are to be consumed.

OBLIGATION LIMITATION - Limitations in appropriations acts on the amount of offsetting collections that can be made available for obligation and counted as budget authority. In the absence of such a limitation, the whole amount of the offsetting collection would be counted as budget authority.

OBLIGATIONS INCURRED - Amounts of orders placed, contracts awarded, services received, and similar transactions during a given period that will require payments during that year or a future year. Such amounts include outlays for which obligations had not been previously recorded and adjustments for differences between obligations previously recorded and actual outlays to liquidate those obligations.

OFF-BUDGET - Transactions that are excluded from the budget totals under law, even though these outlays are part of total government spending. Current law requires that Social Security trust funds and the Postal Service be off-budget.

OFFSETTING COLLECTIONS - Collections from the public that result from business-type or market-oriented activities and collections from other government accounts. These collections are deducted from gross disbursements in calculating outlays, rather than counted as governmental receipts. Some are credited directly to appropriation or fund accounts; others, called offsetting receipts, are credited to receipt accounts. The authority to spend offsetting collections is a form of budget authority.

OFFSETTING RECEIPTS - Amounts deposited in receipt accounts (i.e., general funds, special funds, or trust funds). These receipts generally are deducted from budget authority and outlays by function and/or subfunction, and by agency. Offsetting receipts are subdivided between proprietary receipts from the public and intra-governmental transactions. These receipts do not offset budget authority and outlays at the appropriations account level.

OMB CIRCULAR NO. A-11 – Document that provides detailed guidance to executive departments for preparing and submitting the President's Budget and for budget execution.

OMB HEARINGS - Presentation and justification of a department's budget submission to OMB.

OMB PASSBACK - Process for notifying Executive Branch departments/agencies of OMB's decisions on the budget for the next fiscal year.

ON-BUDGET - Total of transactions for all Federal Government entities except those excluded from the budget totals by law.

ONE-YEAR (ANNUAL) AUTHORITY - Budget authority that is available for obligation only during a specified fiscal year and expires at the end of that time.

OUTCOME - Results of a government program.

OUTLAY RATE - Rate at which budget authority is expended. It is expressed as a percentage of the available budget authority that will be expended in the current year and in each subsequent year.

OUTLAYS - Payments to liquidate obligations (other than repayment of debt), net of refunds and offsetting collections. Outlays are generally recorded on a cash basis, but they also include cash-equivalent transactions, the subsidy cost of direct loans and loan guarantees, and interest accrued on public issues of Treasury debt. Outlays during a fiscal year may be for payment of obligations incurred in prior years (prior-year outlays) or in the same year. The terms expenditure and net disbursement are frequently used interchangeably with the term outlays.

OUTPUT - Level of program activity or effort expressed in a quantitative or qualitative manner.

OUTYEARS - A year (or years) beyond the budget year for which projections are made.

OVERSIGHT COMMITTEE – The congressional committee with general oversight of the operations of an agency or program. Generally, this committee also has authorization responsibility for its constituent agencies and programs.

PAR VALUE SPECIAL – The interest rate performance a department or agency receives on its fund balances that is based on the lowest performing interest amount the U.S. Treasury can offer.

PASSBACK - Generally refers to decisions passed back to a department or agency by the Director of OMB with the concurrence of the President on an agency's total budget level as well as individual program and policy decisions.

PAYGO (PAY-AS-YOU-GO) - Requirement established in the Budget Enforcement Act that requires new direct (mandatory) spending increases or tax reductions in legislation to be offset by legislated reductions in other mandatory spending or by revenue increases. A sequester is to occur if the legislation affecting direct spending or receipts enacted in a fiscal year will increase the estimated deficit (or reduce the surplus) for that fiscal year.

PERFORMANCE GOAL - Target level of performance expressed in measurable terms (standard, value, or rate) that permits comparison with actual achievement.

PERFORMANCE INDICATOR - Value or characteristic used to measure output or outcome. This is a key element in reporting under the Government Performance and Results Act.

PERMANENT APPROPRIATION - Budget authority that becomes available as the result of previously enacted legislation (substantive legislation or prior appropriation act) and does not require current action by Congress. Authority created by such legislation is considered to be "current" if provided in the current session of Congress and "permanent" if provided in prior sessions.

PERMANENT AUTHORIZATION - Authorization without limit of time and, usually, without limit of money. A permanent authorization continues in effect unless changed or terminated by Congress.

PERSONAL CONSUMPTION EXPENDITURE PRICE INDEX - A summary measure of the prices of all goods and services that make up personal consumption expenditures. It is an alternative to the consumer price index as a measure of inflation.

PERSONAL SAVING - Saving by households. Personal saving equals disposable personal income minus spending for consumption and interest payments. The personal saving rate is personal saving as a percentage of disposable personal income.

POCKET VETO - Presidential failure to sign an enrolled bill following the end of the congressional session.

POINT OF ORDER - Procedure by which a member of a legislature (or similar body) questions an action being taken, or that is proposed to be taken, as contrary to that body's rules, practices, or precedents.

PORK BARREL PROJECTS - Special interest funding sponsored by individual members of Congress.

POTENTIAL GDP - The level of real gross domestic product that corresponds to a high level of resource (labor and capital) use.

POTENTIAL LABOR FORCE - The labor force adjusted for movements in the business cycle.

POTENTIAL OUTPUT - The level of production that corresponds to a high level of resource (labor and capital) use. Potential output for the national economy is also referred to as potential gross domestic product.

PRESENT VALUE - A single number that expresses a flow of current and future income (or payments) in terms of an equivalent lump sum received (or paid) today. The calculation of present value depends on the rate of interest.

PRESIDENTIAL APPEAL - Departmental appeals of OMB Passback decisions to the President when appeals to OMB have not been resolved to the satisfaction of the department or agency head.

PRESIDENT'S BUDGET - Document sent to Congress by the President no later than the first Monday in February. It sets forth the President's comprehensive financial plan and indicates the President's policy/program priorities and proposed spending levels for the Federal Government.

PRESIDENT'S BUDGET PRESS RELEASE - Press release highlighting significant measures included in the President's proposals to Congress. It is coordinated by the Director of OMB, the Chairman of the Council Economic Advisors, and the Secretary of the Treasury.

PRIVATE SAVING - Saving by households and businesses. Private saving is equal to personal saving plus after-tax corporate profits minus dividends paid.

PRODUCTIVITY - Average real output per unit of input. Labor productivity is the average real output per hour of labor. The growth of labor productivity is defined as the growth of real output that is not explained by the growth of labor input alone. Total factor productivity is average real output per unit of combined labor and capital inputs. The growth of total factor productivity is defined as the growth of real output that is not explained by the growth of labor and capital. Labor productivity and total factor productivity differ in that increases in capital per worker raise labor productivity but not total factor productivity.

PROGRAM - Organized set of activities directed toward a common purpose, or goal, undertaken or proposed by an agency in order to carry out its responsibilities. In practice, the term program has many uses and thus does not have a well-defined, standard meaning in the legislative process. Program is sometimes used to describe an agency's mission, programs, functions, activities, services, projects, and processes.

PROGRAM ACCOUNT - A budgetary account associated with a credit program that receives an appropriation for the subsidy cost of that program's loan obligations or commitments as well as, in most cases, the program's administrative expenses. From the program account, the subsidy cost is disbursed to the applicable financing account.

PROGRAM ACTIVITY - Specific activity or project listed in the program and financing schedules of the annual Budget of the United States Government. Under the Government Performance and Results Act, performance goals and indicators are to be developed for program activities.

PROGRAM AND FINANCING SCHEDULE - Schedule in the Appendix to The Budget of the United States that includes detailed budget data. The schedule consists of three sections: (1) Program by Activities; (2) Financing; and (3) Relation of Obligations to Outlays.

PROGRAM EVALUATION - In general, the process of assessing the options for meeting program objectives. Specifically, program evaluation is the process for appraising the manner and extent to which programs:

- Achieve their stated objectives,
- Meet the performance expectations of Federal officials and other interested groups, and
- Produce other significant effects of either a desirable or undesirable character.

PROGRAM ASSESSMENT RATING TOOL (PART) – A series of questions used to evaluate the management of Federal programs that were created by the Office of Management and Budget. PART reviews, overseen by OMB, help identify programs' strengths and weaknesses to inform funding and management decisions aimed at making Government programs more effective.

PROPRIETARY RECEIPTS FROM THE PUBLIC - Collections from the public, deposited in receipt accounts, that arise from market-oriented or business-type activities of the Federal Government.

PUBLIC ENTERPRISE FUNDS - Revolving accounts authorized by Congress to be credited with collections, primarily from the public, that are generated by, and earmarked to finance a continuing cycle of business-type operations.

QUESTIONS & ANSWERS - Written responses not included in the hearing record provided mainly for congressional staff analysis.

QUESTIONS & ANSWERS (AS IF ASKED) - Written responses to be included in the congressional hearing record subsequent to direct testimony.

REAL - Dollar amounts that have been adjusted to remove the effects of inflation. Real output represents the quantity, rather than the dollar value, of goods and services produced. Real income represents the power to purchase real output. Real data at the finest level of disaggregation are constructed by dividing the corresponding nominal data, such as spending or wage rates, by a price index. Real aggregates, such as real GDP, are constructed by a procedure that allows the real growth of the aggregate to reflect the real growth of its components, appropriately weighted by the importance of the components. A real interest rate is a nominal interest rate adjusted for expected inflation; it is often approximated by subtracting an estimate of the expected inflation rate from the nominal interest rate.

REAPPORTIONMENT - Revision by OMB to a previous apportionment of budgetary resources for an appropriation or fund account. Agency requests for reapportionment are usually submitted to OMB as soon as a change in previous apportionment becomes necessary due to changes in amounts available, program requirements, or cost factors.

REAPPROPRIATION - Congressional action to continue the obligational availability, whether for the same or different purposes, of all or part of the unobligated portion of budget authority that has expired or would otherwise expire. Reappropriations are counted as budget authority in the year for which the availability is newly available.

RECEIPTS - Collections that result primarily from the Government's exercise of its sovereign power to tax or otherwise compel payment. Receipts are compared to outlays in calculating a surplus or deficit.

RECEIPT ACCOUNT - An account established within Federal funds and trust funds to record offsetting receipts or revenues credited to the fund

RECESSION - A decline in overall business activity that is pervasive, substantial, and of at least several months duration. Historically, recessions have been identified by a decline in real gross national product for at least two consecutive quarters.

RECONCILIATION - Process used by Congress to reconcile spending amounts contained in tax, spending, and debt legislation for a given fiscal year with the ceilings in the concurrent resolution on the budget for that year. The Congressional Budget and Impoundment Control Act of 1974 provides that the Resolution on the Budget, which sets binding totals for the budget, may direct committees to determine and recommend changes to laws, bills, and resolutions, as required to conform with the resolution's binding totals for budget authority, revenues, and the public debt. Such changes are incorporated into a reconciliation bill. Changes in tax laws are generally contained in a separate bill.

RECOVERY - A phase of the business cycle that lasts from a trough until overall economic activity returns to the level it reached at the previous peak.

REESTIMATES - Changes made in executive or congressional budget estimates due to changes in economic conditions, workload, and other factors but not to changes in policy. From time to time, the reestimates are entered into the scorekeeping system.

REFUND - The return of excess payments to or by the Government.

REFUNDABLE TAX CREDITS - Tax credit for which a taxpayer will receive a payment for the amount that the credit exceeds the taxpayer's tax liability. An example is the Earned Income Tax Credit.

REGULATORY AGENDA - Projected list of regulations under development within the Executive Branch pursuant to substantive law.

REIMBURSABLE OBLIGATION - An obligation in an expenditure account that is financed by an offsetting collection.

REIMBURSEMENTS - Sums received by an agency as payment for services furnished either to the public or to another government account. They are authorized by law to be credited directly to specific appropriation and fund accounts. These amounts are deducted from the total obligations incurred (and outlays) in determining net obligations (and outlays) for such accounts.

REINVENTING GOVERNMENT - A term used to refer to the National Performance Review, a process devised under the direction of former Vice President Al Gore. Reinventing Government generally means challenging basic assumptions and methods for implementing government programs. The objective of Reinventing Government is to change the way government works in order to make it work better and cost less.

REPORT LANGUAGE - Statement of congressional policy included in the report accompanying a bill but not included in the statute. It is an advisory to the Executive Branch.

REPROGRAMMING - Use of funds in an appropriation account for purposes other than those contemplated at the time of appropriation. Reprogramming is generally preceded by consultation between the Federal agencies and the appropriate congressional committees. It involves formal notification and, in some instances, opportunity for disapproval by congressional committees.

RESCISSION - Cancellation of budget authority provided in an appropriations act before it would otherwise lapse (i.e. funds cease to be available for obligation). The Congressional Budget and Impoundment Control Act of 1974 specifies that whenever the President determines that all or part of any budget authority will not be needed to carry out the full objectives or scope of programs for which the authority was provided, the President will propose to Congress that the excess funds be rescinded. Budget authority may also be proposed for rescission for fiscal policy or other reasons. All funds proposed for rescission must be reported to Congress in a special message. Generally, amounts proposed for rescission are withheld for up to 45 legislative days while the proposals are being considered by Congress. If both Houses have not approved action on a rescission proposed by the President within 45 calendar days of continuous session, any funds being withheld must be made available for obligation.

RESOURCE MANAGEMENT OFFICES (RMOs) - Offices within the Office of Management and Budget responsible for developing the budget and implementing management and policy reforms for assigned areas. These offices are headed by Program Associate Directors, known as PADs. There are five RMOs – Natural Resources, National Security, Health,,Education, Income Maintenance, and Labor, and General Government.

REVENUES - Funds collected from the public that result from the Government's exercise of its sovereign or governmental powers. Federal revenues consist of individual and corporate income taxes, excise taxes, and estate and gift taxes; contributions to social insurance programs (such as Social Security and Medicare); customs duties; fees and fines; and miscellaneous receipts, such as earnings of the Federal Reserve System, gifts, and contributions.

REVOLVING FUNDS - Funds for business-type activities in which collections are used to pay for goods and services produced. There are three types of revolving funds — public enterprise, intra-governmental, and trust revolving. The budget reflects the net of collections and outlays.

RISK PREMIUM - The additional return that investors require to hold assets whose returns are more variable than those of riskless assets. The risk can arise from many sources, such as the possibility of default (in the case of corporate or municipal debt).

S CORPORATION - A domestically owned corporation with no more than 75 owners who have elected to pay taxes under Subchapter S of the Internal Revenue Code. An S corporation is taxed like a partnership: it is exempt from the corporate income tax, but its owners pay income taxes on all of the firm's income, even if some of the earnings are retained by the firm.

SAVINGS BOND - A nontransferable, registered security issued by the Treasury at a discount and in denominations from $50 to $10,000. The interest earned on savings bonds is exempt from state and local taxation and is exempt from Federal taxation until the bonds are redeemed.

SCOREKEEPING - Procedures for tracking the status of congressional budget actions. Examples of scorekeeping information include up-to-date tabulations and reports on congressional actions affecting budget authority, receipts, outlays, surplus or deficit, and the public debt limit. Scorekeeping generally compares the spending or receipts caused by legislation with a baseline, such as the budget resolution, the President's Budget, or the current services baselines. Both CBO and OMB have statutory scorekeeping responsibilities.

- **CBO** - Publishes status reports on the effects of congressional actions (and in the case of scorekeeping reports prepared for the Senate Budget Committee, the budget effects of potential congressional actions), and comparisons of these actions to targets and ceilings set by Congress in the Budget Resolution. Periodic scorekeeping reports are required by section 308(b) of the Congressional Budget and Impoundment Control Act of 1974.

- **OMB** - Provides Congress with the estimated costs of legislation within five days of its enactment, including comparisons with discretionary spending caps and pay-as-you-go impact on mandatory spending. OMB also prepares a sequester report at the end of a session of Congress that determines whether a sequester of budget authority is required. These reports are required by the Budget Enforcement Act.

SCORING - The process of estimating the budgetary impact of a legislative proposal, which typically results in a single number for each appropriate fiscal year. Legislation is scored for the purpose of measuring its effects against a baseline, against targets established in the Congressional budget resolution, or against some other budgetary standard. Current scoring procedures take into account microeconomic behavioral responses to the legislation to the extent practicable, but they do not take into account the effects of the legislation on aggregate economic measures such as employment, output, and inflation. The procedures do not take into account the budgetary effects of the changes in interest costs associated with the change in the surplus or deficit.

SEASONAL RATE - The average commitments, obligations, and expenses of one or more of the last five fiscal years used to determine the funding level for an appropriations account under a Continuing Resolution.

SECRETARIAL APPEAL - Program or bureau appeals of the department's budget formulation decisions to the Secretary.

SEIGNIORAGE - The gain to the government from the difference between the face value of minted coins put into circulation and the cost of producing them (including the cost of the metal used in the coins). Seigniorage is considered a means of financing and is not included in the budget totals.

SEQUESTER - Automatic cancellation of budgetary resources provided by discretionary appropriations or direct spending legislation, following procedures prescribed in law. A sequester may occur in response to a breach of the discretionary budget authority or outlay limits, an increase in the deficit resulting from the combined result of legislation affecting direct spending or receipts (referred to as a "pay-as-you-go" sequester), or a deficit estimated to be in excess of the maximum allowable deficit amount.

SEQUESTRATION - The cancellation of budgetary resources available for a fiscal year in order to enforce the discretionary spending limits or pay-as-you-go procedures in that year. The process was first established in the Balanced Budget and Emergency Deficit Control Act of 1985. A discretionary spending sequestration would be triggered if the OMB determined that budget authority or outlays provided in appropriation acts exceeded the applicable discretionary spending limits. Amounts in excess of the limits would cause the cancellation of budgetary resources within the applicable category of discretionary programs. A pay-as-you-go sequestration would be triggered if OMB determined that enacted legislation affecting direct spending and revenues increased the deficit or reduced the surplus. An increase in the deficit or reduction of the surplus would cause the cancellation of budgetary resources available for direct spending programs not otherwise exempt by law. On September 30, 2002, the discretionary spending caps and the sequestration procedure to enforce those caps expired, and OMB (and CBO) were no longer required to record the five-year budgetary effects of legislation affecting direct spending or revenues.

SHORT-TERM INTEREST RATE - The interest rate earned by a debt instrument (such as a Treasury bill) that will mature within one year.

SPECIAL FUNDS - Accounts for receipts earmarked for specific purposes and the associated expenditure of those receipts.

SPENDING AUTHORITY - As defined by the Congressional Budget and Impoundment Control Act of 1974 (P.L. 93-344, 31 U.S.C. 1323), a collective designation for appropriations, borrowing authority, contract authority, and other authority for which the budget authority is not provided in advance by appropriation acts. The latter three are also referred to as backdoor authority.

SPENDING AUTHORITY FROM OFFSETTING COLLECTIONS - Budget authority that permits obligations and outlays to be financed from offsetting collections

SPEND-OUT RATE - Rate at which budget authority is expended. (See Outlay Rates)

SPRING PLANNING REVIEW - OMB reviews by budget function and program to establish presidential policy for the upcoming budget.

STAFFORD ACT – Refers to the Disaster Relief Act (Public Law 93-288, as amended). Under this law FEMA has the authority, based upon the declaration of a disaster by the President, to use Federal funds to provide certain types of assistance to states and local communities.

STATUTORY LIMITATION ON THE PUBLIC DEBT - Maximum amount of public debt that can be outstanding. The limit covers virtually all public debt, including intra-governmental borrowing from trust funds and debt of off-budget entities.

STATUTORY TAX RATE - A tax rate specified by law.

STRATEGIC PLAN - Document required by the Government Performance and Results Act that contains a comprehensive statement of an agency's mission, general goals and objectives, and the resources needed to achieve the goals.

SUBCOMMITTEE/COMMITTEE MARK UP - Meeting of members of a congressional committee and staff to markup a bill, such as an appropriation bill, before it is presented to the whole House or Senate.

SUBSIDY - Payment or charge below market value designed to support the conduct of an economic enterprise or activity, such as ship operations. They also include loans, goods, and services to the public at prices lower than market value, such as interest subsidies. Under credit reform accounting, the subsidy is the present value of unreimbursed outlays by Federal direct and guaranteed loan programs. Subsidy cost became the budget authority measure for loans beginning in FY 1992.

SUBSTANTIVE LAW - Public law other than an appropriation act. Substantive law usually authorizes, in general terms, the Executive Branch to carry out a program of work. For entitlement programs, the substantive law usually provides direct spending authority. For other programs, annual determination of the amount of work to be done is usually embodied in an appropriation act.

SUPER MAJORITY - Sixty Senate votes required to override a breach of the discretionary spending cap or certain points of order defined in the Budget Enforcement Act.

SUPPLEMENTALS - New appropriations enacted after an annual appropriations bill has been enacted when the need for funds is too urgent to be postponed until the next regular annual appropriations act. Under the current Budget Enforcement Act, supplemental funding is possible only if: (1) the cap for that category of funding has not been exceeded; (2) an offset is included in the supplemental; or (3) the President and Congress agree that the supplemental is an emergency and therefore not subject to the cap.

SURPLUS - Amount by which receipts exceed outlays.

TAX EXPENDITURES - Subsidy in the form of a tax law that allows an exclusion, exemption or deduction from gross income or provides a credit or deferral of tax liability with the result that the Federal Government forgoes revenue that would have otherwise accrued to it.

10-YEAR TREASURY NOTE - An interest-bearing note issued by the U.S. Treasury that is to be redeemed in 10 years.

THREE-MONTH TREASURY BILL - An interest-bearing security issued by the U.S. Treasury that is to be redeemed in 91 days.

TRADE-WEIGHTED VALUE OF THE DOLLAR - The value of the U.S. dollar relative to the currencies of U.S. trading partners, with the weight of each country's currency equal to that country's share of U.S. trade.

TRANSFER BETWEEN APPROPRIATION/FUND ACCOUNTS - Transaction that, pursuant to law, withdraws budget authority or balances from one appropriation account and transfers the balance for credit to another appropriations account. Payments to other accounts for goods or services are not transfers but are outlay (expenditure) transactions.

TRANSFER PAYMENTS - Payments made by the Federal Government or business firms to individuals or organizations for which no current or future goods or services are required to be provided in return. Government transfer payments include Social Security benefits, unemployment insurance benefits, retirement and veterans' benefits, and welfare payments. Transfer payments by business firms consist mainly of gifts to nonprofit institutions.

TRANSFER OF FUNDS - Transfer of budget authority in one account to another account as authorized in law.

TREASURY APPROPRIATIONS FUND SYMBOL - The separate Treasury account for each appropriation title consisting of the Federal account symbol and an availability code (e.g., annual, multi-year, or no-year).

TREASURY FINANCIAL MANUAL - The Treasury Financial Manual (TFM) is Treasury's official publication for financial accounting and reporting of all receipts and disbursements of the Federal Government. It provides procedures for the agencies to account for and reconcile transactions occurring within and between each other.

TRUST FUNDS - Accounts, designated by law as trust funds, for receipts earmarked for specific purposes and the associated expenditure of those receipts.

TRUST FUNDS GROUP - The moneys collected and spent by the Government through trust fund accounts.

TREASURY SECURITY – A debt instrument of the Treasury used to finance operations of the Federal Government. Treasury securities fall into three categories depending on the length of their maturity term:

- Treasury bills mature within one year of issue.
- Treasury notes mature in more than one year but less than ten years.
- Treasury bonds mature in ten years or more.

UNDISTRIBUTED OFFSETTING RECEIPTS - Receipts that are deducted from government-wide totals for budget authority and outlays. An example is the collection of rents and royalties on the Outer Continental Shelf lands. Undistributed offsetting receipts are included as a separate category in the Functional Classification.

UNEMPLOYMENT RATE - The number of jobless people who are available for work and are actively seeking jobs, expressed as a percentage of the labor force.

UNEXPENDED BALANCE - The sum of unobligated and obligated balances.

UNFUNDED FEDERAL MANDATES - Provision in legislation, statute, or regulation that would impose an enforceable duty on state, local, or tribal government, or the private sector, except as a condition for participation in a voluntary Federal program. Exceptions are for enforcing constitutional rights, statutory provisions against discrimination, emergency assistance requested by states, accounting or auditing for Federal assistance, national security, presidentially designated emergencies, and Social Security.

UNIFIED BUDGET - Present form of the Budget of the Federal Government that began with the 1969 Budget, in which receipts and outlays from Federal funds and trust funds are consolidated. When these fund groups are consolidated to display budget totals, transactions that are outlays of one fund group for payment to the other fund group (i.e., intra-governmental transactions) are deducted to avoid double counting. By law, budget authority and outlays of off-budget entities are excluded from certain estimates in the President's Budget and the Concurrent Resolution on the Budget. Data relating to off-budget entities are displayed in the budget documents.

UNILATERAL TRANSFERS - Payments from sources within the United States to sources abroad (and vice versa) that are not made in exchange for goods or services.

UNOBLIGATED BALANCES - Budget authority that has not yet been obligated.

USER FEES - Fees, charges, and assessments levied on the people or organizations directly benefiting from or subject to regulation by government programs or activities that are used solely to support the program or activity.

VETO - Presidential disapproval of an enrolled bill.

WARRANTS - Documents issued by the Secretary of the Treasury that establish the amount of money authorized to be withdrawn from the Treasury.

YIELD - The average annual rate of return on a security, including interest payments and repayment of principal, if it is held to maturity.

YIELD CURVE - The relationship formed by plotting the yields of otherwise comparable fixed-income securities against their terms to maturity.

Chapter 18

Key Budget and Financial Management Documents

This chapter provides a compendium of documents relevant to budget formulation, congressional action, budget execution, and program evaluation, as follows:

- Table 18-1 lists the guidance and budget documents concerning formulation of the President's Budget;
- Table 18-2 lists the documents pertaining to Congressional Budget Processes;
- Table 18-3 lists the guidance and reporting documents involved in budget execution; and,
- Table 18-4 lists the guidance and reporting documents related to evaluation of results.

Table 18-1
Formulation of the President's Budget

Document	Issued by	Recipient	Purpose	Availability
			Guidance documents	
Spring Planning Guidance	OMB	Departments	• Provides policy guidance for the agency's budget request – Absent new guidance, outyear estimates included in the previous Budget serve as a starting point for the next Budget	Not publicly available
Circular No. A-11 Preparation, Submission, and Execution of the Budget	OMB	Departments and agencies	Provides detailed instructions for submitting budget data and materials	http://www.whitehouse.gov/omb/circulars/a11/current_year/a11_toc.html
Strategic Plan	Departments and agencies	Congress and the public	• States missions, goals, and objectives • Updates required every three years	Department/agency web sites
			Budget documents	
Budget Request	Departments and agencies	OMB	Provides request by Departments and agencies for resources in new fiscal year	Not publicly available
Issue papers	OMB	OMB Director	Analyzes requests and proposes alternatives	Not publicly available
Passback	OMB	Departments and agencies	Provides OMB decisions on what is to be included in the Budget -Late November	Not publicly available
Appeal letter	Departments and agencies	OMB	Requests reconsideration of OMB passback decisions	Not publicly available
President's Budget	OMB	Congress	Provides details of President's Budget request	http://www.whitehouse.gov/omb/
• Budget of the United States Government	OMB	Congress	Contains the Budget Message of the President, budget and management priorities, and budget overviews by agency	http://www.whitehouse.gov/omb/
• Analytical Perspectives	OMB	Congress	Contains analyses on specified subject areas and presentations of budget data to place the budget in perspective	http://www.whitehouse.gov/omb/
• Historical Tables	OMB	Congress	Provides data on receipts, outlays, surpluses or deficits, Federal debt, and Federal employment over an extended time period	http://www.whitehouse.gov/omb/
• Appendix	OMB	Congress	Contains detailed information on appropriations and funds in the budget and is designed for the Appropriations Committees	http://www.whitehouse.gov/omb/
Congressional Budget Justification	Departments and agencies	Congress	Provides details on each requested program	Department and agency web sites
Treasury Blue Book	Treasury	Congress	Provides details on revenue proposals in Budget	http://www.treasury.gov/offices/tax-policy/

Table 18-2
Congressional Budget Processes

Document	Issued by	Recipient	Purpose	Availability
Economic and Budget Outlook	CBO	Budget Committees	• Includes estimates of spending and revenue levels for the next 10 years under current law • Includes budget baseline that serves as a benchmark for Congress to measure the budgetary effect of proposed legislation	http://www.cbo.gov/.
Analysis of President's Budget Proposals	CBO	Budget Committees	• Provides an independent re-estimate of the President's budget proposals about one month after the President submits his budget • Permits the Congress to compare the President's proposals to other proposals using a consistent set of economic and technical assumptions	http://www.cbo.gov/.
Budget Options	CBO	Congress	• Discusses spending and tax options and discussion for or against it. • Produced in February or March of odd-numbered years to coincide with the beginning of a new Congress	http://www.cbo.gov/.
Unauthorized Appropriations and Expiring Authorizations	CBO	Congress	• Assists Congress in adopting authorizing legislation that should be in place before it considers the regular appropriation • Shows the amount that Congress has provided in appropriation acts for programs whose authorization has expired	http://www.cbo.gov/.
Cost Estimates	CBO	Budget Committees and the Congress	• Provides estimate of how individual legislative proposals would change spending or revenue levels under current law to determine whether those budget effects are consistent with targets in budget resolution (for proposals that would amend the Internal Revenue Code, CBO is required to use estimates provided by the Joint Committee on Taxation.)	http://www.cbo.gov/.
"Views and Estimates"	Authorizing Committees	Budget Committees	Indicates committee preferences regarding budgetary matters for which they are responsible. To be provided within 6 weeks of budget transmittal	Not publicly available
House Budget Resolution	House	Senate	House proposed budget plan	http://www.budget.house.gov/
Senate Budget Resolution	Senate	House	Senate proposed budget plan	http://www.budget.senate.gov/

Table 18-2, Continued
Congressional Budget Processes

Document	Issued by	Recipient	Purpose	Availability
Congressional Budget Resolution	Congress	Congressional Committees	• Provides blueprint for Congressional action on budgetary issues Including 302(a) allocations to Committees • To be issued by April 15th	http://thomas.loc.gov/home/approp/app10.html
Mid-Session Review, Budget of the United States Government	OMB	Congress	Contains revised budget estimates resulting from changes in economic assumptions, technical reestimates, Presidential initiatives, and completed congressional actions that have occurred since transmittal of the budget	http://www.whitehouse.gov/omb/
The Budget and Economic Outlook: An Update	CBO	Congress	Updates baseline projections, incorporating a new economic forecast and the effects of laws that have been enacted to date in that session of Congress	http://www.cbo.gov/
302(b)	Appropriations Committees	Budget Committees	Provides allocation of 302(a) by appropriation subcommittee	Appropriations Committees
Statement of Administration Policy (SAP)	OMB	House or Senate	Provides Administration views on proposed legislation	http://www.whitehouse.gov/omb
Appeal letters	Departments and Agencies	House or Senate	Provides Department and agency views on proposed legislation	Not publicly available
Rules Committee Resolution	House Rules Committee	House	Specifies rules for House floor debate on bill	http://www.rules.house.gov/
Proposed House Bill	House Appropriations Committee	House	Bill adopted by House Appropriations Committee and sent to House for floor action	http://thomas.loc.gov/home/approp/app10.html
Engrossed Bill as Agreed to or Passed by House	House	Senate	Bill passed by House	http://thomas.loc.gov/home/approp/app10.html
Proposed Senate Amendment to House Bill	Senate Appropriations Committee	Senate	Bill adopted by Senate Appropriations Committee and sent to Senate for floor action	http://thomas.loc.gov/home/approp/app10.html

Table 18-2, Continued
Congressional Budget Processes

Document	Issued by	Recipient	Purpose	Availability
Engrossed Amendment as Agreed to by Senate	Senate	House	Senate amended version of House bill	http://thomas.loc.gov/home/approp/app10.html
Conference Report	House and Senate Conferees	House and Senate	Agreement between House and Senate conferees on bill	http://thomas.loc.gov/home/approp/app10.html
Statement of the Managers	House and Senate Conferees	House and Senate	Explains conference report	http://thomas.loc.gov/home/approp/app10.html
Enrolled Bill	House and Senate	President	Bill passed by House and Senate and sent to the President for signature	http://thomas.loc.gov/home/approp/app10.html
Continuing Resolution	House and Senate	President	Provides appropriations for a specified period when regular appropriations bills have not been passed	http://thomas.loc.gov/home/approp/app10.html
Enrolled bill Memo	OMB	President	Provides a summary of the bill and agency comments	Not publicly available
Public Law	President	Public	Bill signed by President	http://thomas.loc.gov/bss/d111/d111laws.html
Signing Statement	President	Public, Congress, Departments	Issued by White House to explain action taken by President on bill including any constitutional concerns	http://www.whitehouse.gov
Veto Message	President	Congress	Message vetoes Congressionally pass of legislation and provides explanation for veto	http://www.whitehouse.gov

Table 18-3
Budget Execution

Document	Issued by	Recipient	Purpose	Availability
			Guidance Documents	
Circular No. A–11 Preparation, submission, and execution of the Budget, Part 4. Instructions on Budget Execution	OMB	Departments and agencies	Provides detailed instructions for budget execution	http://www.whitehouse.gov/omb/circulars/
Treasury Financial Manual (TFM)	Treasury	Departments and Agencies	Provides policies, procedures, and instructions for departments and agencies, Federal Reserve Banks, and other concerned parties in carrying out their fiscal responsibilities	http://fms.treas.gov/tfm/
FAST Book Federal Account Symbols and Titles	Treasury	Departments and Agencies	Supplements Treasury Financial Manual and lists receipt, appropriation, and other fund account symbols and titles assigned by the Department of the Treasury	http://fms.treas.gov/fastbook/index.html
Red Book: Principles of Federal Appropriations Law	GAO	Departments and Agencies	Provide reference work covering areas of law in which the Comptroller General renders decisions	http://www.gao.gov/special.pubs/redbook/.html
			Budget Execution documents	
Warrant	Secretary of the Treasury	Departments and agencies	Establishes the amount of appropriations approved by Congress that can be obligated and disbursed	Not publicly available
SF 132, Apportionment and Reapportionment Schedule	Departments and Agencies	OMB	Requests apportionment of available resources and shows approval by OMB	Not publicly available
Allotment	Department	Bureau	Subdivides apportionment allotments to bureaus and offices	
Rescission Special Message	OMB	Congress, Comptroller General	Provides details of proposed rescission	Not publicly available

Table 18-3, Continued
Budget Execution

Document	Issued by	Recipient	Purpose	Availability
Deferral	OMB	Congress, Comptroller General	Provides details of funds deferred for obligation	Not publicly available
SF 133 Reports on Budget Execution and Budgetary Resources	Departments and Agencies	OMB and House Appropriations Committee	Allows the monitoring of the status of funds that were apportioned on the SF 132 Apportionment and Reapportionment Schedule and funds that were not apportioned	Not publicly available
Anti-deficiency Letter	Departments and Agencies	President, presiding officer of each House of Congress and the Comptroller General	Report on a violations of the Anti-deficiency Act	Not publicly available
Daily Treasury Statement	Treasury	Congress, agencies, public	Summarizes the Treasury's cash and debt operations for the Federal Government on a modified cash basis	http://www.fms.treas.gov/dts/
Monthly Treasury Statement	Treasury	Congress, agencies, public	Summarizes the financial activities of the Federal Government and off-budget Federal entities	http://www.fms.treas.gov/mts/index.html
Combined Statement of Receipts, Outlays, and Balances	Treasury	Congress, agencies, public	Contains receipts and outlays with which all other reports containing similar data must be in agreement	http://www.fms.treas.gov/annualreport/
Financial Report of the United States Government	Treasury	Congress, public	Provides status of financial condition of the Government at end of fiscal year	http://www.fms.treas.gov/fr/index.html
Performance and Accountability Reports	Departments and Agencies	Congress, public	Provides information on funds and program performance for a fiscal year	Department and agency web sites

Table 18-4
Evaluation of Results

Document	Issued by	Recipient	Purpose	Availability
Guidance				
The Yellow Book: Government Auditing Standards, July 2007 Revision (GAO-07-731G)	GAO	Department and Agencies	Provides auditing standards	http://www.gao.gov/govaud/ybk01.htm
GAO/PCIE Financial Audit Manual (FAM)	GAO		Presents a methodology to perform financial statement audits of federal entities in accordance with professional standards	http://www.gao.gov/special.pubs/gaopcie/
M-10-01, Increased Emphasis on Program Evaluations (October 7, 2009)	OMB	Department and Agencies	Provides guidance on program evaluation	http://www.whitehouse.gov/omb/assets/memoranda_2010/m10-01.pdf
Reports				
Analytic Studies	CBO	Congress	• Analyzes policy and program issues related to the budget to explore significant budgetary and economic issues in greater depth • Undertaken at request of the Chairman or Ranking Minority, Member of the relevant committee or subcommittee, the Congressional leadership, or, as time permits, individual Members	http://www.cbo.gov/publications/
Reports and Testimonies	GAO	Congress	Reports on studies of agency plans and operations	http://www.gao.gov/docsearch/repandtest.html
Inspector General Reports	Department and Agency IGs	Department and Agency heads	Reports on audits of agency operations	Department and agency IG web sites
Program Assessment Rating Tool (PART)	OMB		• Assesses program performance • Identifies program's strengths and weaknesses to inform funding and management decisions aimed at making the program more effective	http://www.whitehouse.gov/omb/performance/
Federal Financial Management Report	OMB	Congress, Departments	Provides report on progress in improving financial management and a five-year improvement plan	http://www.whitehouse.gov/omb/assets/about_omb/2009_fin.pdf
CRS Studies	CRS	Members of Congress	Provides analyses on specific issues requested by Members of Congress. Studies are held in confidence.	Not generally available

Chapter 19

Directory of Budget Officials

This chapter provides contact information[1] for key stakeholders in the Federal budget process, including:

- Principal people in the department or agency responsible for Budget development; and
- Key staff people in the:

  - Office of Management and Budget (OMB)
  - Congressional Budget Office (CBO)
  - Government Accountability Office (GAO), and
  - Appropriations Subcommittees that handle budget and appropriations issues concerning that department or agency.

The information is organized to include Executive Branch budget stakeholders at the departmental level (e.g., Secretary's Office of Budget), stepping down to selected sub-departmental levels. Each department and agency has a key stakeholder who is responsible for the formulation and execution of the budget.

Appropriations Committees

Each of the House and Senate Appropriations Committees and Subcommittees have a majority and a minority staff headed by a clerk that examines the Administration's Budget proposals from the perspectives of the majority and minority parties. Full committee stakeholders are listed below; subcommittee information is provided by department/agency.

Members of the Committee ultimately recommend an appropriation level and direct the priorities of the department/agencies under their jurisdiction (e.g., House Committee on Appropriations and the House Appropriations Subcommittee on Interior, Environment, and Related Agencies; Senate Appropriations Committee and Senate Appropriations Subcommittee on Interior).

Detailed below are the Congressional stakeholders in the budget process. The individuals are involved in the formulation process as a whole, regardless of which Federal Agency or Department is involved.

CONGRESSIONAL BUDGET STAKEHOLDERS

House Appropriations Committee
Majority Staff Director
Beverly Pheto...........................202-225-2771
Minority Staff Director
Jeffrey Shockey...........................202-225-3481
Senate Appropriations Committee
Majority Staff Director
Charles Houy...........................202-224-7363
Minority Staff Director
Bruce Evans...........................202-224-7257

Shown below is a detailed listing of the various Appropriations Subcommittee stakeholders in the budget process. Each Appropriations Subcommittee is tasked with oversight of the various Federal agencies and departments

AGRICULTURE BUDGET STAKEHOLDERS

House Subcommittee on Agriculture, Rural Development, FDA, and Related Agencies
Majority Clerk
Martha Foley........................202-225-3638
Minority Staff Assistant
David Gibbons........................202-225-3481
Senate Subcommittee on Agriculture, Rural Development, FDA, and Related Agencies
Majority Clerk
Galen Fountain........................202-224-8090
Minority Clerk
Fitz Elder........................202-224-5270

COMMERCE BUDGET STAKEHOLDERS

House Subcommittee on Commerce, Justice, Science, and Related Agencies
Majority Clerk
John Blazey........................202-225-3351

Minority Staff Assistant
Mike Ringler....................202-225-3481
Senate Subcommittee on Commerce, Justice, Science, and Related Agencies
Majority Clerk
Gabrielle Batkin.....................202-224-5202
Minority Clerk
Arthur Cameron................202-224-7277

COMMISSION ON CIVIL RIGHTS BUDGET STAKEHOLDERS
House Subcommittee on Commerce, Justice, Science, and Related Agencies
Majority Clerk
John Blazey....................202-225-3351
Minority Clerk
Mike Ringeler....................202-225-3481
Senate Subcommittee on Commerce, Justice, Science, and Related Agencies
Majority Clerk
Gabrielle Batkin.....................202-224-5202
Minority Clerk
Arthur Cameron................202-224-7277

DEFENSE BUDGET STAKEHOLDERS
House Subcommittee on Defense
Majority Clerk
Paul Juola.....................202-225-2847
Minority Staff Assistant
Tom McLemore 202-225-3481
Senate Subcommittee on Defense
Majority Clerk
Charles J. Houy................202-224-7363
Minority Clerk
Stuart Holmes 202-224-7255

EDUCATION BUDGET STAKEHOLDERS
House Subcommittee on Labor, HHS, Education and Related Agencies
Majority Clerk
David Reich.....................202-225-3508
Minority Staff Assistant
Steve Crane.....................202-225-3481
Senate Subcommittee on Labor, HHS, Education, and Related Agencies
Majority Clerk
Erik Fateni....................202-224-9145
Minority Clerk
Bettilou Taylor..................202-224-7230

ENERGY BUDGET STAKEHOLDERS

House Subcommittee on Energy and Water Development
Majority Clerk
Taunja Berquam................202-225-3421
Minority Clerk
Rob Blair.......................202-225-3481
Senate Subcommittee on Energy and Water Development
Majority Clerk
Douglas Clapp...................202-224-8119
Minority Clerk
Carrie Apostolou.......…………202-224-7260

EPA BUDGET STAKEHOLDERS

House Subcommittee on Interior, Environment, and Related Agencies
Majority Clerk
Delia Scott...........…..…………202-225-3081
Minority Deputy Director
Dave LesStrang.....................202-225-3481
Senate Subcommittee on Interior, Environment, and Related Agencies
Majority Clerk
Peter Keifhaber.....................202-224-3542
Minority Clerk
Leif Fonnesbeck.....................202-224-7233

EQUAL EMPLOYMENT OPPORTUNITY COMMISSION BUDGET STAKEHOLDERS

House Subcommittee on Commerce, Justice, Science, and Related Agencies
Majority Clerk
John Blazey.......................202-225-3351
Minority Clerk
Mike Ringler.......................202-225-3481
Senate Subcommittee on Commerce, Justice, Science, and Related Agencies
Majority Clerk
Gabrielle Batkin.......................202-224-4654
Minority Clerk
Arthur Cameron.......................202-224-7277

EXPORT-IMPORT BANK BUDGET STAKEHOLDERS

House Subcommittee on State, Foreign Operations, and Related Programs
Majority Clerk
Nisha Desai Biswal.................202-225-2041
Minority Staff Assistant
Anne Marie Chotvacs..............202-225-3481

Senate Subcommittee on Commerce, Justice, Science, and Related Agencies
 Majority Clerk
   Gabrielle Batkin.......................202-224-4654
 Minority Clerk
   Arthur Cameron...................................202-224-7277

FEDERAL COMMUNICATIONS COMMISSION BUDGET STAKE-HOLDERS

 House Subcommittee on Commerce, Justice, Science, and Related Agencies
 Majority Clerk
   John Blazey....................................202-225-3351
 Minority Clerk
   Mike Ringler...............................202-225-3481
 Senate Subcommittee on Commerce, Justice, Science, and Related Agencies
 Majority Clerk
   Gabrielle Batkin.............................202-224-4654
 Minority Clerk
   Arthur Cameron...202-224-7277

FEDERAL ELECTIONS COMMISSION BUDGET STAKEHOLDERS

 House Subcommittee on Commerce, Justice, Science, and Related Agencies
 Majority Clerk
   John Blazey....................................202-225-3351
 Minority Clerk
   Mike Ringler................................202-225-3481
 Senate Subcommittee on Transportation, Housing and Urban Development and Related Agencies
 Majority Clerk
   Alex Keenan.................................202-224-7281
 Minority Clerk
   Jon Kamarck................................202-224-5310

FEDERAL RESERVE SYSTEM BUDGET STAKEHOLDERS

 House Subcommittee on Transportation, Housing and Urban Development, and Related Agencies
 Majority Clerk
   Kate Hallahan...............................202-225-2141
 Minority Staff Assistant
   Dena Baron.............................202-225-3481
 Senate Subcommittee on Transportation, Housing and Urban Development and Related Agencies
 Majority Clerk
   Alex Keenan...................................202-224-7281
 Minority Clerk
   Jon Kamarck...................................202-224-5310

FEDERAL TRADE COMMISSION BUDGET STAKEHOLDERS
House Subcommittee on State, Foreign Operations, and Related Programs
Majority Clerk
Nisha Desai Biswal...........................202-225-2041
Minority Staff Assistant
Anne Marie Chotvacs.....................202-225-3481
Senate Subcommittee on Commerce, Justice, Science, and Related Agencies
Majority Clerk
Gabrielle Batkin.......................202-224-4654
Minority Clerk
Arthur Cameron.....................202-224-7277

GENERAL SERVICES ADMINISTRATION BUDGET STAKEHOLDERS
House Subcommittee on Transportation, Housing and Urban Development, and Related Agencies
Majority Clerk
Kate Hallahan.......................202-225-2141
Minority Clerk
Dena Baron........................202-225-3481
Senate Subcommittee on Transportation, Housing and Urban Development and Related Agencies
Majority Clerk
Alex Keenan........................202-224-7281
Minority Clerk
Jon Kamarck.......................202-224-5310

HEALTH & HUMAN SERVICE BUDGET STAKEHOLDERS
House Subcommittee on Labor, HHS, Education, and Related Agencies
Majority Clerk
David Reich.......................202-225-3508
Minority Staff Assistant
Steve Crane.......................202-225-3481
Senate Subcommittee on Labor, HHS, Education, and Related Agencies
Majority Clerk
Erik Fateni.......................202-224-9145
Minority Clerk
Bettilou Taylor.......................202-224-7230

HOMELAND SECURITY BUDGET STAKEHOLDERS
House Subcommittee on Homeland Security
Majority Clerk
Stephanie Gupta.......................202-225-5834
Minority Clerk
Ben Nicholson.......................202-225-3481

Senate Subcommittee on Homeland Security
Majority Clerk
Charles E. Kieffer.............................202-224-8244
Minority Clerk
Rebecca Davies....................................202-224-4319

HOUSING & URBAN DEVELOPMENT BUDGET STAKEHOLDERS

House Subcommittee on Transportation, Housing and Urban Development, and Related Agencies
Majority Clerk
Kate Hallahan.....................................202-225-2141
Minority Clerk
Dena Baron...202-225-3481
Senate Subcommittee on Transportation, Housing and Urban Development and Related Agencies
Majority Clerk
Alex Keenan.......................................202-224-7281
Minority Clerk
Jon Kamarck.......................................202-224-5310

INTERIOR BUDGET STAKEHOLDERS

House Subcommittee on Interior, Environment, and Related Agencies
Majority Clerk
Delia Scott.......................................202-225-3081
Minority Deputy Director
Dave LesStrang....................................202-225-3481
Senate Subcommittee on Interior, Environment, and Related Agencies
Majority Clerk
Peter Keifhaber...................................202-224-3542
Minority Clerk
Leif Fonnesbeck...................................202-224-7233

JUSTICE BUDGET STAKEHOLDERS

House Subcommittee on Commerce, Justice, Science, and Related Agencies
Majority Clerk
John Blazey.......................................202-225-3351
Minority Clerk
Mike Ringler......................................202-225-3481
Senate Subcommittee on Commerce, Justice, Science, and Related Agencies
Majority Clerk
Gabrielle Batkin..................................202-224-4654
Minority Clerk
Arthur Cameron....................................202-224-7277

LABOR BUDGET STAKEHOLDERS

House Subcommittee on the Department of Labor, HHS, Education, and Related Agencies

Majority Clerk

David Reich......................................202-225-3508

Minority Staff Assistant

Steve Crane.....................................202-225-3481

Senate Subcommittee on Labor, HHS, Education, and Related Agencies

Majority Clerk

Erik Fateni......................................202-224-9145

Minority Clerk

Bettilou Taylor...................................202-224-7230

NASA BUDGET STAKEHOLDERS

House Subcommittee on Commerce, Justice, Science, and Related Agencies

Majority Clerk

John Blazey......................................202-225-3351

Minority Clerk

Mike Ringler.....................................202-225-3481

Senate Subcommittee on Commerce, Justice, Science, and Related Agencies

Majority Clerk

Gabrielle Batkin...................................202-224-4654

Minority Clerk

Arthur Cameron..................................202-224-7277

NATIONAL TRANSPORTATION SAFETY BOARD BUDGET STAKE-HOLDERS

House Subcommittee on Transportation, Housing and Urban Development, and Related Agencies

Majority Clerk

Kate Hallahan....................................202-225-2141

Minority Clerk

Dena Baron......................................202-225-3481

Senate Subcommittee on Transportation, Housing and Urban Development and Related Agencies

Majority Clerk

Alex Keenan......................................202-224-7281

Minority Clerk

Jon Kamarck.....................................202-224-5310

NUCLEAR REGULATORY COMMISSION BUDGET STAKEHOLDERS

House Subcommittee on Energy and Water Development

Majority Clerk

Taunja Berquam...................................202-225-3421

Minority Clerk

Rob Blair..202-225-3481

Senate Subcommittee on Energy and Water Development
    Majority Clerk
            Douglas Clapp...202-224-8119
    Minority Clerk Professional Staff Member
            Carrie Apostolou..202-224-0335

OFFICE OF PERSONNEL MANAGEMENT BUDGET STAKEHOLDERS
    House Subcommittee on Transportation, Housing and Urban Development, and Related Agencies
        Majority Clerk
                Kate Hallahan.................................202-225-2141
        Minority Clerk
                Dena Baron....................................202-225-3481
    Senate Subcommittee on Transportation, Housing and Urban Development and Related Agencies
        Majority Clerk
                Alex Keenan...................................202-224-7281
        Minority Clerk
                Jon Kamarck..................................202-224-5310

POSTAL SERVICE BUDGET STAKEHOLDERS
    House Subcommittee on Transportation, Housing and Urban Development, and Related Agencies
        Majority Clerk
                Kate Hallahan.................................202-225-2141
        Minority Clerk
                Dena Baron....................................202-225-3481
    Senate Subcommittee on Transportation, Housing and Urban Development and Related Agencies
        Majority Clerk
                Alex Keenan...................................202-224-7281
        Minority Clerk
                Jon Kamarck..................................202-224-5310

SECURITIES EXCHANGE COMMISSION BUDGET STAKEHOLDERS
    House Subcommittee on Commerce, Justice, Science, and Related Agencies
        Majority Clerk
                John Blazey...................................202-225-3351
        Minority Clerk
                Mike Ringler..................................202-225-3481
    Senate Subcommittee on Transportation, Housing and Urban Development and Related Agencies
        Majority Clerk
                Alex Keenan...................................202-224-7281
        Minority Clerk
                Jon Kamarck..................................202-224-5310

SMALL BUSINESS ADMINISTRATION BUDGET STAKEHOLDERS
House Subcommittee on Commerce, Justice, Science, and Related Agencies
Majority Clerk

John Blazey...................................202-225-3351

Minority Clerk

Mike Ringler..................................202-225-3481

Senate Subcommittee on Commerce, Justice, Science, and Related Agencies
Majority Clerk

Gabrielle Batkin.............................202-224-4654

Minority Clerk

Arthur Cameron............................202-224-7277

SOCIAL SECURITY ADMINISTRATION BUDGET STAKEHOLDERS
House Subcommittee on Labor, HHS, Education, and Related Agencies
Majority Clerk

David Reich...................................202-225-3508

Minority Staff Assistant

Steve Crane...................................202-225-3481

Senate Subcommittee on Labor, HHS, and Education, and Related Agencies
Majority Clerk

Erik Fateni....................................202-224-9145

Minority Clerk

Bettilou Taylor................................202-224-7230

STATE BUDGET STAKEHOLDERS
House Subcommittee on Commerce, Justice, Science, and Related Agencies
Majority Clerk

John Blazey...................................202-225-3351

Minority Clerk

Mike Ringler..................................202-225-3481

Senate Subcommittee on State, Foreign Operations, and Related Programs
Majority Clerk

Tim Rieser....................................202-224-4242

Minority Clerk

Paul Grove....................................202-224-2104

TRANSPORTATION BUDGET STAKEHOLDERS
House Subcommittee on Transportation, Housing and Urban Development, and Related Agencies
Majority Clerk

Kate Hallahan.................................202-225-2141

Minority Clerk

Dena Baron 202-225-3481

Senate Subcommittee on Transportation, Housing and Urban Development and Related Agencies
- **Majority Clerk**
  - Alex Keenan....…..................................202-224-7281
- **Minority Clerk**
  - Jon Kamarck…..............….............…....202-224-5310

TREASURY BUDGET STAKEHOLDERS

House Subcommittee on Transportation, Housing and Urban Development, and Related Agencies
- **Majority Clerk**
  - Kate Hallahan…...............…...............…202-225-2141
- **Minority Clerk**
  - Dena Baron...........….............…...........202-225-3481

Senate Subcommittee on Transportation, Housing and Urban Development and Related Agencies
- **Majority Clerk**
  - Alex Keenan…...............….................…202-224-7281
- **Minority Clerk**
  - Jon Kamarck…...............…...............…...202-224-5310

USAID BUDGET STAKEHOLDERS

House Subcommittee on State, Foreign Operations, and Related Programs
- **Majority Clerk**
  - Nisha Desai Biswal…...........................202-225-2041
- **Minority Staff Assistant**
  - Anne Marie Chotvacs…................…......202-225-3481

Senate Subcommittee on Transportation, Housing and Urban Development and Related Agencies
- **Majority Clerk**
  - Alex Keenan…......…......................................202-224-7284
- **Minority Clerk**
  - Jon Kamarck…......…......................................….202-224-2104

VETERANS AFFAIRS BUDGET STAKEHOLDERS

House Subcommittee on Military Construction, Veterans Affairs, and Related Agencies
- **Majority Clerk**
  - Tim Peterson (Acting)….........…...........….202-225-3047
- **Minority Clerk**
  - Martin Delgado…....…...............…......….202-225-3481

Senate Subcommittee on Military Construction and Veterans' Affairs, and Related Agencies
- **Majority Clerk**
  - Christina Evans…..............….............…......202-224-8224
- **Minority Clerk**
  - Dennis Balkham…...............................…202-224-5245

Office of Management and Budget

The White House Office of Management and Budget (OMB) maintains an ongoing presence throughout the budget formulation process. Each individual Federal agency or department is overseen by one of the five our Resource Management Offices:

- General Government Programs,
- Health Programs,
- Education, Income Maintenance, and Labor Programs,
- National Security Programs, and
- Natural Resources Programs.

Within each Resource Management Office there are budget divisions, organized by branches that focus on specific program areas. Branch budget examiners are responsible for the evaluation, formulation and coordination of the budget, management procedures, and program objectives affecting Federal agencies and departments (e.g., OMB's Natural Resources Division/ Interior Branch/ Fish & Wildlife Service Examiner).

OMB also has a management component that is focused on improving the management of Government programs. The Office of Information and Regulatory Affairs maintains a detailed presence in the regulatory process. A list of OMB offices and key non-career officials follows:

OFFICE OF MANAGEMENT AND BUDGET

Natural Resource Programs
Program Associate Director
Sally Ericsson...............................202-395-3120
Non-Career

General Government Programs
Program Associate Director
Xavier Briggs..............................202-395-1217
Non-Career

Health programs
Program Associate Director
Keith Fontenot....................202-395-5178
Non-Career

Education, Income Maintenance, and Labor Programs
Program Associate Director
Robert Gordon....................202-395-5178
Non-Career

National Security Program
 Program Associate Director
  Steve Kosiak........................202-395-4657
   Non-Career

OIRA

 Administrator
  Cass Suntien.........…....…... 202-395-4852
   Senate Confirmed

Departments and Agencies

Each Federal agency and department has budget officials who maintain a watchful eye regarding the budget formulation and execution process. Below is a listing of each Federal agency and department's budget officials and the OMB, CBO and GAO officials that review their programs and budgets.

AGRICULTURE BUDGET STAKEHOLDERS

 USDA

 Office of the CFO
  Chief Financial Officer
  Jon Holladay
   202-720-5539
    (Acting)

  Deputy Chief Financial Officer
  Jon Holladay
   202-720-5539
    Senate -Confirmation

  Budget Division Director
  Donald Bice
   202-720-1885
    Senate-Confirmed

 Office of Budget & Program Analysis
  Director
  W. Scott Steele
   202-720-3323
    Senate-Confirmed

<u>**OMB**</u>

Natural Resources Division
Agricultural Branch Chief
Adrienne Erbach-Lucas
202-395-3446
Career

<u>**CBO**</u>

Budget Analysis Division
Natural & Physical Resources Cost Estimates
Unit Chief
Kim Cawley
202-226-2860
Career

<u>**GAO**</u>

Natural Resources & Environment
Managing Director
Patricia Dalton
202-512-3841
Career

COMMERCE BUDGET STAKEHOLDERS

<u>**DEPARTMENT OF COMMERCE**</u>

Office of the Chief Financial Officer and Assistant Secretary for Administration
Chief Financial Officer and Assistant Secretary for Administration
Scott Quehl
202-482-4951
Career

Office of Financial Management
Deputy Chief Financial Officer and Director for Financial Management
Lisa Casias
202-482-1207
Career

Office of Budget
Director for Budget and Performance Improvement
Neil K. Shapiro
202-482-4648
Career

<u>**OMB**</u>

Housing, Treasury, and Commerce Division
Commerce Branch Chief
Randolph Lyon
202-395-5800
Career

CBO

State and Local Government Cost Estimates Unit
Unit Chief
Leo Lex
202-225-3220

GAO

Financial Management and Assurance Team
Managing Director
Jeanette Francel
202-512-2600
Career

COMMISSION ON CIVIL RIGHTS BUDGET STAKEHOLDERS

COMMISSION ON CIVIL RIGHTS

Office of Management
Budget Director
John Ratcliff
202-376-8364
Career

OMB

Transportation, Homeland, Justice & Services Division
Justice Branch Director
James Boden
202-395-7241
Career

CBO

Budget Analysis Division
    Natural & Physical Resources Cost Estimate
    Unit Chief
        Kim Cawley
            202-226-2860
                Career

GAO

Financial Management and Assurance Team
    Managing Director
        Jeanette Franzel
            202-512-2600
                Career

DEFENSE BUDGET STAKEHOLDERS

DOD

Office of the Under Secretary of Defense (Comptroller)
    Under Secretary (Comptroller) and CFO
        Robert Hale
            703-695-3237
                Senate-Confirmed

Program Budget Office
    Deputy Comptroller
        John Roth
            703-695-3950
                Career

Air Force

Financial Management & Comptroller
    Assistant Secretary and Comptroller
        Dr. Jamie Morin
            703-697-1974

Army

Financial Management & Comptroller
    Assistant Secretary and Comptroller
        Mary Matiella
            703-614-4356
                Senate-Confirmed

NAVY

Financial Management
Assistant Secretary and Comptroller
Gladys Commons
703-697-2325

Office of Budget
Deputy Assistant Secretary of the Navy for Budget
Rear Adm Joseph Mulloy
703-697-7105

Associate Director
Ed Cochrane
703-614-7105
Career

OMB

National Security Division
Deputy Associate Director
Kathleen Peroff
202-395-3884
Career

CBO

Budget Analysis Division
Defense, International Affairs & Veterans Affairs
Unit Chief
Sarah Jennings
202-226-2840
Career

GAO

Defense Capabilities & Management
Managing Director
Janet St. Laurent
202-512-4300
Career

ENERGY BUDGET STAKEHOLDERS

DEPARTMENT OF ENERGY

Office of Budget
  Director
      Neile Miller
          202-586-4180
              Career

FEDERAL ENERGY REGULATORY COMMISSION

Office of the Executive Director
  Deputy CFO
      Anton Porter
          202-502-8728
              Career

OMB

Energy, Science, and Water Division
  Energy Branch Chief
      Kevin Carroll
          202-395-1486
              Career

CBO

Budget Analysis Division
  Natural & Physical Resources Cost Estimate
  Unit Chief
      Kim Cawley
          202-226-2860
              Career

GAO

Natural Resources & Environment
  Managing Director
      Patricia Dalton
          202-512-3841
              Career

EDUCATION BUDGET STAKEHOLDERS

DEPARTMENT OF EDUCATION

Office of the Secretary
Chief Financial Officer (Acting)
Thomas Skelly
202-401-0085
Senate-Confirmed

Office of the CFO
Deputy CFO
Hugh Hurwitz
202-245-6555
Career

Budget Service
Director
Thomas P. Skelly
202-401-1700
Career

OMB

Education & Human Resources Division
Education Branch Chief
David Rowe
202-395-3846
Career

CBO

Budget Analysis Division
Natural & Physical Resources Cost Estimated
Unit Chief
Kim Cawley
202-226-2860
Career

GAO

Education, Workforce & Income Security
Managing Director
Barbara Bovbjerg
202-512-7215
Career

ENVIRONMENTAL PROTECTION AGENCY BUDGET STAKEHOLDERS

EPA

Office of the CFO
Chief Financial Officer
Barbara Bennett
202-564-1151
Senate-Confirmed

Office of the CFO
Deputy CFO
Maryann Froehlich
202-564-1152
Career

OMB

Natural Resources Division
Environment Branch Chief
Janet Irwin
202-395-6827
Career

CBO

Budget Analysis Division
Natural & Physical Resources Cost Estimate
Unit Chief
Kim Cawley
202-226-2860
Career

GAO

Natural Resources & Environment
Managing Director
Patricia Dalton
202-512-3841
Career

EQUAL EMPLOYMENT OPPORTUNITY COMMISSION BUDGET STAKEHOLDERS

EEOC

Office of the CFO
Chief Financial Officer
Jeffrey Smith
202-663-4200
Career

Office of the CFO
Planning and System Services Division
Director
Germaine Roseboro
202-663-4238
Career

OMB

Transportation, Homeland, Justice & Service Division
Transportation and GSA Branch Chief
Andrew Abrams
202-395-3823
Career

CBO

Budget Analysis Division
Natural & Physical Resources Cost Estimate
Unit Chief
Kim Cawley
202-226-2860
Career

GAO

Education, Workforce & Income Security
Managing Director
Cynthia M. Fagnoni
202-512-7215
Career

EXPORT-IMPORT BANK BUDGET STAKEHOLDERS

EXPORT-IMPORT BANK

Office of the CFO
Chief Financial Officer and Senior Vice President
John Simonson
202-565-3250
Career

OMB

International Affairs Division
Economic Affairs Branch Chief
Christa Cappazola
202-395-4595
Career

CBO

Budget Analysis Division
Natural & Physical Resources Cost Estimate
Unit Chief
Kim Cawley
202-226-2860
Career

GAO

International Affairs & Trade
Managing Director
Jacquelyn Williams-Bridgers
202-512-3101
Career

FEDERAL COMMUNICATIONS COMMISSION BUDGET STAKE-HOLDERS

FCC

Office of Financial Operations
Duputy CFO and Budget Center Chief
Kim Bassett
202-418-1953
Career

OMB

Transportation, Homeland, Justice & Services Division
    Transportation and GSA Branch Chief
        Andrew Abrams
            202-395-3823
            Career

CBO

Budget Analysis Division
    Natural & Physical Resources Cost Estimate
    Unit Chief
        Kim Cawley
            202-226-2860
            Career

GAO

Physical Infrastructure Team
    Managing Director
        Katherine Siggerud
            202-512-6570
            Career

FEDERAL ELECTIONS COMMISSION BUDGET STAKEHOLDERS

FEC

Office of the Staff Director
    Budget Planning and Management
    Director
        Richard Kodl
            202-694-1216
            Career

OMB

Transportation, Homeland, Justice & Services Division
    Transportation and GSA Branch
        Andrew Abrams
            202-395-3823
            Career

CBO

Budget Analysis Division
Projection Unit
Chief
Jeff Holland
202-226-2880
Career

GAO

Homeland Security and Justice Team
Managing Director
Cathleen Berrick
202-512-3404
Career

FEDERAL TRADE COMMISSION BUDGET STAKEHOLDERS

FEDERAL TRADE COMMISSION

Office of the Executive Director
Chief Financial Officer
Steven Fisher
202-326-2116
Career

Office of the Executive Director
Assistant Chief Financial Officer for Budget
James Baker
202-326-3168
Career

OMB

Housing, Treasury, and Commerce Division
Commerce Branch
Branch Chief
Randolph Lyon
202-395-5800
Career

CBO

Budget Analysis Division
    Projection Unit
    Chief
      Jeff Holland
        202-226-2880
        Career

GAO

Homeland Security and Justice
    Managing Director
      Kathleen Berrick
        202-512-3404
        Career

GENERAL SERVICES ADMINISTRATION BUDGET STAKEHOLDERS

GSA

Office of the CFO
    Chief Financial Officer (Acting)
      Micah Cheatham
        202-501-1721
        Career

    Deputy Chief Financial Officer
      Douglas Glenn
        202-501-0562
        Career
Budget Office
    Director
      Micah Cheatham
        202-501-0719
        Career

OMB

Transportation, Homeland, Justice & Service Division
    Transportation and GSA Branch Chief
      Andrew Abrams
        202-395-3823
        Career

GAO

Physical Infrastructure Team
Managing Director
Katherine Siggerud
202-512-6570
Career

HEALTH & HUMAN SERVICES BUDGET STAKEHOLDERS

HEALTH & HUMAN SERVICES

Office of the Assistant Secretary for Financial Resources
Assistant Secretary and CFO
Ellen G. Murray
202-690-6396
Senate-Confirmed

Office of Budget
Principal Deputy Assistant Secretary for Budget
Norris Cochran
202-690-7393
Career

Budget, Policy, Execution & Review Division
Director
Andy Baldus
202-690-6151
Career

OMB

Health Division
HHS Branch Chief
Phil Ellis
202-226-2666
Career

CBO

Budget Analysis Division
Natural & Physical Resources Cost Estimate
Unit Chief
Kim Cawley
202-226-2860
Career

GAO

Health Care
 Managing Director
  Majorie Kanof
   202-512-7114
    Career

HOMELAND SECURITY BUDGET STAKEHOLDERS

DHS

Office of the CFO
 Chief Financial Officer (Acting)
  Peggy Sherry
   202-447-5751
    Senate-Confirmed

OMB

Transportation, Homeland, Justice and Services Division
 Homeland Branch Chief
  Steve Mertens
   202-395-4935
    Career

CBO

Budget Analysis Division
 Natural & Physical Resources Cost Estimate
 Unit Chief
  Kim Cawley
   202-226-2860
    Career

GAO

Homeland Security and Justice Team
 Managing Director
  Cathleen Berrick
   202-512-3404
    Career

HOUSING & URBAN DEVELOPMENT BUDGET STAKEHOLDERS

HUD

Office of the CFO
Chief Financial Officer (Acting)
Douglas Criscitello
202-402-6399
Senate-Confirmed

Office of the Assistant CFO for Budget
Assistant Chief Financial Officer
Anthony Scardino
202-402-6801
Career

Program Budget Development Division
Director
Kenneth Leventhal
202-402-6849
Career

OMB

Housing, Treasury & Commerce Division
Housing Branch Chief
Michelle Enger
202-395-7874
Career

CBO

Budget Analysis Division
Natural & Physical Resources Cost Estimate
Unit Chief
Kim Cawley
202-226-2860
Career

GAO

Financial Markets and Community Investment Team
Managing Director
Richard Hillman
202-512-8678
Career

INTERIOR BUDGET STAKEHOLDERS

DEPARTMENT OF INTERIOR

Office of the Assistant Secretary
Assistant Secretary of Policy & Management and Budget/Chief Financial Officer
Rhea Suh
202-208-1927
Senate-Confirmed

Office of Financial Management
Director and Deputy CFO
Don Geiger
202-208-5225
Career

Office of Budget
Director
Denise Flanagan
202-208-5308
Career

OMB

Natural Resources Division
Interior Branch Chief
Craig Crutchfield
202-395-4806
Career

CBO

Budget Analysis Division
Natural & Physical Resources Cost Estimate
Unit Chief
Kim Cawley
202-226-2860
Career

GAO

Natural Resources and Environmental Team
Managing Director
Patricia Dalton
202-512-3841
Career

JUSTICE BUDGET STAKEHOLDERS

DEPARTMENT OF JUSTICE

Executive Offices for US Attorneys
Chief Financial Officer
Lisa Bevels
202-616-6886
Career

Office of Justice Programs
Chief Financial Officer
Larry Ferguson
202-307-2820
Career

Office of the Budget & Management Services
Budget Division Associate Chief Financial Officer
Ralph Martin
202-305-1802
Career

OMB

Transportation, Homeland, Justice & Services Division
Justice Branch Chief
James Boden
202-395-7241
Career

CBO

Budget Analysis Division
Natural & Physical Resources Cost Estimate
Unit Chief
Kim Cawley
202-226-2860
Career

GAO

Homeland Security & Justice Team
Managing Director
Cathleen Berrick
202-512-3404
Career

LABOR BUDGET STAKEHOLDERS

DEPARTMENT OF LABOR

Office of the CFO
Chief Financial Officer (Acting)
Daniel Lacey
202-693-6800
Senate-Confirmed

Office of the CFO
Deputy Chief Financial Officer
VACANT
202-693-6800
Career

OMB

Education & Human Resources Division
Labor Branch Chief
Melissa Benton Bomberger
202-395-7887
Career

CBO

Budget Analysis Division
Natural & Physical Resources Cost Estimate
Unit Chief
Kim Cawley
202-226-2860
Career

GAO

Education, Workforce & Income Security Team
Managing Director
Barbara Bovbjerg
202-512-7215
Career

NASA BUDGET STAKEHOLDERS

NASA

Office of the CFO
Chief Financial Officer
Elizabeth Robinson
202-358-0978
Senate-Confirmed

Office of the CFO
Deputy Chief Financial Officer
Terry Bowie
202-358-0978
Career

Office of the CFO
Comptroller
VACANT
202-358-4489
Career

OMB

Energy, Science and Water Division
Science and Space Branch Chief
Paul Shawcross
202-395-3807
Career

CBO

Budget Analysis Division
Natural & Physical Resources Cost Estimate
Unit Chief
Kim Cawley
202-226-2860
Career

GAO

Acquisition and Sourcing Management
Managing Director
Paul Francis
202-512-4841
Career

NUCLEAR REGULATORY COMMISSION BUDGET STAKEHOLDERS

NUCLEAR REGULATORY COMMISSION

Office of the CFO
Chief Financial Officer
James Dyer
301-415-7322
Career

Office of the CFO
Deputy Chief Financial Officer
Milton Brown
301-415-7501
Career

OMB

Energy , Science and Water Division
Energy Branch Chief
Kevin Carroll
202-395-1486
Career

CBO

Budget Analysis Division
Natural & Physical Resources Cost Estimate Unit Chief
Kim Cawley
202-226-2860
Career

GAO

Natural Resources & Environment
Managing Director
Patricia Dalton
202-512-3841
Career

OFFICE OF PERSONNEL MANAGEMENT BUDGET STAKEHOLDERS

OFFICE OF PERSONNEL MANAGEMENT

Office of the CFO
Chief Financial Officer
Mark Reger
202-606-1918
Career

Office of the CFO
Associate CFO
Daniel Marella
202-606-2638
Career

Office of the CFO
Budget Chief
Edward Callicott
202-606-1268
Career

OMB

Housing, Treasury & Commerce Division
Treasury Branch Chief
Lin Liu
202-395-3308
Career

CBO

Budget Analysis Division
Projection Unit Chief
Jeff Holland
202-226-2880
Career

GAO

Strategic Issues Team
Managing Director
J. Christopher Mihm
202-512-6806
Career

POSTAL SERVICE BUDGET STAKEHOLDERS

POSTAL SERVICE

Office of Finance
CFO/Executive Vice President
Joseph Corbett
202-268-5272
Non-Career

Budget & Finance Analysis Manager
Tony Mazzei
202-268-2967
Non-Career

OMB

Housing, Treasury & Commerce Division
Treasury Branch Chief
Lin Liu
202-395-3308
Career

CBO

Budget Analysis Division
Projection Unit Chief
Jeff Holland
202-226-2880
Career

GAO

Physical Infrastructure Team
Managing Director
Katherine Siggerud
202-512-6570
Career

SECURITIES & EXCHANGE COMMISSION BUDGET STAKEHOLD-ERS

SECURITIES & EXCHANGE COMMISSION

Office of Financial Management
  Assistant Director for Finance and Accounting
    Zayra Okrak
      202-551-7856
        Career

  Assistant Director for Planning and Budget
    Diane Galvin
      202-551-7853
        Career

  Budget Officer
    Mark D. David
      202-551-7852
        Career

OMB

Housing, Treasury & Commerce Division
  Treasury Branch Chief
    Lin Liu
      202-395-3308
        Career

CBO
Budget Analysis Division
  Projection Unit Chief
    Jeff Holland
      202-226-2880
        Career

GAO

Financial Markets & Community Investment Team
  Managing Director
    Richard J. Hillman
      202-512-8678
        Career

SMALL BUSINESS ADMINISTRATION BUDGET STAKEHOLDERS

SMALL BUSINESS ADMINISTRATION

Office of the CFO
Chief Financial Officer
Jon Carver
202-205-6449
Career

Deputy Chief Financial Officer
Tong Qin
202-205-6449
Career

Office of Planning & Budgeting
Budget Officer
David Lippold
202-205-6447
Career

OMB

Housing, Treasury & Commerce Division
Treasury Branch Chief
Lin Liu
202-395-3308
Career

CBO

Budget Analysis Division
Projection Unit Chief
Jeff Holland
202-226-2880
Career

GAO

Financial Markets & Community Investment Team
Managing Director
Richard J. Hillman
202-512-8678
Career

SOCIAL SECURITY ADMINISTRATION BUDGET STAKEHOLDERS

SOCIAL SECURITY ADMINISTRATION

Office of Budget, Finance and Management
Deputy Commissioner
Michael Gallagher
410-965-3148
Non-Career

Office of Budget
Assistant Deputy Commissioner
Stephanie Hall
410-965-9704
Career

OMB

Education & Human Resources Division
Labor Branch Chief
Melissa Benton Bomberger
202-395-7887
Career

CBO

Budget Analysis Division
Natural & Physical Resources Cost Estimate
Unit Chief
Kim Cawley
202-226-2860
Career

GAO

Education, Workforce & Income Security Team
Managing Director
Barbara Bovbjerg
202-512-7215
Career

STATE DEPARTMENT BUDGET STAKEHOLDERS

DEPARTMENT OF STATE

Bureau of Financial Management & Policy
   Assistant Secretary for Resource Management/CFO (Acting)
      James L. Millette
      202-647-7490
         Senate-Confirmed

Office of State Program, Operations and Budget
   Deputy Assistant Secretary
      Barbara Retzlaff
      202-647-8517
         Career

OMB

International Affairs Division
   State Branch Chief
      Joe Pipan
      202-395-1470
         Career

CBO

Budget Analysis Division
   Natural & Physical Resources Cost Estimate
   Unit Chief
      Kim Cawley
      202-226-2860
         Career

GAO

International Affairs and Trade
   Managing Director
      Jacquelyn Williams-Bridgers
      202-512-3101
         Career

TRANSPORTATION BUDGET STAKEHOLDERS

DOT

Office of the CFO
  Assistant Secretary for Budget and Program and CFO (Acting)
    Chris Bertram
      202-366-9191
        Senate-Confirmed

  Deputy Assistant Secretary
    Lana Hurdle
      202-366-9192
        Career

OMB

Transportation, Homeland, Justice & Service Division
  Transportation and GSA Branch Chief
    Andrew Abrams
      202-395-3823
        Career

CBO

Budget Analysis Division
  Natural & Physical Resources Cost Estimate
  Unit Chief
    Kim Cawley
      202-226-2860
        Career

GAO

Physical Infrastructure Team
  Managing Director
    Katherine Siggerud
      202-512-6570
        Career

TREASURY BUDGET STAKEHOLDERS

DEPARTMENT OF TREASURY

Management and CFO Office
Assistant Secretary and CFO
Dan Tangherlini
202-622-0410
Senate-Confirmed

Deputy Chief Financial Officer
Al Runnels
202-622-0750
Career

OMB

Housing, Treasury & Commerce Division
Treasury Branch Chief
Lin Liu
202-395-3308
Career

CBO

Budget Analysis Division
Projection Unit Chief
Jeff Holland
202-226-2880
Career

GAO

Homeland Security and Justice
Managing Director
Cathleen Berrick
202-512-3404
Career

USAID BUDGET STAKEHOLDERS

USAID

Bureau for Management
    Chief Financial Officer/Director
        David Ostermeyer
        202-712-0988
           Career

OMB

International Affairs Division
    Economic Affairs Branch Chief
        Christa Cappazola
        202-395-4595
           Career

CBO

Budget Analysis Division
    Natural & Physical Resources Cost Estimate
    Unit Chief
        Kim Cawley
        202-226-2860
           Career

GAO

International Affairs & Trade
    Managing Director
        Jacquelyn Williams-Bridgers
        202-512-3101
           Career

VETERANS AFFAIRS BUDGET STAKEHOLDERS

DEPARTMENT OF VETERANS AFFAIRS

Office of the Assistant Secretary
    Assistant Secretary for Management and CFO (Acting)
        Todd Grams
        202-461-6600
           Senate-Confirmed

Office of Budget
    Deputy Assistant Secretary
        Daniel Tucker
            202-461-6630
                Career

OMB

National Security Division
    Veteran Affairs and Defense Health Branch Chief
        Narahari "Hari" Sastry
            202-395-3124
                Career

CBO

Budget Analysis Division
    Defense, International Affairs & Veterans' Affairs Cost Estimates Unit Chief
        Sarah Jennings
            202-226-2840
                Career

GAO

Health Care Team
    Managing Director
        Marjorie Kanof
            202-512-7114
                Career

Appendix

History of the Income Tax

The Founding Fathers recognized that the Government could not function without the authority to raise taxes. Today, the power to tax and spend is one of the most important of all Federal powers.

The Constitution endowed the Congress with the power to "[l]ay and collect taxes, duties, imposts, and excises, pay the Debts and provide for the common Defense and general welfare of the United States."

Initially, the collection of taxes was the responsibility of state governments; however, the Federal Government did levy excise taxes to pay the debts of the Revolutionary War.

Prior to passage of the Sixteenth Amendment to the Constitution, the Government's taxing powers were generally limited to tariffs, excise taxes, customs duties, and direct taxes in proportion to the population in the states. Congress did attempt to tax income on several occasions before the Amendment was passed but each time the tax was either repealed or held to be unconstitutional.

The Federal tax system has been marked by significant changes over the years in response to changing circumstances and changes in the role of the Government. Wars and the state of the economy have been driving factors for tax policy.

- **War of 1812**. Customs duties fell due to a lack of trade and the Government had to borrow funds and adopt new taxes including taxes on dwelling houses, lands, and slaves which were apportioned among states. These were repealed after the war.

- **Civil War (Revenue Acts of 1861 and 1862).** Tariffs were increased, new excise taxes were levied, taxes were again placed on land and dwelling houses, an inheritance tax was enacted, and income taxes were levied on individuals and corporations.

  - These were the first Federal income tax acts. The Act of 1861 provided that "there shall be levied, collected, and paid, upon annual income of every person residing in the U.S. whether derived from any kind of property, or from any professional trade, employment, or vocation carried on in the United States or elsewhere, or from any source whatever."
  - The 1862 Act provided that income tax was to be withheld by the employer and it established a permanent tax collection agency (the office of the Commissioner of Internal Revenue).
  - These Acts were significant because it was the first time that Congress had levied tax on citizen's wages to cover the Federal Government's expenditures. Both Revenue Acts allowed deductions for business expenses, interest, taxes, and other items. The income tax was repealed 10 years later.

- **Depression in the 1870s.** Support grew for an income tax on the belief that it would be fairer than tariffs that hit farmers and laborers especially hard. The Democratic Party in 1894 added to a tariff bill a section providing an income tax on the income of individuals and corporations. In 1895, the Supreme Court declared it unconstitutional in *Pollock v. Farm Loan and Trust Co.* on the grounds that the tax had to be apportioned among the states on the basis of population.

- **1909 Federal Budget Deficit.** The Congress was considering an income tax to increase receipts when President Taft recommended an amendment (the 16th amendment) to the Constitution that would permit an income tax without apportionment among the states based on population. The amendment gave Congress the authority to enact (or reinstate) an income tax. In 1913, Wyoming ratified the 16th Amendment, providing the three-quarter majority of states necessary to amend the Constitution. That same year an income tax provision was included in the Underwood-Simmons Tariff Act, signed by President Wilson on October 3, 1913. The tax was:

  - A base tax rate of one percent on individual and corporate income up to $20,000 with graduated rates up to a top rate of seven percent on income over $500,000,[1] and
  - An exemption of $3,000 for individuals and $4,000 for married couples.

---

[1] Due to the high exemption, only two percent of households paid any tax.

Historically, the income tax has been a progressive tax levied at rates based upon an individual or corporation's so-called "ability to pay"; that is higher income people are assessed a higher percentage of tax than lower income people. This is in contrast with a regressive (flat) tax, such as excise or sales taxes and tariffs that are levied uniformly regardless of income.

The appropriate levels of taxes and the distribution of the tax burden among income groups, especially the rates for the highest income people, have been continuing issues since the income tax was first imposed in 1913. In general, rates have been increased to pay for wars and reduced to stimulate the economy in recessions. A summary of the major changes since they were first imposed is contained in Table A-1.

Table A-1

Major Changes in Income Tax Policy Since They Were First Imposed

Problem	Actions to resolve problem	Subsequent actions
World War I Financing	• Tax rates were increased; top rate went from 15% in 1916 to 77% in 1918 • An estate tax was created • 8% excess-profits tax levied on business income • New excise taxes levied	• Top rate dropped, reaching 24% in 1929 • Transportation and some other excise taxes reduced or eliminated • Excess profits tax terminated
Depression (Low Federal receipts)	• 1932 act increased tax rates and reduced exemptions • Excise taxes added on specified manufacturers focused on automobiles and gasoline	
World War II Financing	• Tax bands broadened by dropping exemption for single person to $500 and by increasing initial tax rate to 23% • Top individual tax rate increased to 94% in 1944 and 1945 • Top corporation rate rose to 40% • Excess profits tax enacted of almost 90% • Deductions allowed, such as medical and investment expenses • Excise tax rates raised and new categories added such as transportation of freight and passengers, jewelry, and furs	• Taxes reduced • Revenue Act of 1945 reduced individual income tax rates (top rate fell from 94% to 86%) • Another tax reduction in 1948 • Excess profits tax repealed
Korean War Financing	• Individual and corporation taxes increased across the board in 1950 and 1951 • Excess profits tax enacted	• Excess profits tax ended
1960's Economic Stimulation (Kennedy tax cuts)	• 1964 act reduced top individual tax rate from 91% to 70%, and top corporate rate from 52% to 48%	
Vietnam War Financing	• 10% surtax in 1968 and 1969; 5% for first 6 months of 1970	
1970's Economic Stimulation	• Repeal of 7% auto excise tax • 1975 act provided rebate on 1974 individual income taxes equal to 10% of earned income up to maximum of $400 for low-income families with children • Business taxes reduced • 1978 act widened tax brackets, reduced number of tax rates, and dropped top corporate rate to 46%	

Table A-1, continued
Major Changes in Income Tax Policy Since They Were First Imposed

Problem	Actions to resolve problem	Subsequent actions
1980's Economic Stimulation (Reagan tax cuts)	• 1981 act phased in 23% cut in individual tax rates across the board, with the top rate dropping from 70% to 50% • 1986 act decreased highest marginal rate from 50% to 28% for individuals and from 46% to 34% for corporations	
1990's Deficit Reduction	• 1990 act raised top rate to 31% and limited deductions and personal exemptions • 1993 act created 36% and 39.6% tax brackets	
Early 2000's Economic Stimulation (Bush tax cuts)	• 2001 act provided $300 rebate to most taxpayers, reduced rates across the board (top rate reduced to 36%), and reduced the number of brackets • 2002 and 2003 acts reduced taxes on corporation and small business owners	Expire in 2011

EOP Foundation Book Order Form

EOP Foundation, Inc.

DATE: ___/___/___ (MM/DD/YY)

819 7th St. NW. Suite 400, Washington, DC. 20001
Phone 202-833-8940 Fax 202-833-8945

CUSTOMER INFORMATION

Name: _____

Organization: _____

Mailing Address: _____

City: _____ State: ___ Zip Code: _____

Phone Number: _____

QTY	ITEM #	DESCRIPTION	UNIT PRICE	LINE TOTAL
_____		Understanding the Budget Policies and Processes of the United States Government 14th Edition (Hard Cover)	$74.99	_____
_____		Understanding the Budget Policies and Processes of the United States Government 14th Edition (Soft Cover)	$49.99	_____
_____		Understanding the United States Government's Regulatory Policy 1st Edition	$29.99	_____
_____		Understanding the Ethics Policy of the U.S. Government 1st Edition (Hard Cover)	$54.95	_____
_____		Understanding the Ethics Policy of the U.S. Government 1st Edition (Soft Cover)	$39.95	_____
_____		Understanding Effective Writing in the Government 1st Edition (Soft Cover)	$49.95	_____
_____		Understanding Effective Writing in the Government 1st Edition (Hard Cover)	$64.95	_____
		Understanding the Presidential Transition Process 1st Edition (Hard Cover)	$69.95	
_____		Shipping and Handling Fees (per item)	$1.50	_____
			Total Amount	_____

For additional information, Contact the EOP Foundation at 202-833-8940.
Make the check or money order payable to: **EOP Foundation, Inc.** Please do not send cash through the mail.
Please fax/email the order form and mail your payment to:

> The EOP Foundation – Publications Department
> 819 7th St. NW
> Suite 400
> Washington, DC. 20001
> Fax: 202-833-8945
> Email: wmyurgaites@819eagle.com

Please contact us for Quantity Discounts for Government Agencies and Educational Institutions